# AMERICAN POLITICS IN HOLLYWOOD FILM

Ian Scott

Edinburgh University Press

*This book is dedicated to
my mother, Irene Scott*

© Ian Scott, 2000

Edinburgh University Press Ltd
22 George Square, Edinburgh

Typeset in Palatino Light
by Pioneer Associates, Perthshire, and
printed and bound in Great Britain by
MPG Books Ltd, Bodmin

A CIP record for this book is available from the
British Library

ISBN 0 7486 1246 7 (paperback)

# AMERICAN POLITICS IN HOLLYWOOD FILM

# CONTENTS

# LIST OF ILLUSTRATIONS

# ACKNOWLEDGEMENTS

———◁▷———

As all authors are aware, a book of virtually any kind cannot be produced without an army of colleagues, advisers and friends pushing the writer towards the final goal and passing on invaluable advice and support along the way. I consider myself fortunate that so many have offered their time and help with this project that there just is not enough space to thank everyone here by name, much as I would like to. At the outset then, let me acknowledge all my friends and family who have been generous with their encouragement for more years than I can remember. I would particularly like to thank all at the Department of English and American Studies at Manchester, and most especially Richard Francis, Helen Johnson, Ian McGuire, Alex Sherwood (for translation) and Ian Walker who have helped in an assortment of ways. For additional constructive thoughts and valuable insight on the text I should like to thank Kevin Felstead and David Brown; and I would also like to thank those who have been generous in granting me time to present or offer articles that have gone on to inspire the book, namely Philip Davies, Liam Kennedy and Robert Rosenstone. I should also like to pass on gratitude to the students at Manchester who have taken my course, written up work and offered thoughts that have always made me go away and think about my writing again. Finally I would also like to offer my thanks to all at Edinburgh University Press, but most of all to Nicola Carr whose faith in this project never wavered and who put up with my excuses and frustrations throughout.

# INTRODUCTION

The typical reaction to any comment that your work is about film and politics is usually that polite enquiry: aren't all films about politics? At first my stock answer used to be invariably yes, all films are 'political'. Now, however, having thought about the question many times in preparation for writing this book, I have recently come round to a different explanation: 'no, not all films are "political", but they are all ideological'.

While admitting that Hollywood's influence on the cultural and historical landscape of America has been immense during the course of the twentieth century I am keen to demonstrate in this book that films have also dramatically shaped the democratic and institutional agenda of the United States; that Hollywood has, in the words of Peter Rollins: 'turn[ed] out films consciously designed to change public attitudes towards matters of social and political importance'.[1]

Therefore, in Hollywood's film history I have found that the distinction between the 'political' and 'ideological' paradigm is not only useful but, in some cases, quite necessary. This book is indeed a consideration of film and ideology, but it is more especially about American politics and in particular political ideas in film and why they are, in fact, much more prevalent and important than has previously been noted, or, at the very least, acknowledged. It is certainly the case that a few of the films discussed in this book – a book that self-consciously includes the words 'film' and 'politics' in its title – actually have no 'politics' in them at all. For example, Clint Eastwood's 1997 film *Absolute Power*, follows a structural and ideological path whereby the central character, President Alan Richmond (Gene Hackman) reveals neither his party identity, his political background, current policies, nor any kind of institutional belief system whatsoever; to the degree that the plot – rich, powerful man becomes implicated in murder of beautiful girl

1

while ensuing cover-up fails to gloss over the cracks in the conspiratorial alibi – might just as well not have a political setting at all. Displace the President of the United States with a famous actress and the story could just as easily have been Jane Fonda in Sidney Lumet's *The Morning After* (1986).

Of course interpretations are never quite as simple as that, because *Absolute Power*, like all other films with a political 'motif', does have an agenda, an agenda that is distinctly political, and one that Marxist theorists would interpret as originating within the realms of the ruling elite. It is engaged in, as Hollywood has been throughout its history, what Robert Ray identifies as 'elaborating American mythology'.[2] To put this in even more strident, Gramscian terms, Hollywood has a hegemonic set of values that reflects the conformities of American democracy. Hollywood is, as Richard Maltby asserts, a 'social institution'; and outside of films that have no character references or institutional connections to American politics the ability to transmit ideology within a social framework is what adds the 'political' dimension to such widely disseminated recent movies as, for example, *Field of Dreams* (1989), *Thelma and Louise* (1991) or *Falling Down* (1992).[3]

This societal context of 'politics' in Hollywood films is a recognised and much discussed area of research, but assessing ideological and institutional politics has often been a more difficult concept for film writers and historians. Does this refer to initiatives, debate and legislation at state or federal level concerning cinema in America? Does it refer to periods of seemingly overt propagandist control of the medium such as the Hays Office or the investigations of the Dies Committee and later the House Un-American Activities Committee? Or is it the way Hollywood has become complicit in the actual making of propaganda films, during World War Two for example?

One would be fairly naive to suggest that all of these areas have not had at least some impact on Hollywood's cinematic and, by definition, political outlook. This book refers to all of the above at various times. Through its transmission of social and democratic dialogue it has been as much Hollywood's task to placate institutions as it has had to infuse its own output with their ideological vision periodically. With this in mind the focus on an examination of American political institutions and figures specifically, and on the ideology that has been a part of the history of American democracy, is even more pertinent. As a result, Chapter 1 outlines key theoretical and analytical concepts associated with political films, and the ways in which narrative and stylistic treatments have governed the presentation of such ideas.

Structurally this book then sets out to reflect on historical change in both a cinematic and political context by addressing the era of the 1930s and 1940s in Chapter 2, and the contemporary period of the 1990s in the final section of the book, Chapter 6. Both chapters are concerned to show the way Hollywood has approached political subjects by means of didactic screenplays and visual composition. Both are also joined by a recognition of the 1990s' homage to the legacy of classic 1930s' and 1940s' screwball, romantic comedies. Retaining many of the key features of the earlier period, more contemporary political films similarly seek to engender subtle and carefully plotted outlines of populist, liberalist and communitarian tradition in their storylines.

In-between these two chapters, however, I have attempted to address political films, I believe, in their proper generic forms. Thus Chapter 3 considers election films through Hollywood's history; Chapter 4 seeks to advance a new set of observations concerning action, adventure and political conspiracy thrillers; and Chapter 5 analyses political biography as a separate and critical subgenre of this cinematic field of study. Each of these chapters countenances historical change while offering explanations as to why particular stylistic and structural treatments have been engaged, and how directors, screenwriters and actors have formulated, and been informed by, periodic political and institutional re-evaluation.

In the final chapter a number of these themes are brought together to elaborate on the view that, as we enter the twenty-first century, Hollywood and Washington are closer partners than ever in the arena of political discourse and in the debates about the continuing efficacy of the American polity. It is almost certainly true, as this book underlines, that Hollywood has somehow been complicit in the simplification of democratic debate in the United States, particularly since the mid-1970s. But I feel strongly that in its own way Hollywood has also served to ground many of the fundamental principles and beliefs of the nation into the consciousness of its citizenry through symbolic as well as pedagogic means. This book aims to show how these dual tracks have run, sometimes parallel, sometimes in convergence, but always with lessons to be learnt and messages of change and evaluation for the American democratic experience.

## NOTES

1  Peter C. Rollins, 'Introduction', in *Hollywood as Historian: American Film in a Cultural Context*, ed. Peter C. Rollins (Lexington: University of Kentucky Press, 1983) p. 1.
2  Robert Ray, *A Certain Tendency in Hollywood Film* (Princeton: Princeton University Press, 1987) p. 13.
3  Richard Maltby, *Hollywood Cinema* (Oxford: Blackwell, 1995) p. 361.

*Chapter 1*

# FILM, IDEOLOGY AND
# AMERICAN POLITICS

—⊃⊂—

'Movies reflect political choices' as one commentator recently observed.[1]
But these choices are often distorted and clouded by a medium that,
after all, places before its audience a commodity emphasising entertainment. Within the fields of communication studies, film theory and
cultural studies the deconstruction of messages that exemplify the
conflicts and ideas within society is the clue that leads us towards a
construction of 'political' meaning within films. But such deconstruc-
tionalism, together with the language of Gramscian Marxism, has in
addition accentuated the debate between the elite and subordinate
groups in society as regards the product and meaning of culture as a
whole.

No longer the domination of one over the other, popular film has
been the territory of resolution for conflicting ideologies in the wider
community and Hollywood has increasingly regarded its role very
seriously in this context. It has, for instance, been perceived more often
than not as a champion of democracy, in both political and social
terms, more actively so than any other medium or institution.[2] By this
argument, Hollywood has actually become an active participant in
the debates inherent in American political life. Those debates have
often involved simplification of ideals and have been grounded in the
dialogue of traditional narrative structuralism; nevertheless they have
reflected upon, and been contiguous of, political and institutional
progression in its own right and in a core set of values exemplifying
twentieth-century American politics.

I believe there are two ways in which Hollywood has been able to
present the American polity as an active inculcate of cultural discourse:
one is the actual pervasive nature of democratic ideology in film – the
themes, beliefs and values that are part of the American creed, stretching
back into its history, and which sweep through films about politics with

5

a far greater force than has ever really been acknowledged; the second element is the mythological determinant that politics and political culture play in the creation of the *idea* of America, the thoughts and feelings, scenes and rhetoric, which create symbolic imprints and allow American politics to be considered relative and relevant to its citizenry, even though its processes and laws are often far more complex and abstract, certainly than some Hollywood depictions would have its audience believe. In other words, politics has always played, and Hollywood came along to enhance, a game of spectacle and idealisation. Hollywood reflects and indeed encourages the kind of mythmaking that American politics itself has constantly engaged in, and for this reason alone its politics have an acute sensibility to the cinematic medium that is worth investigating and deciphering in greater depth.

## HOLLYWOOD: THE SIGNIFIER OF AMERICAN DEMOCRACY

In many ways the mythology of democracy is a very appropriate form of cultural identification for politics in film because America's own democratic symbols are as much tied together by its iconic political structures as are all other forms of Americanism. Hollywood has been careful to utilise this imagery as a signifier of political discourse in many genres of movie-making. Again one could construct a whole list of films that are outside the confines of this book but nevertheless elaborate upon this idea with the use of institutional backdrops, most usually in Washington DC: from Hitchcock's *Strangers on a Train* (1951) and Robert Wise's *The Day the Earth Stood Still* (1951) to, more recently, Sidney Pollack's *The Firm* (1993) or James Cameron's *True Lies* (1995).[3] Recent work by Albert Boime has further elaborated upon the notion of iconography as a strong ideological principle, resonant to a populace who locate its significance alongside that of key documents like the Constitution, or strongly distinctive political figures like Franklin Roosevelt or John F. Kennedy.[4]

Boime identifies a model of patriotic, right-wing appropriation of key monuments and memorials through history where the authoritarian instinct of the elite has rested on the maintenance of social and economic controls vested in such iconic symbols as the Stars and Stripes or the Statue of Liberty. 'Those who attempt to control the nation's history through visual representations as well as through texts are regulators of the social memory and hence of social conscience', he says. 'In learning about the original history of our national monuments and icons, Americans can come to understand that the democratic rhetoric surrounding them has been manipulated for political purposes.'[5]

In fact the historical origins of this intercourse, as Boime makes clear, stretches well back into the past, and its extended relationship has served to make iconographic representation a part of mainstream critical parlance in the present, irrespective of right- or left-wing connotations. Indeed it has long been the province of America's cultural elite to establish and deconstruct the effigies of American exceptionalism. One only has to think in artistic terms of painters such as Robert Rauschenberg, who borrowed the image of John Kennedy during the 1960s and 1970s for use in paintings like *Retroactive* and *Signs*, or Jasper Johns, whose series of works in the 1950s centred around the Stars and Stripes, to appreciate the perpetuation of this theory of nationalistic iconography down through many American cultural forums. Critic Robert Hughes described the devotion of Johns as 'aesthetic, not patriotic' and one, on the face of it, could similarly ascribe the same kind of sentiment – the deconstruction of formalism – to the political imagery of Hollywood films.[6]

It is not just symbolic forms of identification, however, that Hollywood has used to link scenes of the White House or Washington Monument or Capital Dome to a representation of American politics. In Hollywood's language, these structures *literally* tell the story of America's democratic heritage and thus literal and metaphoric dimensions of ideological discourse sit neatly side by side in these cinematic presentations.

In *Mr Smith Goes to Washington* (1939), arguably the most famous and talked-about film on American politics, Frank Capra's hero Jefferson Smith embarks on a trolley bus tour of the capital as soon as he arrives to see the sights and hear the sounds of the city. He finds himself ultimately, as another one thousand and one movie politicians have, at the steps of the Lincoln Memorial. The grandeur of Henry Bacon's architectural style and Daniel Chester French's imposing sculpture of the man embodies iconic symbolism itself, but what Smith, and through him Capra, is really drawn to is the education of the young boy, accompanied by his grandfather, and following him the black man who takes off his cap and listens while the child recites the

Gettysburg Address on the south wall of the monument. The memorial is thus a school for the child – as it later proves to be for Jeff also – and a place of learning as well as one of worship. The boy could go home and read the address in any history book, but being there *is* history, a time and place where he can be at one with those who shaped the direction of the nation. The Lincoln Memorial therefore overwhelms the foreground of iconic structures and becomes symbolic in many Hollywood films of solemnity, of theological contemplation, a place to seek sanctuary and find inspiration. Such is the power of its visual depiction that John Ford utilised the statue in his closing soliloquy for *Young Mr Lincoln* (1939), a direct homage itself to the final scene of the memorial, following the assassination, incorporated in D. W. Griffith's own *Abraham Lincoln* (1930). Both directors were undaunted by the crossing of nearly sixty years of history between the closing of their stories and the erection of the Lincoln Memorial itself, dedicated as recently as 1922, when the metaphoric iconography in both pictures appeared spatially seamless.

For Capra, the focus upon the Gettysburg Address at the memorial was also an inbuilt recognition of the nature of political principles embodied in the words carved there. As political theorist Michael Foley explains, 'government of the people, by the people, for the people' was the composition of liberty, equality and democracy all in the space of a few lines, and it remains at the heart of the ideology of American democracy.[7] Capra recognised the need to reinforce 'text' with the 'iconography of text', and to take on board implicitly the debates in society concerning the real and impressionistic state of ideas and principles. He reiterates the point later in the film when Smith, while trying to construct his Boys Camp Bill for consideration by the Senate, points to the Capitol Dome outside his office window and explains to his secretary Saunders that that symbol is what he wishes to see incorporated into his bill.

*Mr Smith Goes to Washington* thus created a framework upon which, as Eric Smoodin has argued, the audience were offered not only an aesthetically plausible democracy but also a guide to the rigours of good citizenry.[8] In this guise it has not only been the ideological doctrines underpinning *Mr Smith* that have stood the test of time but the impressionistic connotations of the film's title and, by implication, its central character. Allen Rostron's article, for example, 'Mr. Carter Goes to Washington', self-consciously equates the Smith persona with the former president who saw himself as a kind of Horatio Alger-like figure, a source of strength for his 1976 campaign when Americans were searching for healing and renewal, but, as Rostron pointedly remarks, the sand bank upon which his presidency was ultimately marooned four years later.[9]

More significant still, Lauren Berlant's analysis of a contemporary iconic product, *The Simpsons*, in an episode entitled 'Mr. Lisa Goes to Washington', is for her proof that 'the activity of national pedagogy' is alive and well, building upon elements of Hollywood's classical history, and finding a reception even in the ironic world of 1990s' postmodern culture.[10]

Capra's film, therefore, acts as a dual conduit both for the perceptions of democratic theory that it translates and for the patented logo of American polity that its title and principal character represent. From the pre-war years until now Hollywood has attempted to build upon this construct of democracy: it has tried to infuse its output on politics with a sense of history, to proffer a democratic tradition that, it claims, has no equal; in other words, to offer its own version of exceptionalism and manifest destiny. In the 1930s, when the discussion of political films really begins, this was of course predicated upon a very vital need; the United States was fighting an ideological battle, a battle for the hearts and minds of a people who had begun to suspect that America's great democratic experiment was, in the face of the Depression, all washed up. Political films during the decade countered this in a way that was part triumphalist, part nationalistic, but almost wholly recognisable as a fragment of the mythic landscape upon which American history had been built. This is why the features of Abraham Lincoln, if not his words, crop up in almost all political films of the era. Lincoln tied together the Depression era with the 1860s because he was associated with triumph in the face of adversity, with sacrifice, and with preservation of the republic in a time of great upheaval.

Even by the 1950s, when any portrayal of political institutions could be interpreted as a codified attack on American life, the era of anti-communism could still allow Hollywood to accommodate a re-examination of the early life of President Andrew Jackson – a neat parallel with his reputation as a purger of 'undesirables' in his relations with Native Americans during the early nineteenth century – with Henry Levin's *The President's Lady* (1953) (see Chapter 5).

With each proceeding decade, from the 1930s onwards, Hollywood

has followed almost precisely the same formula of encrypting democratic patriotism within familiar symbols, regardless of real life crisis or
consensus, and that formula has found a cultural receptiveness that no
other art form has been able to touch in the twentieth century. What is
striking about the collection of films on view in this book is the way
one can separate those that were commercially successful from those
that were largely ignored at the box office, and see the ideological
pathways that have governed such commercial viability. Such an
analysis of consumption and production leads one down the road of
examining Hollywood, in the term that culturalists Theodor Adorno
and Max Horkheimer have used, as the 'culture industry'. To these
1940s' German critics, mass production of material – the Hollywood
studio system – would lead to mass consumption of a standardised
product that encouraged conformity and relegated consciousness. The
result, at the time, was the possibility of fascist takeover in a society
where the means of cultural control was safeguarded by the elite.[11]

This notion of a kind of aesthetic guardianship of highbrow culture
may have been partly realised in films about politics but it is important
to understand how audiences have selected certain pictures, while
rejecting others, and to discover how this both supports the capitalist
functions of the film industry, and invokes the values and aspirations
of the watching public. Only by channelling this investigation in such
a way do we, I believe, get to the exceptionally important concept of
Hollywood as purveyor of real and mythical political discourse.[12]

Scholars looking at the 1930s, for instance, have pointed to the fact
that social consciousness cinema was terribly unpopular (escapist films
did far better at the box office) and that the political creed was diluted
by populist demands.[13] Brian Neve even suggests that general intuition
considered that 1930s' films in the second half of the decade at least
had little 'social or political relevance'.[14] If one were to accept the pure
comparison of financial returns as a means to demonstrate influence,
then this was certainly true. Films about politics were not box office
gold for the studios. But Chapter 2 in this book makes a strong case *for*
the transmittable nature of politics and *against* the diminution of ideas
and values in 1930s' cinema. I argue that Hollywood was actually well
aware of the potential for the medium to spread political notions and
ideals, and that audience reception of political films revealed a more
deep-seated sense of ideological and didactic intercourse taking place,
and a consciousness of the position of these films relative to the wider

dissemination of political and sociological thought. In other words, the surface interpretation, and dismissal, of political films, I would argue, needs some sharp revision in this context.

*Mr Smith Goes to Washington* did very well for Capra in 1939, amassing takings of more than $3 million in America despite scathing attacks from the political establishment (see Chapter 2).[15] And yet it remains true that his 1948 film *State of the Union* – a more recalcitrant and, because of this, vital examination of politics at the time – was far less popular and was given far less media attention. Likewise in the 1990s, Hollywood's two most conspicuously Clintonesque movies (and the two most reminiscent of the classic 1930s' era), *Dave* (1993) and *The American President* (1995), cleaned up at the box office in comparison to Tim Robbins's witty and caustic *Bob Roberts* (1992). The question is not solely why one film would prove more popular than another but whether some encase the resolution of political conflict and the transmission of values within recognisable indicators for their audience more than other pictures perhaps do.

Both from a cinematic tradition, and from the perspective of more contemporary cultural theory, one answer lies in a critical ideological debate. It would be amiss of us, for example, to neglect the discourse of 'nostalgia' that permeates the recent films mentioned above, certainly has commercial ramifications in the present Hollywood era, and which provides a suitably convenient comparison of political films sixty years apart. *Dave* and *The American President* are fine examples of a cultural medium's positioning of an idealised past focused in the lens of a dispassionate observer. These two films do embed their observations with knowing references, not only to a 'kinder, gentler era', but also to the 1930s' screwball cinematic tradition they pay homage to (Reiner's film *The American President* keeps the Capra theme active with a reference to both the director and *Mr Smith*). This then is less a manipulation of the source of cultural iconography, as with *The Simpsons*, than an updated photocopy of the original article. Critics such as Christopher Lasch have warned of the problems inherent in this societal approach to what he terms as 'nostalgia culture' but there are two observations I think that should be made in response given the subject matter in this instance.[16]

The first is that this mythical idealisation is not new in Hollywood's history and was as representative of 1930s' films, and their own recurrent historical traditionalism, as much as it is today. The picture of communitarianism that runs through many of the political films here as a source of democratic discourse is a visual construction that needs more debate, and an argument that is constantly re-examined in this book. The second point though is that the connection *Mr Smith, Dave* and *The American President* share – rooted in the simplicity of a nostalgic populism that appears to be their calling cards – is not that they fail to take on board a sophisticated critique of democratic ideology, and thus their popularity is perceived to be predicated upon a simplistic comfortable exhortation of the political process, but that like many other light, comedic narratives set within political frameworks they play to the strength of democratic 'signifiers' which are already persuasive sounding boards for political values.

Jefferson Smith, Dave Kovic and Andrew Shepherd are already identifiable political figures for the audience because they are in fact the type of men the American electorate really does want. They have not replicated a particular creed of politician or leader, but have served to define that role model, they have patented it, reworked it, and then cast it out into the political ether and watched it flourish and multiply. Franklin D. Roosevelt, Dwight Eisenhower, John Kennedy, Ronald Reagan, John Glenn, Jack Kemp and Colin Powell, to name only a few, are all real figures who had, or have, certain resemblances and beliefs not unlike their fictional counterparts. They have all benefited from name recognition, from heroic status, from positive personality traits, from the realisation that style and image matter at least as much, if not far more, than content and ideology. This book argues that Hollywood has not reflected this trend in characterisation, it has not merely copied but influenced and shaped this distinctive political character.

As critic Michael Kelley has observed, the faith in image has been a cumulative growth that has increasingly sidelined the traditions of professionalism (in political administration at least) and ideology in Washington. Actions have become judged according to the presentation of their handling rather than the real consequences of those actions.[17] In such a climate what is the reporter of public affairs but a critic of a piece of theatre? As Kelley states, 'If perception is reality, what is the point of any differences at all between Republicans and Democrats, between journalists and government officials, between ideologues and copywriters, between Washington and Hollywood?'[18]

Of course it must also be conceded that this is a direction in American politics that has never really been restricted to just the media age of the twentieth century, for Thomas Jefferson, Andrew Jackson, Abraham Lincoln and Teddy Roosevelt could all lay claim to be populist image and style gurus for their time long before Hollywood, and television, was established.

But, as well as having historical precedents on their side, the key for the modern political figures in the first list is that they have been the guardians of an essential consensus in American public life which dates back to these earlier, now venerated public icons. In other words, there is a linear connection to the present day that is, in effect, the *lingua franca* of American politics. Hollywood, it should be stressed, has always been aware of this and that is why Washington, Jefferson and Lincoln have been so constantly referenced by political films.

This connection to the 'real' and the 'constructed' in the presentation of politics is perhaps best exemplified by cultural theorist Allan Lloyd Smith. He talks about the 'element of spectacle' involved in American politics and about politicians' desire to create 'scenarios of power and ideology'.[19] It is almost the quintessential abstraction of the realities of discourse from the processes of governance. It is the real and mythical morphing to become one and the same; Hollywood has become the centre of ideological discourse, Washington has become the breeding ground for the entertainment culture. As Joan Goodman has observed: 'Washington and Hollywood are two cities divided by a common ambition. Each has what the other craves.'[20] Reflecting on political films such as *The Best Man* (1964) and *The Candidate* (1972) (both extensively discussed in Chapter 3) at the beginning of the 1980s, Philip Davies and Brian Neve commented that Hollywood had correctly surmised the new route to power seeking. 'Just as politicians must become celebrities in order to gain power, so celebrities are halfway to becoming politicians; indeed in a country lacking a debate about public philosophies, style may be everything.'[21]

The nature of this relationship has undoubtedly changed over the years. In the 1920s and 1930s the Hollywood moguls, the epitome of first- or second-generation New York Lower East Side immigrant stock, demanded the acceptance of Washington and the wider society for their part in the construction of the American Dream. In the 1940s and 1950s the studios sought to prove that loyalty and purge themselves of any ill-gotten values. In the 1980s and particularly the 1990s Hollywood personalities carry political consultants with them as much as they do filofaxes, no cause is too bold or too ennobling, and

Hollywood studios, although becoming less reverential towards their portrayal of the institutional establishment, have fixed the attention of both (real and fictionalised political characters), as Neve and Davies predicted, to presentation and image in the global era of communication.

Hollywood has been acutely susceptible to recognising the media and connecting them to the source of all political messages in this modern age. In its 1930s' films the press and radio were still a means to convey and debate policy and ideology. In the contemporary era, television means simply to be a name, a badge, an identification of personality and candidacy; it is the receptacle by which politics survives and plays out a game the public can observe but barely participate in. The oft quoted source of this relocation of messages and understanding for the tribal community, as Tom Wolfe once described it, is in the seminal work of Marshall McLuhan, whose 1960s' book *Understanding Media* took to heart and pre-dated the 1990s' passivity for seeing the media, and especially TV, as a mediating and interactive force that has subsumed the masses.[22] Hollywood has driven a narrative course whereby almost all political films have been assuaged with the need to confront the machinations of media influence and control, and, as this book argues strongly, this has tracked and finally become the vanguard of 'real' political actions in the modern age. The representation of journalistic endeavour in 1933's *Gabriel over the White House*, for example (see Chapter 2), has transmogrified into the propagandist possibilities of global deception in 1998's *Wag the Dog* (see Chapter 6).

Art and life have therefore closely tailed each other in Hollywood political films. As outlined in Chapter 2, Warner Brothers got cold feet in early 1933 because of the radical tendencies invoked in director Gregory La Cava's *Gabriel*, its release coming hot on the heels of the attempted assassination of Franklin Roosevelt in Miami prior to his inauguration that year. This is nicely juxtaposed with the reflections on Mike Nicholls's *Primary Colors* in early 1998 where the candidate, Jack Stanton, sees his campaign for President almost blown off course by backstage dalliances with various members of the opposite sex. The film's release coincided with the revelations over President Bill Clinton and the Monica Lewinsky affair.

Of course *Primary Colors*, the adaptation of Joe Klein's previously anonymous novel, *is* Clinton, for the book and film cannot avoid the templates of character that Klein loaded into the story from Clinton's own 1992 campaign staff, and it therefore falls for the *Citizen Kane*-like veiled biography approach. Nevertheless, the film delves into the deconstructionist 1990s' vogue that searches for synchronous links to truth, fiction, fact and mythology in current society. As one reviewer commented:

> *Primary Colors* isn't simply a case of art imitating life. It's a matter of art improving on life. [Nicholls's] film starts out as a shrewd, razor-sharp political satire, then slowly, inevitably deepens into something darker. Something, as the Kathy Bates character says, 'human and sad'.[23]

In other words, is *Primary Colors* – the fictionalised account of a southern governor's campaign for the presidency in the 1990s – actually the 'truth' about Clinton after all; and is it a 'better truth' than can ever be gleaned or interpreted by actual analysis of the real man? Questions like these have increasingly excited film scholars who are interested in history and real life characters as a topic of film. Robert Rosenstone, for instance, has been interested to excavate the historical interpretation and the relative tensions between fact and fiction in Hollywood presentations, and these arguments are further elaborated on in Chapter 5's assessment of political biography.[24] More recent analysis has also acknowledged the strong interest and seriousness with which audiences react to such material. Robert Toplin argues that the public consider films like *All the President's Men* (1976) and *JFK* (1991) (both discussed in Chapter 4) to be important social commentaries and therefore worthy of vociferous debate.[25] In the context of the reaction to *Primary Colors* this would appear to be a vital perspective to consider in any analysis of the impact of political films.

The postmodern cultural environment has seen film become not only a separate, but integrated source of discourse for a pluralistic community. Its holistic tendencies allow for scholars, reviewers and commentators from many fields to come together and find themselves adept at being able to extricate social and political realism from fictionalised politics played out in Hollywood films.[26] When real political figures are involved, however – Nixon and Kennedy are the most obvious examples – the quest has been more often to see whether history is being rewritten, whether this is a genuine and 'truthful' account of a life, and the history that surrounded it, or whether it is merely the rantings of a megalomaniac director. The recent analysis of political films needs to come to terms with a collage of personality traits that make fictional characters palatable for film audiences whereas biographical re-enactments are often dismissed as conjecture at best, and damnable subversion at worst.

The aim of this book is to make sense of these currents that weave between cultural and historical interpretation of textual material. The understanding of visual composition and the way public perceptions reinforce the acceptance of symbolic references, while all the time recognising particular democratic signs that construct an identifiable pattern of acceptance and conformity, is one way that the following chapters attempt to do this.

## HOLLYWOOD AND THE PORTRAYAL OF AMERICAN POLITICAL IDEAS

If Hollywood has constructed a pattern of mythical and abstract thinking that is able to instruct our analysis of the real political world through imagery and perception, then it is also critical to our understanding of the medium's influence to recognise its contribution to the representation of political ideas; ideas that have long been an intrinsic part of American society. I wish to argue here that it is not enough simply to convey a line of thinking that declares Hollywood political films as the harbingers of postmodern discourse, a marriage of Hollywood visual sensibilities with spin doctoring soundbite wisdom, though this seems clearly apparent in itself. Political culture in its most familiar state, as a collection of the themes that represent the American political tradition, is also much in evidence in all these films and vital, I would stress, to this real and mythical debate precisely because of a pervasive ideological agenda that Hollywood has consistently relayed.

As was noted in the introduction, and has been reinforced by many American political commentators, one can produce a list of values and doctrines that Americans subscribe to in a way that, as Graham Wilson has observed, appears to be just not possible for the British or French.[27] The ideals of liberalism, democracy, egalitarianism, pluralism, populism and messanism, to name only the most obvious, are themes that suggest social equity, the value of the economic market and the limited role of government, and which form the collective nucleus that is Americanism. From D. W. Griffith's *The Birth of a Nation* in 1915 to

Mike Nicholls's *Primary Colors* in 1998, these ideals are the substantive ideological precepts upon which political films operate. As a recent commentator has observed, Hollywood does not go to Washington for the mind-numbing minutiae of committee work or constituency meetings; it is not there to provide a literal depiction of Congress at work.[28] But if the definition of a great political movie is the way it pertains to show how political power is exercised, it *is* a literal investigation into the theories of American political culture.

This is exactly why a line of great political figures perceived as consensual theoreticians – from Washington to Roosevelt and Kennedy, by way of Jefferson, Jackson and Lincoln – has been drawn by Hollywood through its own history. These men represent the moments when democracy has suffered critical tests or been subject to re-evaluation. Hollywood has offered their words and deeds as explanations for the endorsement of these ideological traditions as well as providing a convenient reading of their individual interpretations of American philosophical thought.

Liberalism and democracy, for example, are only two such ideologies that highlight the tensions at work in American politics and these have been constantly restated in explicit and implicit form during the history of Hollywood's portrayal. On the one hand American liberalism draws its influence from the law of natural rights as envisaged by seventeenth-century philosopher John Locke. Locke took on board the individualist argument of Thomas Hobbes together with the egalitarian thoughts of Hobbes' contemporary James Harrington.[29] Wedded together Locke foresaw the property-owning classes as having the means to control legislative power but that a 'contract' also needed to be established between the governed and the government. So instrumental has liberal thought been in American society that in the 1950s Louis Hartz, in his famous book, considered the 'liberal tradition' in the United States to be a pervasive theory that had confined political debate within a fairly narrow range.[30]

On the other hand American democracy has always been a source of tension for this theory – rather than a compliment to it which is how it is often portrayed – because it has feared the kind of majority rule that strikes down minority thought and opinion.[31] The Founding Fathers sought to maintain both these ideas within a single framework when they wrote the American Constitution in 1787, and Hollywood films implicitly grapple with these fundamentals of the American way through the vast majority of their narratives. The heroes, Jefferson Smith, Long John Willoughby, Judson Hammond, B. G. Brown, Dave Kovic, Andrew Shepherd and Jay Bulworth, all embody a humanist tradition, all recognise and have to battle majority and tyrannical opposition, and all seek to reaffirm the relationship of the establishment with the people, to mend the betrayals that Hollywood films interpret as being at the heart of the institutional malaise.[32]

Egalitarianism is also an intrinsic part of the Hollywood agenda just as it is for American politics as a whole, underlined by J. R. Pole's view that equality is central to democratic beliefs in the United States.[33] How are the poor, the needy, the disenfranchised to be represented in public life; how do women and minorities coexist and find a voice? Hollywood's role in this area may be more subconsciously defined, but it has found itself intertwined with the debates in twentieth-century society between justice and consent and this, as John Zvesper argues, is the critical tension within the idea of equality itself.[34]

With the exception of Eddie Murphy in *The Distinguished Gentleman* (1992), Adrian Lester in *Primary Colors*, and Glenn Close in *Air Force One* (1997), all the chief political protagonists in the films discussed are white, male and wealthy/privileged/middle class (itself an accurate reflection of elitist tendencies in national politics in America down through the ages). Race and gender are, though, two areas that have had little attention in films about politics and yet their visible and non- visible presence has an important legacy to play in assimilationist and segregationist ideals within the American polity. A surprising number of strong female roles have been constructed in a variety of political film genres (from Jean Arthur as Clarissa Saunders in *Mr Smith* through to Annette Benning as Sidney Ellen Wade in *The American President*, by way of real-life Pat Nixon played by Joan Allen in *Nixon* (1995)) but their positions relative to political ideology, and in the context of Hollywood's own gender position, deserve further attention. As the analysis of each of the above films will show, Hollywood has been at pains to demonstrate its own, and the establishment's, attempts to refine the constitutional system in order to establish a more equal or just society, even in the light of antithetical forces and varying interpretations of what equality means. But at the heart of these and other theoretical considerations are debates concerning pluralist and elite control in American society and this is an important signal of the position of Hollywood in the wider political

landscape and the strong democratic and consensual messages that it
has striven to represent.

Through messianism, Hollywood has ascribed a particularly religious
zeal to America's colonising, investment and redirecting of the world
towards its own self-interested virtues. This has a strong nationalist
streak to it, as the foreign policy subplots of *Washington Merry-Go-
Round* (1932), *Gabriel over the White House, The American President* and
*Wag the Dog* ably demonstrate; but there is also a theological treatment, reflected in the vibrant Christian and religious iconography, that
sees fictional and factual political heroes as saviours and Christ-like
figures, not only of their own people but of the entire world. Again
Gregory La Cava's 1933 film *Gabriel over the White House* merged these
themes in the dual persona of President Judson Hammond to produce
an excellent early example of the agency of Hollywood ideology. Frank
Capra's *Meet John Doe* (1941) achieves much the same effect for its
principal character, Long John Willoughby, and Henry King followed
on from this with his biographical and idealised portrait *Wilson* in 1944
(see Chapters 2 and 5 respectively).

More than this, the political culture has combined these and other
theoretical attributes to produce a resonant civic and moral pride – what
Benjamin Franklin called 'the art of virtue' – but with it a particular
distrust of government, and politics in general.[35] Hollywood's treatment of politics has long reflected a nagging suspicion about the
integrity of institutions – Willoughby's speeches in *Meet John Doe*,
Dave Kovic's innocent idealism in his closing speech in the Senate in
*Dave*, or even Jeff Johnson's desire to get a 'slice of the financial action'
in *The Distinguished Gentleman* all highlight an outsider's perturbation
and cynicism at the system – but its attention, the need for dramatic
structure, has always seemingly dragged filmmakers towards the prevailing battles between good and evil, as director Rod Lurie explains.

> Hollywood is not a subtle place. Hollywood is an area of extremes.
> When you look at the Kennedy–Nixon TV debates, it is a presen-
> tation of bad on the one hand and good on the other in terms of
> their politics and their physical appearances. Good verses Evil
> [sic]. Which is why Hollywood either goes Nixon or Kennedy.[36]

Laurie emphasises the tendency to regard Hollywood political ideas
as rather naive and merely centred around questions of personal

moralism. The integrity of the individual is certainly at stake in many political narratives, and Hollywood could most assuredly be charged with feeding its ideology through the personality traits of sincerity and a strong righteous dignity. But that would be to fall into the trap of accusing Hollywood of simply being too artless, too belittling and restrictive in its process and performance to allow serious political dialogue to emerge.

It would also be to ignore the crucial ideological framework that has been built around individualism at the core of political thinking in America. Individualism has been the driving force for liberty and equality, as principal theorists in this field such as Daniel Bell have observed, and these two themes have also been at the heart of Hollywood's individualistic and heroic ideological representation.[37] In a world where liberal individualism has held such sway, it becomes less surprising to find a clamour for a return to the core spirit of community.[38]

As further elaborated within the work of Glenn Alan Phelps, there are greater issues at stake here than good neighbourly values or the triumph of the underdog; and his analysis is perhaps the most telling in trying to ascribe the political values and American democratic theory of individualism and liberalism to Hollywood's tradition in this area. In particular, his work on the 'populist' films of Frank Capra is importantly one of the few that takes up the theoretical arguments concerning elite and pluralist forms of democracy in Hollywood presentation.[39]

Comparing the models of elite and pluralist power that were most forcefully espoused by the likes of C. Wright Mills and Nelson Polsby in the 1950s and 1960s, Phelps has grafted the analytical debates about where power lies in America onto the four (in his eyes) most socially conscious films of Capra's career: *Mr Deeds Goes to Town* in 1936, *Mr Smith Goes to Washington* (1939), *Meet John Doe* (1941), and finally *It's a Wonderful Life* from 1946. His thesis argues that Capra's background and his somewhat 'privileged' position in the 1930s' studio system, of being a director with considerable weight and control over his output, made him an artist who augmented his films with strong social statements. Chapter 2 examines the Phelps thesis in greater depth, but his revelations about Capra's portrayal of 'the masses' in his films, their input into the political arena, and the closures that allowed for the triumph of what he calls the 'lone, democratic, patriotic individualist' over the wider, and sometimes unforeseen, forces of authority and control, is a valuable addition to the literature on political films. More importantly it demonstrates the influential nature of Capra's political thesis which has become a template for the (comedic at least) political film ever since.[40]

Indeed the ideology inherent in Capra's films that Phelps describes could be equated with a more recent theory of individualism that Herbert Gans has outlined. His arguments for 'middle American individualism' are just the sort of abstract themes that relate to the thoughts and lifestyle of the 'masses' Capra once portrayed in his stories.[41] Among other things, Gans makes a play for this 'popular individualism' as he defines the set of ideas that middle Americans hold as being a strong desire for personal control, a theoretical framework that identified with audience feelings over not just Capra's political representation, but many other filmmakers' as well.[42]

Therefore the central questions that this book sets out to tackle are: how has Hollywood portrayed politics in the United States; what is the philosophical and ideological basis of this portrayal; and how have the basic tenets of this philosophy changed over time and with the alterations and power struggles that have taken place within institutional circles as well as the film industry itself? The history of films about political institutions, leaders and events cannot avoid a legacy that has seen mixed reactions at the box office and this notion of political economy, outlined earlier in the chapter, needs to be aware of the many and varied political and social forces beyond the textual reading that hinder objective analysis. It is the intention, however, to dispel at least one notion that financial takings must initially predispose one to regard this as a rejection of any fundamental political philosophy gaining kudos with the audience. In addition, it would be hard to contest fully the aesthetic underpinning of these films in Maltby's reading of political texts as often being ones that conform to previous generic forms, be it western or gangster or screwball traditions.[43]

Yet the palatability of Hollywood politics is the strength of its ideological form; its politics is a stealthy progress of thought and persuasion moving towards a set of ideals that are themselves recognisable and yet have remained debatable within American society. Terry Christensen's criticism that Hollywood is reduced to articulating only general and consensual politics would, in fact, be a triumph of singular conformity in itself, if it were true.[44] The ability to manufacture a consensual political dialogue is no small feat, and in actual fact Hollywood's history tells us

that this has, in any case, not been possible. Hollywood has followed
the fashion for debate about contemporary political ideas, and moved
with the changing times as much as scholars and politicians themselves have. But values and principles that constitute the exceptionalism
of the republic are a different matter. They tend to be more endemic
and reflective of societal convention rather than simply ideological
assertion, and as such their appearance within this artistic medium
should surprise no one.

Christensen's further contention that 'politics is trivialized, reduced
to the need for occasional individual action to regulate an essentially
good, smoothly functioning process by pointing out flaws in the form
of bad individuals and sometimes bad organizations likes gangs,
machines and corporations' is a fine argument for the debate about
individualism in Hollywood film and political society, but his focus is
as much about ideology through narrative convention and character
realisation of the heroic protagonists as it is about other, equally
important, structural and stylistic elements.[45]

This book attempts to fashion both a history of political ideology
through film, and a history of cultural politics that demonstrates
Hollywood as having political depth as well as moving towards a
postmodern discourse of what Federic Jameson has described as
'depthlessness'.[46] The iconic visual spectacle and rhetorically simplistic
individual discourse, I would argue, is matched by the strong presence
of ideological and institutional political ideas. This history and ideology
is represented in the book by a roughly chronological, but more or less
thematic investigation into films on politics. Thematic because 'films
about politics' as opposed to merely 'political films' have a particular
set of sub-genres that have never really been defined and located
within film theory, or by film historians. Films dealing with elections
for instance, or biographies of political personalities, have often been
categorised together with other fictional accounts, rather than discussed on their own terms, and those categorisations now deserve
special attention.

American politics has been operating under an assumed artificiality
in Hollywood for most of its history. Some of that artificial nature is the
overblown effect of thematic convention and genre personification.
Hollywood, of course, makes sweeping gestures towards its democratic
heritage. But while the seeming desire to neglect or refute 'isms' in
American life appears a play for dogged self-reliance upon Hollywood's

part, its adoption of political rhetoric has continued the debate about the aesthetics of pluralist democracy and its institutions in the United States, as Beverly Kelley persuasively argues, and it serves to elucidate the notion that the political structure is a complex and constantly shifting collective.[47] In its purest form, Hollywood exists to legitimate those dominant institutions and their value systems, as Ryan and Kellner have argued, and it is the form, content and possible divergence from that legitimation that the following chapters set out to examine.[48]

## NOTES

1  Steve Allen, 'Foreword', in *Reelpolitik: Political Ideologies in '30s and '40s Films*, ed. Beverly Merrill Kelley with John J. Pitney, jun., Craig R. Smith and Herbert E. Gooch III (Westport, CT: Praeger, 1998) p. xv.

2  In particular see Andy Willis, 'Cultural Studies and Popular Film', in *Approaches to Popular Film*, ed. Joanne Hollows and Mark Jancovich (Manchester: Manchester University Press, 1995) pp. 178–84.

3  George Perry, 'Power Cuts', *The Sunday Times* Magazine, 10 January 1999, pp. 70–3.

4  Albert Boime, *The Unveiling of National Icons: A Plea for Patriotic Iconoclasm* (Cambridge: Cambridge University Press, 1998).

5  Ibid. p. 9.

6  Robert Hughes, 'Behind the Sacred Aura', *Time Magazine*, 11 November 1996, pp. 104–6.See also Boime, *The Unveiling of National Icons*, p. 3.

7  Michael Foley, *American Political Ideas* (Manchester: Manchester University Press, 1991) pp. 151–2.

8  Eric Smoodin,'"Compulsory" Viewing for Every Citizen: *Mr. Smith* and the Rhetoric of Reception', *Cinema Journal*, vol. 35, no. 2, Winter 1996, pp. 3–23.

9  Allen Rostron,'Mr. Carter Goes to Washington', *Journal of Popular Film and Television*, vol. 25, no. 2, Summer 1997, pp. 57–67.

10  Lauren Berlant, 'The Theory of Infantile Citizenship', *Public Culture*, vol. 5, no. 3, Spring 1993, pp. 395–410.

11  Theodor Adorno and Max Horkheimer, 'The Culture Industry: Enlightenment as Mass Deception', in their *The Dialectic of Enlightenment* (London: Verso, 1979).

12  For a more comprehensive overview of 'political economy' in film, see Joanne Hollows,'Mass Culture and Political Economy', in *Approaches to Popular Film*, ed. Hollows and Jancovich, pp. 153–6.

13  Phil Melling, 'The Mind of the Mob', in *Cinema, Politics and Society*, ed.

Philip Davies and Brian Neve (Manchester: Manchester University Press, 1981) pp. 21–4.

14 Brian Neve, *Film and Politics in America: A Social Tradition* (London: Routledge, 1992) p. 2.

15 Joseph McBride, *Frank Capra: The Catastrophe of Success* (London: Faber & Faber, 1992) p. 424.

16 Christopher Lasch, *The True and Only Heaven: Progress and Its Critics* (New York: Norton, 1991) pp. 82–119.

17 Michael Kelley, 'The Game and The Show', *The Guardian*, Weekend, 20 November 1993, pp. 6–16.

18 Ibid. p. 8.

19 Allan Lloyd Smith, 'Is there an American Culture?', in *Culture*, ed. Richard Maidment and Jeremy Mitchell (London: Hodder & Stoughton, 1994) p. 307.

20 Joan Goodman, 'How Hollywood Whispers', *The Sunday Times Magazine*, 23 March 1997, p. 18.

21 Davies and Neve, *Cinema, Politics and Society*, p. 16.

22 Marshall McCluhan, *Understanding Media* (New York: Signet, 1964).

23 Eleanor Ringel, 'Boomers Go Bust in too True Colors', *Atlanta Journal Constitution* on the Net, www.accessatlanta.com 25 March 1998.

24 Robert Rosenstone, *Revisioning History: Film and the Construction of a New Past* (New Jersey: Princeton University Press, 1994).

25 Robert Brent Toplin, *History by Hollywood: The Use and Abuse of the American Past* (Chicago: University of Illinois Press, 1996).

26 Among many reviews and commentaries that have appeared in recent years, two of the most interesting that take up the themes of the contemporary era and link them to fictional Hollywood material are: Martin Walker, 'Clinton's Hollywood', *Sight and Sound*, September 1993, p. 19; Mark Steyn, 'Whiter-than-White House', *Daily Telegraph*, 6 December 1995.

27 Graham K. Wilson, *Only in America: The Politics of the United States in a Contemporary Perspective* (Chatham, NJ: Chatham House, 1998) p. 11.

28 Tom Curry, 'Hollywood's Take on Politics', *MSNBC* on the Net, www.msnbc.com

29 Locke's *Second Treatise on Government*, published in 1690, became the work that was to dominate American thinking in later generations. It took its influence from Hobbes's *Leviathan* published in 1651 and Harrington's *Commonwealth of Oceana* in 1656. See Kenneth M. Dolbeare, *American Political Thought*, 2nd edn (Chatham, NJ: Chatham House, 1989) pp. 19–20.

30 Louis Hartz, *The Liberal Tradition in America* (New York: Harcourt Brace, 1955).

31 Tim Hames and Nicol Rae, *Governing America* (Manchester: Manchester University Press, 1996) pp. 47–9.

32 Ian Scott, 'Mr Innocence Goes to Washington: Hollywood and the Mythology of American Politics', in *Representing and Imagining America*, ed. Philip Davies (Keele: Keele University Press, 1996) p. 238.

33 J. R. Pole, *The Pursuit of Equality in American History* (Berkeley: University of California Press, 1978).

34 John Zvesper, 'Ethnicity and "Race" in American Politics', in *Democracy*, ed. Richard Maidment (London: Hodder & Stoughton, 1994) pp. 159–82.

35 Benjamin Franklin, *The Means and Manner of Obtaining Virtue* (London: Penguin, 1995).

36 Jeff Dawson, 'All the President's Mien', *The Times*, 9 March 1998, p. 20.

37 Daniel Bell, 'The End of American Exceptionalism', in *The American Commonwealth*, ed. Nathan Glazer and Irving Kristol (New York: Basic, 1976) p. 209.

38 Steven Kautz, *Liberalism and Community* (Ithaca, NY: Cornell University Press, 1995) p. 28.

39 Glenn Alan Phelps, 'The Populist Films of Frank Capra', *Journal of American Studies*, vol. 13, 1979. pp. 377–92.

40 Ibid. p. 389.

41 Herbert Gans, *Middle American Individualism* (New York: Free Press, 1988).

42 Ibid. p. 211.

43 Richard Maltby, *Hollywood Cinema* (Oxford: Blackwell, 1995) p. 368.

44 Terry Christensen, *Reel Politics: American Political Movies from Birth of a Nation to Platoon* (New York: Blackwell, 1987) p. 212.

45 Ibid. p. 212.

46 Federic Jameson, *Postmodernism: or, The Cultural Logic of Late Capitalism* (London: Verso, 1991).

47 Kelley, *Reelpolitik*, p. 164.

48 Michael Ryan and Douglas Kellner, *Camera Politica: The Politics and Ideology of Contemporary Hollywood Film* (Bloomington: Indiana University Press, 1988).

*Chapter 2*

# POLITICAL FILMS IN
# THE CLASSIC STUDIO ERA

———— ⇒⊂ ————

People . . . All of them coming to Washington to get something. Why
does nobody come to Washington to give something?

B. G. Brown in *Washington Merry-Go-Round*

The stock market crash on Wall Street in October 1929 changed the
United States forever. The ensuing Depression created an era as
enriching and vibrant culturally, as it was shattering and despondent
economically. It heralded the arrival of New York Democrat Franklin
Delano Roosevelt (FDR) as president and the 1930s became a decade
when the cult of political personality finally surfaced as the dominant
force in public life. Roosevelt's leadership of America stood not only in
sharp contrast to the proceeding Republican era of Harding, Coolidge
and Hoover, but to almost all other eras as well. By sheer force of will
he manœuvred himself on to the pedestal previously occupied only by
those pantheon of immortals, Washington, Jefferson and Lincoln.

It was in no small way the very personal nature of his campaigning
and leadership that quickly established Roosevelt as a forceful, but also
a divisive figure in a nation where interpretations of his vision veered
between conservative capitalism and dangerous socialism with equal
alacrity. But his methods gave politicians a whole new public identity,
and one that has gone on to be cloned in American politics ever since.
As Tony Badger has explained, Roosevelt 'delighted in the open exercise
of his personal political skills' and he was not alone either in making
character, style and rhetoric the chief reference points for any examination of his aims and record.[1] Figures like Huey Long, Alben Barkley,
and members of Roosevelt's own cabinet such as Harry Hopkins
and Frances Perkins, all brought an individual, self-contained slant to
politics in America during these years. Fronting an administration that
treated communication as a policy tool, the New Deal became an

exercise in pragmatic and, often, dispassionate political management, rather more than complex Keynesian economics which Roosevelt only vaguely comprehended and largely disavowed.

In maintaining a very direct contact with the people through his fireside chats – weekly radio broadcasts to the nation – Roosevelt helped to reinvigorate that which he considered most dangerous both to his own success and to the future of American democracy: public faith in political institutions. As Phil Melling notes, the 'theatrical' style of the President on radio, or film, generated a sympathy and support for his presidency that kept more dangerous intellectual forces at bay.[2] It may have been true that the United States was on the verge of revolution in 1932, but it was a revolution borne out of frustration and indifference on Washington's part to certain very vocal members of the population.[3] Roosevelt's revolution, following his election, was a much quieter affair, a steady, unrelenting, but more or less conservative reformulation that, as Carl Degler has explained, 'purged the American people of their belief in the limited powers of the federal government and convinced them of the necessity of the guarantor state'.[4]

Culturally the most visible sign of the New Deal's burgeoning commitment to the arts came with the federal projects in painting, theatre and especially writing, all components of the larger Works Progress Administration (WPA).[5] These projects recognised the needs of struggling companies and individuals and they would later be seen as the training ground for many of America's leading exponents in the arts. The one field that the New Deal had no reason to aid was of course movies. A number of writers who benefited from New Deal projects like the Federal Theatre – especially in New York where talent was strong – would later graduate to Hollywood, and the studios generally supported agencies like the National Recovery Act (NRA), although mainly on the pretext of returning prosperity and successful capital entrepreneurship rather than egalitarian redistribution; a critical distinction in a town where the moguls were almost uniformly Republican in outlook.

Hollywood, however, was by no means immune to economic difficulties and the effect of the Depression was certainly apparent, particularly during 1931 and 1932. RKO and Paramount Studios were put in the hands of receivers at this time, as Colin Shindler notes, and Warner Brothers lost a combined total of $22 million in just two years, having made a combined profit of $24 million in 1929–30.[6] The prophets of doom, however, soon became just profits again. Roosevelt's long-standing notification of his passion for movies, together with his constant refuelling of unabashed optimism, helped Hollywood out of its depression long before the time of his first re-election in 1936. The administration had forged a partnership with the film community and one that came to reveal itself ever more forcefully in Hollywood output during the 1930s. As Shindler has surmised: 'Together they metaphorically sang and danced through the decade, echoing each other's ringing declarations of confidence and pointing to each other as inspiring symbols of recovery from past troubles and optimism for the future.'[7]

In 1932 Roosevelt had considered that partnership important enough to coax Jack Warner on board for the election campaign, and, although a long-standing Republican, the problems for his studio, and the mess in the country at large, encouraged Warner to feel that FDR was the strong man needed to lead America out of the Depression. The studio even took out an advertisement in *Variety* in January 1933 proclaiming that the United States was on the verge of a 'new start' with a new leader at the helm.

Artistically Warners took on the New Deal imagery almost straight away with William Wellman's film, *Heroes for Sale*, in July 1933. Using a familiar plot structure replicated in such classics as *I am a Fugitive from a Chain Gang* (1932), the studio forged a growing reputation for tackling social issues with the story of a forgotten man enduring the worst effects of the Depression.

Ironically enough, by the time the film was released, Roosevelt had practically patented his own version of heroic optimism and *Heroes* was viewed, remarkably enough, as rather cautious in its endorsement of New Deal principles. Russell Campbell's detailed analysis of the film points not only to a somewhat confused narrative structure but also to its poor box-office returns.[8] He determines that this was not down to the mere rejection of social realism on the public's part, but actually the slow beginning of an attempt to mould public perceptions in the direction of social debate and 'forestall any radical sentiment among the dispossessed'.[9] The relationship with government has thus begun to be cemented and Hollywood proceeded to envelop itself more and more in New Deal values as a symbolic and literal metaphor for a number of its vehicles as the decade progressed.

Many scholars like Melling are, however, critical of placing too much emphasis on the 1930s in general, and the New Deal in particular, as the active inculcate of a new cultural consciousness. Richard Maltby sees the moguls merely as simplistic artisans who ravaged history for the defining concepts of American populist tradition, and then gave it a refined cultural identity. Such notions cannot be easily dismissed. One would have to accept, for instance, that Hollywood's awakening to the possibility of narratives on politics was hardly a concerted movement as the number of films going into production at the time testifies to; and Maltby is surely correct in thinking that a combination of the moguls' moderate ideological stance, the overseeing facility of the Production Code, and the public's lacklustre response to ideologically thought-provoking cinema, was a sure dilution of any enforced trend.

Yet whether commercially successful or not, ideologically liberated to pursue their causes or otherwise, films with political themes centred on Washington did go into production in greater numbers, and whilst these projects may have appeared populist or even escapist in tone, pervasive democratic ideas seeped through their storylines and infiltrated their visual spectacle in a concentration sufficient to engage public consciousness and liberate political thought from the shackles of Hollywood regulation. Indeed the attention given in recent years to audience reception as theoretical study demonstrates a public, even in the 1930s, whose capacity for social and political drama was far more exacting than has previously been acknowledged. Scholars in this field, such as Eric Smoodin, have noted how the reaction through official and fan correspondence, to 1930s' films like *Mr Smith Goes to Washington*, opened debates among audiences about the efficacy of American democracy.[10]

Much of the output concerned with politics and society in the 1930s also came to resemble President Roosevelt's own intuitive recognition of that crisis of confidence in the public mind towards their democratic experiment: had the institutions of the Founding Fathers let them down in their hour of most need? Hollywood in the Depression cried out with a resounding no! Shady businessmen, crooked politicians, and misunderstood patriots were all brought centrestage in films that portrayed them as the harbingers of America's economic misery, and not the sacred scriptures of the Constitution. This in a decade when, for the first time, the studios and directors contemplated Washington as the setting for a new genre; that of the political drama.

The New Deal, therefore, became the major inspiration for the establishment of the social problem film because, as Roffman and Purdy explain, 'a hungry and insecure audience needed the psychic relief and rejuvenation of entertainment films but also demanded that filmmakers give at least token recognition to the ever-pressing realities of the time'.[11] But the New Deal influence not only challenged the political elite on the economics of the American Dream in films like *Heroes for Sale* and King Vidor's *Our Daily Bread* (1934); it also challenged the theoretical and institutional doctrines upon which the republic itself had been founded. In order to do this political films of the 1930s encompassed history, played on the patriotic triumphalism of the populace towards their iconic symbols, and educated the audience (electorate) in the complexities of legislative representation: in short, they taught political science.

This should not allow us to get carried away by suddenly interpreting the studios as political neophytes. Hollywood remained very wary of taking on board the responsibilities for social regeneration and crisis management in the Depression, it certainly increased its output even more in the staples of comedy and musicals, and it almost certainly never regarded itself at this particular time as a haven for the kind of European cinematic neo-realism that would infuse Hollywood immediately after the war. But social thought in the United States was changing during these years and influential writers like John Dewey subjected the notion of community to rigorous examination and forcefully argued for public participation in moving the 'Great Community' on towards a 'Great Society' as he described it.[12] This was the essence of democracy in Dewey's eyes, the widespread participation and interaction of the public in social and organisational functions of the state.

Hollywood was one such organisational structure. Then as now its actions as a collective forum and its ability to preach participatory discourse promoted what Richard Maltby has described as 'restrained respectability' for society.[13] Such an analysis might easily lead us on a path back to populist sentimentality, the ideology of fond recollection for times past, as the driving force in 1930s' political and social films. Dewey for one reflected upon the need to distinguish between social and political democracy, between the practitioners of policy and the enveloping ideals of historical nationhood.

But Hollywood, in its political films of the 1930s and 1940s, also consciously blurred the lines of that distinction in attempting to make populism an active inclusory ideal. It did not simply hark back to a bygone agrarian era therefore, nor immerse itself in a parochial neigh-bourly cause as is often determined, but sought to examine the social pathology that had seemingly caused drift and distraction in America, the roots of a divisive agenda that had sensed political participation on the wane. In defence of a political tradition that had experienced crisis before, Hollywood reminded its audience of the force of personality through history, and thus traced the roots of great men that had shaped its history and, indirectly of course, gave a boost to the elevation of FDR into that company. It should be regarded as no coincidence that two of the finest and most influential directors of their generation should begin and end the decade with biographies of Abraham Lincoln. Both D. W. Griffith's eponymously titled 1930 portrait and John Ford's epic examination of the sixteenth president's early life, *Young Mr Lincoln*, are joined by their saintly invocation of a new Lincoln figure – that is, Roosevelt – a plea for and praise given for the arrival of a similar political saviour.

Political biography might have appeared the most credible and effective way to convey the power of democratic experience and yet, apart from these two conspicuous examples, it was not the genre that Hollywood made extensive use of in the 1930s. It was instead going to implant melodrama upon Washington, but also come to realise that the staples of comedy and romance were the real keys to a stealthy ideological support of liberal democracy.

In the first instance Hollywood's dive into the political maelstrom was not a commercial godsend in the early part of the decade. Indeed the rise of what became the social problem film looked distinctly threadbare when set against the popularity of musicals (Busby Berkeley leading the way and exploiting the early fascination with sound), westerns, or romantic, screwball comedies. But the offshoot of an increased political awareness had already initially raised its head in other genres than those directly to do with politics. Most particularly in gangster movies the notion of state power, political infighting and the long-established battles in machine politics gave an authenticism to *The Public Enemy* (1931), *Scarface* (1932) and later *Angels with Dirty Faces* (1938). The legalistic and social examinations that had connections to the gangster genre were most carefully intimated in courtroom dramas like *Public Defender* (1931), and in moral presentations like the aforementioned *I am a Fugitive from a Chain Gang* (1932). Carefully because studios like Warner Brothers, who made *I am a Fugitive*, were

well aware of the delicate political debates they were entering into and
how any attack on what might be considered a pillar of the American
community could bring the attention of state or federal politicians to
film content, or the studios own hired gun, Will Hays, overseer of the
Production Code.[14]

The figure of 'Czar' Hays and the directionalism of the body he
oversaw, the Motion Pictures Producers and Distributors of America
(MPPDA), were two variables that came to affect political films most
readily. As early as 1915, the Supreme Court in the *Mutual Film
Corporation* vs. *Ohio* ruling effectively stated that the movies did not
have the protection of the first amendment to the Constitution. They
therefore could not say what they liked, and further they had to be
purveyors of ideas and events in the public domain, not as a force for
their own independent values that could be somehow deemed 'evil'.[15]
Later legislation such as the Hudson and Neeley Pettigell anti-trust
Bills in the 1930s hammered home this mantra of responsibility and
morality upon the studios as well as attacking its economic monopoly.

Even before this time, however, any link to examinations of the
democratic process was, at the very least, being dubiously frowned
upon. The precursor to the Hays Office, the self-regulatory National
Association of the Motion Picture Industry, had its president, William
A. Brady, publicise its thirteen points, first introduced in March 1921.[16]
Point nine of the thirteen talked of the need to avoid stories or scenes
'which ridicule or deprecate public officials, officers of the law, the
United States army, the United States navy, or other governmental
authority, or which tend to weaken the authority of the law'.[17]

The MPPDA (Hays Office) already had a blueprint then for the pillars
of decency and taste as well as the means to curb extremist political
sentiment. By the 1930s, they added direct intervention to their repertoire by making statements about the content of certain pictures and
forcing 'artistic' changes. And yet the outlook of the studios and Hays
himself towards filmmaking was actually quite similar. As Hays himself
said, self-regulation was his goal and beyond that he really wanted to
educate the movie-going public.[18] He recognised the capacity within
films for peddling what could be construed as dangerous social dogma,
and thus he shared a critical position with the studios in supporting
the overtly educational nature of the presentation of institutional
structures.

Although almost all films framed their narratives within the contemporary era, their slights at recent economic collapse and political incompetence amounted to only half the story. Many sought to reaffirm the doctrines of institutional authority and content themselves with the perceived menace of rogue, dictatorial ambition among reckless charlatans. Early restrictions on the portrayal of public figures in the 1930s were flouted therefore, as many were portrayed as weak and corrupt, but the pay-off was a steadfast loyalty to the system itself.

The studios, critics, congress and indeed the general public all had their own reasons for being suspicious of directors and/or producers who embarked on political films but, in retrospect, many, if not all, films of the era upheld and even reinforced the status quo. Not a great surprise perhaps when the chair of the California Republican Party was Louis B. Mayer, a man who helped to scupper the challenge of left-wing writer Upton Sinclair in his bid for the governorship of the state in 1934.[19] The tarnishing of Sinclair as a radical communist only helped to feed the reactionary and fearful mentality of the studios at this time.[20] The result of such conservatism may have still been a long way from producing an anodyne presentation of politics at work, but the difficulty lay in extracting an ounce more political commentary out of the films they were championing for more daring producers like Darryl Zanuck.

Zanuck could easily be equated with a sentimentalist ethos represented by his production of John Ford's *The Grapes of Wrath* (1939) – the apotheosis of cinematic New Dealism – but, although it does contain slices of trifling emotion, his presentation of *Wilson* (1944) five years later was in many ways a more virtuous achievement. This is because, like his contemporaries Griffith, Capra and Ford, Zanuck encouraged director Henry King to put at the forefront of this endorsement of democratic righteousness the moral foundations of upstanding heroic characterisation, channelled through the fundamental American ideology of individualism.

The protagonists of 1930s' political films are invested with a similar gravitas, and thus the heroes of *Washington Masquerade* (1932), *Washington Merry-Go-Round*, *Gabriel over the White House* and *Mr Smith Goes to Washington* all plea for justice and accountability, and above all for faith in the political system realised through the moral principles of individual self-reliance and attainment. These heroes do at times seek outcomes which produce moral and democratic ambiguities; and in undeniably setting out to destroy what Roffman and Purdy call the 'shyster cycle' of double-dealing financiers and entrepreneurs that are causing social and political breakdown, they are conscious of manipulating the process and breaking the rules to pursue their causes successfully.[21]

Publications of the time like *Variety* conveniently viewed these films as merely treating politicians as noble statesmen (which was the trade paper's assertion about *Washington Merry-Go-Round* for example) but really Hollywood was undertaking the greater task of displaying to its audience the viability of their institutions more than the wholesome goodness of politicians who inhabited Washington. The heroes were not the real guardians of democracy in these films, the Founding Fathers and the Constitution were. The words, sentiments and doctrines of American democracy infuse all of the pictures discussed below and if, as Hollywood opined, the heroes could ride in and out of town in time to rescue their honour and fall in love with the heroine, that did not disguise the fact that the Constitution remained their bible of faith.

In essence then political films of the 1930s became not only a template for this genre of Hollywood movie down through the ages, but soon broke away from the economic remit of depression era social anxiety films like *Heroes for Sale* and *Our Daily Bread*, towards a conscious genre that amplified a more solid endorsement of democratic principles and institutional ascendancy.

## INSIDE THE CORRIDORS OF POWER

In its 1932 review of the film, the magazine *Photoplay* described *Washington Merry-Go-Round* as a story that 'tears the veil from conditions in this country' and goes on to depict James Cruze as a director, 'hammering home his truths with brass knuckles'.[22] Appreciated for its no holds barred stance on the political system even then, *Washington Merry-Go-Round* made quite a stir in Hollywood and the capital in what was a presidential election year. Adapted by Jo Swirling, from a stageplay by Maxwell Anderson, the film was subject to exhaustive scrutiny by executives of Columbia Pictures, including the head Harry Cohn, resulting in the final cut deleting, for example, one potentially inflammatory scene showing a politician being flung onto the Capitol steps by a lynch mob. Although it was made just prior to the more rigid enforcement of the Production Code, Columbia were well aware of the advance publicity the film was getting and felt obliged to indulge in the sort of compromise cuts needed to make the picture acceptable, resulting in a pale imitation of what might have been.[23]

In actual fact *Washington Merry-Go-Round* already had a significant cinematic precedent before it and one that had revealed the difficulty of commercial viability for the political film. MGM's early 1932 vehicle for Lionel Barrymore, *Washington Masquerade*, took a not dissimilar route through Capitol graft and deceit to reveal a system wracked by duplicitous gold-diggers. Barrymore played prospective man of the people Jefferson Keane, who is elected to the Senate on a promise to expose corruption but who is caught in a web of blackmail himself when seduced by classic vamp Consuela Fairbanks (Karen Morley). Keane, armed with the symbolism of his historical name, and an equally Jeffersonian background from rural Kansas, really does love Fairbanks, gives up his position and marries her, but comes to regret his choice. He resolves to return to Washington and get the Senate Investigation Committee to hold hearings into procedure but tragedy ensues in the final reel.

While the film's potential audience in Britain was isolated by its intricate portrayal of the workings of Washington, as a number of reviews noted, in America the comments were foreshadowed by the predicament of the Depression.[24] *Variety* summed up the feeling in their review by noting that the anticipated box-office nosedive of the movie would be predicated upon the fact that the people were left sour at this time to portrayals of federal politicians honourably looking to rejuvenate the political system.[25] In addition, the MGM connection and Keane's grandiose speeches – a reference to Valley Forge is directly copied by President Judson Hammond in 1933's *Gabriel over the White House* – seemed to suggest a possible covert Republican agenda in the film, and a not unsympathetic nod to the problems befalling Herbert Hoover at that very time.[26]

Despite the lacklustre reception to this film, and possibly because they were still a poverty row 'B' movie studio with less to lose than the majors, Columbia went ahead less than a year later and produced *Washington Merry-Go-Round*, a film that still retains all the classic hallmarks of the archetypal political film. Although characterisation – particularly the similarities of Keane to B. G. Brown – could be seen to be disseminated from *Washington Masquerade*, *Merry-Go-Round* really had the prototype political narrative and one that was a personal influence on Frank Capra's own classic *Mr Smith Goes to Washington* later in the decade.

B. G. Brown (Lee Tracey) is elected to the House of Representatives playing to the whims of his home state's political machine. Set against the backdrop of the Bonus March in Washington in 1932, we learn of Brown's own war veteran status and he is given the opportunity, as hero and self-made spokesperson for the cause, to address the campaigners in the Hoovervilles set up only a few blocks from the White House itself, thanks to a chance meeting with an old buddy, 'Beef' Brannigan.[27] Brown though uses the informal address as a platform on which to lambast the audience of ex-veterans and dropouts for their shoddy patriotism and lack of personal responsibility. 'You call yourselves ex-servicemen, well why don't you become *servicemen* [my emphasis]', he cajoles the audience.

The premise of the narrative ensures that Brown's arrival in Washington is not designed as the return of a saviour, a true reformer; but that it is one who seeks redemption by setting out to destroy the machine that got him elected in the first place. Brown admits that he won his race because of the fraudulent buying of votes in his state by political boss Kelleher, and he further admits that he doesn't really understand the workings of the political system, despite the fact that he rails about the need to protect its key documents in a scene set inside the National Archive. In fact, Brown's election is not one that climaxes in the triumph of crusading populism at all, as a conventional interpretation might imply. Rather, his motive is revenge, and a revenge that becomes personal by the conclusion, thanks to the evil tycoon Norton who ruthlessly dispatches opponents like Brown's friend, the Prohibition Department official Tilden, and the corrupted Senator Wylie.

Aware of the ambiguous nature of the hero's agenda, Cruze frames his story always with the backdrop of historical convention and democratic symbols in mind. The early scenes, for example, relay the heritage of Brown's name, B. G., standing for Button Gwinnett, thus revealing that his ancestry dates back to one of the actual signatories of the Declaration of Independence. Cruze also establishes the presence of iconic symbolism early in the piece – Brown's chance meeting with Brannigan is relocated to the steps of the Capitol with the dome in the background – and, together with his set-piece address to companion Alice while gazing at the Declaration of Independence, the director also uses Brown's objections in the House to the Digger Bill as a chance to relay the ideological libertarian sentiment within the film. Brown clearly opposes the bill (HR417) to build a monument – a running commentary itself in the film on the significance of heritage – to some unknown (a fictitious General Digger) whom he describes as a man who merely went round 'killing Indians', and yet he despises the lack of debate over the bill even more. It presents the audience with a tacit example of pork-barrelling and of its kind is a more illicit and shocking denunciation of congressional activity than, say, Jefferson Smith's fight against the Willet Creek Dam appropriation in *Mr Smith*.

The denouement sees Brown collate together all the bribery and misdemeanours that Norton has been engaged in around Washington by having him watched using the veterans who Norton is allegedly helping – by sending them food parcels – but who he is really using to put pressure on the administration through prolonging their hopeless protest, and thus camouflaging his foreign mining interests and protection by the US army in South America. Yet all the 'evidence' acquired is not for the purposes of bringing Norton to any kind of legal or approved justice; it is a cyclical narrative device in order for Brown to provide Norton, in conclusion, with the same option he, Norton, offered the discredited Tilden at the beginning of the film, the chance to cheat justice by taking his own life. The closure leaves Brown's position as congressional representative at best unresolved – he has been through the process of a recall election in his state – and the downfall of Norton seemingly creates a void that the film implies could be filled at any minute by any number of other unscrupulous operators in Washington. Add to this Alice Wylie's need to be smothered by Brown in the back seat of the car at the climax of the film – undermining what had been up until that point a remarkably feminist agenda for its time – and *Washington Merry-Go-Round* clearly defines some of the uncertainties of closure at the heart of political movies. Publications like *Photoplay* and the *Cinema Booking Guide Supplement* acclaimed the film for its 'finely fluid direction' and Lee Tracey's 'vigorous and like-able performance' as Brown.[28] Outside the United States, the film was interestingly renamed *Invisible Power* and directed audiences to the more melodramatic aspects of the picture.

The American title concentrated its focus on the social whirl of parties, receptions and gatherings which, as Alice informs Brown, is where the real business of Washington is carried out. The darker

undercurrent of the European title, however, is that the phrase, the
Washington merry-go-round, is used in Tilden's parting confession,
the letter to Brown that is received after his death and is the signal to
him of foul play in the highest circles. Thus the European direction of
the film pointed to its less than ambiguous violent intent only rein-
forcing the spectre of death and sacrificial loss that is never far away in
all of these films. Indeed the gangster genre might be interpreted as
having a far greater impact than at first acknowledged, shown in even
more stark relief by Gregory La Cava's 1933 picture, *Gabriel over the
White House*.

In this film, the narrative draws upon contemporary social dislocation
by pushing political authority towards a widespread clampdown on the
activities of organised crime. Walter Huston plays Judson Hammond,
recently elected as president with a strong Depression-era remit to
solve the economic problems of America. The opening scenes of the
film present not an archetypal 'movie politician' as Roffman and Purdy
argue for, but simply an archetypal politician. Hammond's public
pronouncements about curing the Depression, his rather hollow references to the spirit of Gettysburg, the Argonne and Valley Forge, are the
prophetic initiation of what we would readily interpret today as convenient soundbites for the eager and attentive press corps hanging on
his every word. As Hammond makes clear to his state cronies at the
inauguration reception, he intends to do nothing more than enjoy his
time in the White House and exploit the privileges of the office.

In political terms the film initially puts Hammond in the camp of
Hoover Republicanism offering platitudes to the effect that the
Depression will cure itself, while setting up a plot development that
will see him miraculously, quite literally, turned into a Rooseveltian
(and at the end of the film Wilsonian) Democrat.[29]

Thus La Cava initiates a narrative rite of passage that is bookended
by a road to Damascus conversion for Hammond, the product of a
near fatal car crash that leaves him in a coma. Here he is visited upon
by the Archangel Gabriel and given the chance to seek redemption for
his uncaring actions in a few brief months of life afforded to him. At
first, seemingly zombiefied by his impossible recovery, Hammond goes
about abusing his position by sacking his cabinet and beginning a
vigilante crusade to rid the streets of bootleg gangsterism, the trail of
heavy-handed revenge being taken up where Cruze's *Merry-Go-Round*
left off. With the help of his secretary Beekman, who assumes military

Fig. 1 *Judson Hammond (Walter Huston) addresses notions of fascist dictatorship and totalitarianism in* Gabriel Over the White House *(BFI Films: Stills, posters and designs).*
Gabriel over the White House © 1933 *Turner Entertainment Co.*
*A Time Warner Company. All Rights Reserved.*

status rather suddenly and inexplicably, Hammond ends the reign of arch-villain Nick Diamond, has a kangaroo court try and sentence him to swift execution, and then unites himself with John Bronson's unemployed workers in a New Deal-like programme of welfare and job creation.

This breakneck early narrative pace offers a sympathetic account of a 'good dictatorship' on the one hand, but the film's editing clearly diverts the attention from any more dubious fascistic undercurrents. One ending suggested manslaughter for Hammond to break the chain of totalitarian rule, but the idea of life being spiritually whisked away from him adds a convenient twist for closure of his radical policies. This paradigm is even more considerably diverted in the final third of the film which takes its literal symbolism too far by making Hammond a bullying convertor of the world's imperial powers towards peace, freedom and the democratic values that, as he says, the United States holds so dear.[30] In fine Wilsonian tradition it is to be Hammond's great wish that the world can live in peace and harmony with each other.

Although plainly concerned with the domestically institutional machinations of solving the Depression, *Gabriel*, like *Washington Merry-Go-Round* before it, and *The President Vanishes* (1935) following, also engaged with a contemporaneous foreign policy sub-plot and strong revisionist values extolling America's place in the world. Screenwriter Jo Swirling was extremely careful in *Merry-Go-Round* not wholly to extend Brown's patriotic triumphalism to his service in World War One. He says in his initial speech in the camp that 'maybe some of us didn't know what we were fighting for, maybe this country was never in any danger but man it's in danger now', conveniently pitching the Bonus Army protest into the greater maelstrom of social dislocation that was occurring, but not endorsing America's participation in 1917–18 outright. Brown criticises the marchers – thus towing an official government line – while attaching them to the hidden forces of Norton who has his own foreign policy agenda in Latin America, where troops are stationed to protect his mining interests.

Although only briefly dwelt upon, Norton is envisaged as a scheming pillager of assets in the region which was a familiar and controversial criticism of American policy in Central and Latin America at the time. Significantly the film pre-dates, but almost prophesies, Roosevelt's 'Good Neighbour' policy which he invoked on coming to power and thus removed a significant amount of American military commitment to the region.

## CHRISTIAN SYMBOLISM, ICONOGRAPHY AND REPRESENTATION

*Gabriel over the White House*, by the very nature of its title and composition, built heavily upon the religious ethic that infused other social problem films of the 1930s. John Ford's *The Grapes of Wrath*, as perhaps the most famous example, took the 'biblical' nature of the dust bowl famine, and the 'exodus' it caused, as almost literal depictions of a new spiritual awakening within America. In *Gabriel*, the Depression was still the mainstay of Hammond's Christian mission – as relayed to him through the archangel Gabriel whose spirit he temporarily inherits – but it also suffused the concluding theories on American internationalism at the end of the film; and it was built upon and became intrinsic to many other political pictures through the examination of loyalty and doubt in institutional politics as well as personal relationships.

What I am interested in pursuing here is not a dialogue about Christian moralism *per se*, or any real religious devotion or toleration. Of the films discussed in this chapter, some – one in particular – have been given Catholic rather than Protestant meaning to their symbolic rituals, while others may be seen as appropriately secular in the American tradition. In reference to political films, however, it seems apparent to me that the placement, position and reverence of characters to political institutions, and their wider mythic interpretation, are the broadly defined Christian symbolism at the heart of this genre. These films seek to encourage devotion to the American creed certainly, but are at once the temples on which the education of democratic discourse, and the entreaty to participation, are in addition built.

In *Washington Merry-Go-Round* B. G. Brown rallies and directs his disciples to rise up from their wasteland in the veterans camp and reject their lot in life. In *Gabriel over the White House*, Judson Hammond is redeemed by the ethereal presence of the Archangel Gabriel who teaches not just the need to confront one's own mortality but also to practise a new kind of political statesmanship. Directors like James Cruze and Gregory La Cava thus initiated this particular style of communal activity in their political films. No director, however, honed the technique or revisited the site of this iconic devotionalism as many times as Frank Capra.

Capra's track record as the chronicler of the American condition in the 1930s and 1940s is unparalleled, and all the more impressive for a director who saw his art mainly centred on comedy and romance rather than outright social and political immersion. The effects of the Depression though, and what appears to be a sympathetic eye for the ideals of Roosevelt's New Deal, suffuse the narratives of *American Madness* (1932), *Mr Deeds Goes to Town* (1936), and *You Can't Take It With You* (1938), the final pair winning Capra two of his three best director Academy Awards. Each one helped to cement the notion of populist ideology in his films, a byword for Capracorn, as his sentimentalist outlook was often termed in the eyes of some. The triumph of lone, rural, innocent heroes – the victory of 'democratic man' as Glenn Alan Phelps describes it – over the forces of wealth, power and media megalomania became the ideological cup from which Capra and his audience gained unifying and communitarian comfort during the dark days of the Depression.[31]

Such was the affinity that Capra heroes like Tom Dickson (the upstanding bank manager in *American Madness*) and Longfellow Deeds (the wildly innocent hero who inherits a fortune in *Mr Deeds Goes to Town*) had with the contemporary era that they almost inevitably seemed to be spokesmen for the Roosevelt generation and the 'can do' spirit of a now younger and more vibrant Washington. Yet Capra was not a Democrat, he even disliked Roosevelt, despite a brief meeting between the two in the summer of 1938 after which Capra was left admiring a typically lively press conference given by the President, and he went out of his way to vote for Republican opponents in all four of FDR's election victories.[32] This is partly but not solely the reason why Capra's three most overtly 'political' films, and the populist critique under which they have laboured, need further assessment and critical revision.

The fact was that although Capra had the celebrity clout to be able to criticise FDR publicly, his films took on a guarded account of the social and economic conditions of the time, even sprinkling populist sentiment with doubts about institutional leadership. Beverly Merrill Kelley observes that Capra's ethos closely matched Aristotle's pursuance of happiness through virtue and the conditions of society preordained by others.[33] This is a clear reading of his films as a conservative plea for toleration of the rules that govern people, allied to an inbred sense of decency. Yet beyond the *mise-en-scène* of the democratic hero, Capra's personalities and institutional agendas offer more desperate scenarios for social dislocation than is at first apparent. In *Mr Smith*, for instance, Jeff's father – Clayton Smith – did not merely die as an underdog championing decency, but as an underdog who comprehended the hegemonic forces at work in American society and their all-encompassing will. In short, Capra was able to use the kind of artistic control he had in Hollywood at the end of the 1930s to give himself scope to pursue what was in reality a more complex analysis of democratic values and a rather fatalistic interposition of political mercenaries in his films.

For in *Mr Smith Goes to Washington* (1939), *Meet John Doe* (1941) and *State of the Union* (1948), Capra's political voice is not mere populism, not simply a vision of homely small-town values, but a growing voice for disenchantment, criticism and fears for the future of American democracy. These three pictures are not endowed by a constantly optimistic refinement of democratic politics but are instead progressively constrained by an uncertain future that their settings – either side of World War Two – propagates on to American society itself.

Although it is, as Phelps has expressed, a constant preoccupation with the roots of power and the elite forces of control in American politics, Capra's auteur vision was disrupted by the conflagration of 1939–45 and along the way this troika of films helps to demonstrate why and how he managed to lose that natural affinity he had always had with his audience.

Capra was called into military service by the chairman of the Joint Chiefs of Staff, General George C. Marshall, in 1942. Initially sceptical about his ability to make effective propaganda films, Marshall nevertheless appealed to Capra's sense of patriotism and duty. Attached to the 834th Photo Signal Department, the director went on to make the *Why We Fight* series of films between 1942 and 1945 as well as a number of other influential propaganda efforts, notably *The Negro Soldier* in 1944 and the *Know Your Enemy* pair of films centred on Germany and Japan. Described as vividly clarifying the official government line, Thomas Doherty's analysis of his films went on to add: 'As a wartime historian and director of postwar policy, Frank Capra was there at the creation.'[34] Capra's unflinching democratic faith was an important part of the mix, but Doherty too interestingly spots that the darker undercurrent of the director's work had slowly surfaced in these years, exemplified by the images of totalitarian deception foisted on the common people in *Meet John Doe*.[35] Capra was already fascinated by the force and power of propagandist imagery and, given the sentiments of his 1941 movie before he had actually seen this work, he made extensive use of German filmmaker Leni Riefenstahl's documentary account of the 1934 Nuremberg rallies, *Triumph of the Will* (1935), during *Why We Fight* to magnify that sense of the mastery and terrifying spectacle of control. Indeed her work became a significant reference point for the approaches and technique Capra himself used in his own documentary efforts.

Riefenstahl's part in the Nazi propagandist machine has always been a historically controversial one. Venerated and condemned in equal measure, she maintained a story of aloofness from the Third Reich all the way to her 96th year at the end of the century. Undoubtedly, however, she benefited from privileges associated with the Nazi regime and *Triumph of the Will* was no one-off. She had already begun to hone the technique of symbolic and indeed quasi-religious iconography (Hitler descends to Nuremberg by plane from the heavens at the beginning of *Triumph of the Will*) with *Sieg des Glaubens* (Victory of Faith) in 1933 and continued this style in *Olympia 1* and *2* (*Fest der Völker* and *Fest der Schönheit*) in 1938.[36]

Capra described the visual representation as 'terrifying . . . and blood-chilling'.[37] It seems fair to state that the kind of assertive, ideologically challenging work that a director like Riefenstahl was engaged in made Capra think about the medium all over again. He maintained in his autobiography *The Name above the Title* that his goal after the war was to deal with the heart using compassion and to explore the loss of faith and the need to revaluate that spiritual bond of liberty and freedom with individuals in his audience.[38] He rededicated himself to spirituality and divinity and yet the war had given Capra a harder edge in his fears over the dictating of ideas upon people's lives. *It's a Wonderful Life* (1946) was an attempt to recapture the aura of Capracorn, to set those emotions of religious and democratic freedom into the context of a past Capra vision; a construction of a town, Bedford Falls, that harboured the ghosts of Tom Dickson, Longfellow Deeds and Jefferson Smith.[39] Two years later, however, *State of the Union* revealed how far Capra's social and political realism had been extended, and how hardbitten and rancorous a character like Grant Matthews was now allowed to become. This film became a final watershed for Capra's career and highlighted just how much of a gap had opened up during the 1940s between the director and his audience.

Raymond Carney explains the schism that emerged between Capra and his fans as the product of not only his own self-doubt, but of the inconsistencies that were becoming apparent in pre-, but most particularly post-war American society. Quoting Emerson, Carney argues for a director that became torn between 'imaginative self-reliance and the rival claims of social and institutional responsibility'.[40] He was at once attracted to, and wary of, mavericks invading his pictures who might tear at the foundations of the system as much as nurture and recondition it. His heroes came to reflect this and emphasised for a critic like Carney the spiritual torment that was the centre of Capra's own art. Nevertheless, Capra's energies in these later pictures were devoted to communicating explicitly social and religious ideals through the prism of democratic ideology, but also using Christian symbolism as a cipher for the historical antecedents of Americanism that had been strongly prevalent in much of his career, but especially so in these three films.

Borrowing a phrase from Capra himself, Charles Maland has described the director's later 1930s' period as a time when Capra made films that reflected the 'ecumenical church of humanism'.[41] Jeffrey Richards goes further, suggesting that all of Capra's heroes were Christ figures, an extension of earlier 1930s' character references to Keane, Brown and Hammond, although based on the pretext of their representation of populist mythology which, as explained below, I only partly share.[42] But it is this strong identity with religious principles that becomes the backbone of Jeff Smith's plea to Joseph Paine in the Senate in *Mr Smith* when Jim Taylor's political machine has seemingly crushed Smith's fight to clear his name of the fraudulent land deal associated with Willet Creek. In 'loving thy neighbour' Smith pleads with Paine on the floor of the chamber that this rule places a great trust upon a man, and this forces Paine's belated confession of his own misdemeanours. In *Meet John Doe*, Willoughby's radio broadcast is a propaganda exercise for neighbourly communitarian ideals as he confidently begins to believe in the words placed before him, concluding, 'The meek shall inherit the earth when the John Does start loving their neighbours'. While in *State of the Union*, Grant Matthews' own simultaneous radio and telecast, made in his family's front living room, becomes a confessional explanation of his debt to family and friends whose respect and company he lost sight of while chasing the presidency.

Coming in the middle of this triumvirate, *Meet John Doe* has more often been invoked with religious ideology than its companion films primarily because of its overt biblical narrative – although Matthews and Smith could be equated with similar features in their respective films, the poverty-stricken, faded Bush League baseball player, Long John Willoughby, is more often ascribed Christ-like status by virtue of his actions.

Willoughby (Gary Cooper) answers an advert in a newspaper, *The Bulletin*, which is looking for somebody to act as a stooge for a series of letters being placed in the paper by an anonymous John Doe who is protesting the injustices of the world by threatening to jump off the roof of the City Hall on Christmas Eve – six months hence in the story. The letters are written by columnist Ann Mitchell (Barbara Stanwyck) who saves her job from impending redundancy by the stunt, encourages her

editor, Connell, to take Willoughby on, falls in love with him, and sees
the product of their manufactured ideals – Ann constructs the letters
using the thoughts of her deceased father's correspondence thus
invoking the spirit of some higher presence – realised in the John Doe
Clubs that spring up around the country.[43] Unbeknown to Ann and
Long John, however, the new owner of *The Bulletin*, the dictatorial D.
B. Norton, has his own plans for the clubs and aims to use them as a
springboard for his assault on the presidency and the beginning of
what Capra presents as fascistic control in America.

Glenn Alan Phelps's specific reading of *Meet John Doe* suggests that
Willoughby undergoes an epiphany in the film that reveals to him the
strong presence of a political ideology of Christian communalism as
practised by the John Doe Clubs.[44] In short, it is not only the actions of
the hero as a saviour figure but the conceptual theories encompassed
within the narrative that are vital for Phelps in revealing the political
ideals of Capra in this film in particular. The appearance of strong
Christian identity as basis for political theory also tapped into the mood
of progressivism that formed the backbone of social regeneration in
America in the early part of the twentieth century. Although outwardly
radical and innovative, its concealed conservative tendencies and
WASPish outlook seemed to provide a suitable comparison to the
moderately liberal tendencies of some parts of the Hollywood community in the 1930s and 1940s.

*Meet John Doe*, moreover, has also often been debated as a film with
particular Catholic sentiments. Joseph McBride described how Capra
had problems with the Catholic Church while shooting the film still
basing his finale on the original suicide ending for Willoughby.[45] He
understood how nervous the Church was about the idea of a film with
a man having a lengthy preordained determination to take his own
life, and in later years Capra became less sure of his choice of ending.
Other readings have focused on a possible suicide for Willoughby as
the mainstay of any redemptive conclusion and thus a rebirth of his
spirit through the John Doe Clubs, in other words a closure that
encourages a demonstratively Catholic reading of the film.[46]

In the end Capra and collaborator Robert Riskin managed to incorporate both aspects of this pedagogic Christian sentiment by allowing
Willoughby to survive and giving the redemptive power of his communal message a chance. Ann Mitchell claims that Long John's sacrifice
will live on in the John Doe Clubs and the members from the small

town of Millville crowd along with her to the site of John's redemption, the City Hall rooftop scene on Christmas Eve, to tell him this is so. She reminds him that a saviour died two thousand years before for his ideals and like his, Long John's teachings – that is, her father's – will continue to prosper.

The interpretation of Phelps also points out possibly the most important ethos at work in the film, and that is the joining of the religious and democratic strands of the narrative through the moral conscience of the colonel, Willoughby's companion and alter-ego. The colonel spends the film denouncing what he refers to as the 'helots': the bankers, the money men, the politicians, in other words the establishment that controls people's lives and dictates their actions.[47] He is presented as the alternative asocial answer to Norton's individualistic greed and despotism on the one hand, and Willoughby's inclusive communalism on the other. As Phelps points out, the colonel represents the type of put-upon citizen that Theodore Lowi's work on the cultural condition of participants in modern society perceives as dropping out of the mainstream.[48] We are meant ultimately to reject such notions, society cannot function if too many colonels are left wondering around. Yet the message is appealing in *Meet John Doe* and while many highlight its contradictory nature given the communitarian pitch of Willoughby the hero, it does show how Capra's ideological feelings were altering steadily at this time. The John Doe Clubs themselves are in their own way exclusory, like the colonel's message, because they specifically do not allow politicians to join. The very link of the people to the pillars of establishment control is therefore severed in *Meet John Doe*, and Capra's ironic Christian message is not transposed through the ruthless character of Norton – that is, that fascism is heretical – but in his ever increasing fear about the manipulation, gullibility and dispassionate detachment of the voters, the masses. In other words, their devotion to principles and social, as well as personal and religious, values, he argues, is being diluted by the weight of a modern technologically persuasive community, incorporated into the colonel's near 'hedonistic' contemplation of society.[49]

Capra's fascination with the mindset of the people in his films, and the ideas that they are imbued with, again stretches back to the early 1930s. The run on Tom Dickson's bank in *American Madness* is an early sign of collective mentality and fear for Capra. He repeats almost exactly the same trick in arguably his most enduring film, *It's a*

*Wonderful Life*, with a similar run on the Bailey Building and Loan Company. His most overtly dramatic realisation of the power of the masses comes towards the close of *Meet John Doe*, but its most interesting manifestation for political theory occurs in *Mr Smith Goes to Washington*.

Quite literally by the toss of a coin Jefferson Smith (James Stewart) is chosen by his state's political machine to be their new senator in Washington replacing the deceased incumbent Sam Foley. Wide-eyed and utterly raw, Smith marvels at the chance not only to 'visit' his nation's capital but to work with one of his murdered father's great friends, the 'silver knight' himself, Senator Joseph Paine (Claude Rains). Smith's respect and devotion to Paine, and the other's fatherly entreaty of Smith, mask the fact that Paine is in the pocket of the political machine headed by 'big' Jim Taylor (Edward Arnold), and his job is to make sure Smith does nothing that will harm their mutual interest. Paine attempts to occupy Smith's time by having him draw up a bill for his one great plan, a boys camp in his home state. As luck would have it Smith earmarks exactly the same piece of land that Taylor and Paine have ringed for a fraudulent land deal attached to an appropriations bill, Willet Creek. The refusal by Smith to back down from the idea and the subsequent discrediting of him in a Senate investigation sets up the final confrontation with Smith's odds against filibuster attempting to block the passage of the bill, and expose the corruption at the heart of institutional politics.

This film presents critics with the classic Capra ideology dilemma of popular individualism versus collective responsibility. Phelps resolves the problem in his own critique by merely presenting the Capra heroes like Smith as idealistic possibles of individual spirit backed by small free-thinking people.[50] This is what can be achieved even if the narrative on offer cannot wholly resolve the conditions of elite control, he suggests. Joyce Nelson argues that Capra's portrayal of 'crowds' in *Mr Smith* is ambiguous at best, but underlines the notions of populism through strong individual leadership.[51] One could not simply dismiss either proposition here but both hint at the deeper political dimensions and problems that Capra had in resolving his closure. Has elite power been destroyed at the end of *Mr Smith*; is Smith a triumphant political figure; has the public been vindicated for its views/support/belief in the system?

The answer to all three questions is almost certainly no and has been spotted by scholars and critics alike many times. In the original trailer for *Mr Smith*, Capra included scenes of a homecoming for Smith and the reconstituted Paine as a form of healing for the state, party and system of government. But, like the dismantling of the Taylor machine, this epilogue did not make it into the final cut and what the audience are left with is the banshee howl of Saunders (Jean Arthur), Smith's secretary and romantic interest, into the chaotic chamber below as the Senate descends towards disruption after Smith's collapse in front of the Vice-President.

The animalistic excitement of the people – for what Saunders is reclaiming for herself is a life as part of the masses not the Washington establishment – is certainly a message of duplicity and acceptance on the public's part for any amount of propaganda that they might hear. That propaganda is promulgated by Capra's usual fifth column, the press, which is controlled in this case by Jim Taylor in much the same way that Norton has control in *Meet John Doe*. Yet there is something fundamental in the concluding scenes to *Mr Smith* that aids the democratic reading of the film. Nelson is surely right to highlight the distance between the governed and the government.[52] It is the pretext of the whole picture. Whether by excuse or frustration, it is this lack of bonding that encourages Joseph Paine to throw his lot in with Taylor, to take the money and seek patronage for higher office, not from his constituents but from the elite forces of power and wealth. He tells Jeff that the people don't really care who is in Washington because 'half the time they don't vote at all'.

Capra's ideology therefore is about the relationship between 'the masses' and their political system, it is not just about representation and elite control, but the way the constitution and the institutions of state are part of the American people's history, and their best guide to its future. The vast part of the middle section of the film is an educational directive in procedure, in the ways that the system can work, and Jeff's education in that procedure by Saunders is his means to representation and democratic applicability. It is through Saunders that we, the audience, get to endorse Smith's ideological underpinnings of democracy and individualism, even though, as both Poague and Gallagher have asserted, those acts of speech and language eventually become the shackles by which Saunders' individual ascendancy is curbed by her love – and silence punctuated by gestures in the filibuster scene – for Jeff.[53] Nevertheless, Jeff's fulfilment of his potential as an orator in the filibuster scene is richly embellished with the Lockian sense of individual liberty and the American Protestant impulse towards direct commitment to God.[54] The procedural nature of the text in *Mr Smith*, and the educational initiatives derived from it, are also crucial to an ideological concept of individualism. This calls more often than not for heroic individualism pitting one against the masses or the state and where 'they have to embody the virtues of negative liberty, by which the removal of restriction leads ineluctably to the maximisation of freedom'.[55]

These values are perfectly demonstrated during Jeff's filibuster. First, the possible undemocratic nature of this tactic – that an individual can talk a bill out of the chamber by hijacking the procedure and arguably denying free speech – is cleverly subverted by having famous radio journalist H. V. Kaltenborn comment on 'democracy's finest show, the filibuster' taking place in the Senate at the outset of the scene. Second, Smith resorts not to idle or innocuous chat or some personal rant at the injustice of his position, but instead gives himself over to an indefatigable reading of the whole of the Constitution and the Declaration of Independence, largely to a disinterested Senate chamber. Capra argues here that the relationship between the voters and representatives has broken down precisely because neither is interested in what the Constitution has to say anymore. It is no longer the imperious document it once was, and yet Capra reminds his audience, through political iconography at the Lincoln Memorial in the beginning and climax to the film, that the words, symbols and meaning of the Constitution is a vital induction into their means of becoming and identifying themselves as Americans. History, in other words, is on Jeff's side when he reminds the Senators that the Boys Camp is there because those boys 'will sit in these seats' one day as the generations pass.

Capra's unleashing of mass chaos at the end of *Mr Smith* was magnified wholesale by his dramatic convention rally, shot at Wrigley Field, Chicago, for the conclusion of *Meet John Doe*. His demonstration of the people's culpability was nearly complete but Capra did return to this theme after his service in World War Two with his final great film, *State of the Union*. Now, however, the melodrama and power of the tragic forces that he saw in his own career as well as American life overwhelmed the itinerant beliefs of his hero, Grant Matthews. Having taken on the burden of his own production company Liberty Films with George Stevens and William Wyler, Capra witnessed a post-war

America that had lost his sense of comedic value and social interaction in his pictures. Hollywood was being touted as an important force for a new social order that was going to reformulate the national cultural and political conditions of the country, and Capra's style appeared to him perfunctory to such a cause.[56] *It's a Wonderful Life* might therefore be seen as a last hurrah for the director playing, as it did, to the timeless Capra strengths, and yet its settings and even characters seemed to antedate their contemporary period. The film received five Oscar nominations but in critical and box-office terms paled against the success in the same year, and at the 1947 Academy Awards, of Wyler's returning veterans drama *The Best Years of Our Lives*.[57]

Capra, therefore, resolved to return to the political arena as subject-matter in 1948 with his second feature for Liberty, the adaptation of Howard Lyndsey and Russell Crouse's stageplay *State of the Union*. The film was as pertinent for its timing – going into production just as the House Un-American Activities Committee (HUAC) arrived in Hollywood – as it was for the storyline. On the face of it, the plot followed a familiar Capra route. Grant Matthews (Spencer Tracy) is a successful businessman but an amateur in politics who wishes to get involved and change the system. He allies himself with a ruthless, career-minded media tycoon, Kay Thorndyke (Angela Lansbury), who has the means to put Grant in the White House and forces her own views into national prominence.

Yet under this basic premise all is not as it seems in the film. Grant's comfortable and secure family life is in fact a sham. He is in effect separated from his wife, Mary (Katherine Hepburn), and is actually carrying on an affair with his patron, Kay. Matthews' sense of time and location is compromised by a career in plane manufacturing that has left him without a spiritual home but a personal ambition to serve that is worthy, although increasingly driven by self-interest as the film develops. Capra never allows his hero any interaction with the public, save for some one-to-one meetings, and many scenes are deliberately located after set piece speeches that are meant to spread the word about Matthews' impending candidacy around the country. The director even emphasises the point about detachment in the long final denouement that takes place in Matthews' house by having the audience virtually composed of media folk, and including television cameras as an indicator of political development and the reach of propaganda to a wider audience in the post-war years.

Fig. 2 *Grant Matthews (Spencer Tracy) confronts professional ambition and family responsibility in* State of the Union *(BFI Films: Stills, posters and designs).*
State of the Union © 1948 Liberty Films, for Loews Inc.

The culmination of a concerted pre-campaign to put Matthews on the Republican ticket (political allegiances are clearly expressed in the film unlike any other work by the director) is undone by his nagging conviction that not only do the public not know all the facts about Grant Matthews, but that he is also not worthy of them. Matthews' public uncertainty was an allegorical interpretation of Capra's own indifference. As he is quoted in his autobiography he thought the film would get crucified by HUAC, he was suspicious as to why President Truman would like it when it pointedly criticised him, and Capra was already aware, having made the picture, that Liberty could not go on sustaining the debts it had and he would have to forsake his independence. '*State of the Union* would be my last Frank Capra film, my last burst of autumn colours before the winter of artistic slavery to the major studio hierarchy at Paramount Pictures', he said.[58]

Yet I share Leland Poague's view that politics in *State of the Union* is more explicit than any of Capra's other accounts and the honesty of its human dilemmas, choreographed with a ideological pretext that pulled few punches, makes it a crucial chapter in the director's repertoire.[59] Given that Capra had fears about HUAC, the political sensibilities of the cast and the problems with Liberty, it is amazing that the film works at all. As screwball comedy it is not really in the class of *It Happened One Night* (1934), as heroic melodrama laced with Christian symbolism it does not really match up to *Mr Smith* or *Meet John Doe*; but as an example of value-oriented ideals reflecting the social machinations of the time, *State of the Union* perfectly sums up the way the political film had traversed across many new aspects of the genre since *Washington Merry-Go-Round* sixteen years earlier.

Charles Maland argues for a structural piece that does resemble earlier Capra philosophy. The break between professional and amateur politics, and the strains of realist and idealist agendas, are certainly noteworthy similarities, but Capra also blurs the lines of earlier distinctions, and most especially with character.[60] Jim Conover (Adolf Menjou) is not a villain as definable as Jim Taylor or D. B. Norton, wife Mary offers a far more complicated reading of romantic entanglement than Saunders or Ann Mitchell, and Matthews himself does not emanate from the same loosely conceived agrarian philosophy that the likes of Deeds, Smith or George Bailey could all claim as their own.

Most of all Kay Thorndyke is a more richly complicated villainess than other Capra figures, symptomatic for Poague of the strong manipulation of gender roles in the film, and illustrative generally of a pattern of inclusive establishment dominance in female roles as the era rolled on.[61] Alice Wylie in *Washington Merry-Go-Round* becomes a Washington insider by virtue of her family connections as well as her charm, while Clarissa Saunders and Ann Mitchell are portrayed as career women knocking at the gates of a male-dominated society. Pendola Malloy (Karen Morley) is a similarly ill-defined mix of the two in *Gabriel over the White House*, and in Stanley Logan's 1937 film *First Lady*, Kay Francis plays a scheming Secretary of State's wife, claiming influence for high-level politics initiated where the real power is, at her breakfast table.

All contest and yet similarly reaffirm the position of women in Washington life, and American politics generally in the 1930s and 1940s, that of loyal wives or dismissive concubines. But Kay Thorndyke in *State of the Union* has not only a harder edge to her but a brittle realisation that time and life are marching on, that her career and consolidation of

Fig. 3 *Mary Matthews (Katherine Hepburn) contemplates the forces of power and propaganda in the shape of Jim Conover (Adolphe Menjou) and Kay Thorndyke (Angela Lansbury) in Frank Capra's* State of the Union *(BFI Films: Stills, posters and designs).*
State of the Union © *1948 Liberty Films, for Loews Inc.*

power are the gateways to a newer and more powerful world in the second half of the twentieth century. Her respect for her father is encapsulated by one of Capra's most powerful ever scenes, right at the beginning of the film when Kay closes the door on Sam, aware that the cancer that is killing him is now too much to bear. As she warns the nurse not to go into the room, Capra hones in on an extreme close-up of Kay – somewhat stylistically drawn from Eisenstein who Capra greatly admired – briefly shuddering as a gunshot goes off inside, and then walking down the stairs pausing only briefly to gaze out of the window concealing a protected emotion as camera flashes allow Capra to dissolve the scene into one of Kay shaking hands with her new editors as she assumes control of the Thorndyke Press. Capra brings vehemently female qualities of intuition and drive to this scene, and to the film as a whole. With Jean Arthur, Barbara Stanwyck and Angela

Lansbury, he alluded to a distinctive new setting for gender politics in Hollywood and American society in the second half of the twentieth century. The role of women was now changing and politics had become hard-nosed business, not simply idealistic fulfilment. Yet it was this very direction for politics which was going to restrict the ability of women to pursue social causes and political careers. Politics was assuming the cloak of image, position, style and rhetoric, and the ideological foundations of the Hollywood studio years, and American public life in general, were about to be torn up and rebuilt with different values.

## NOTES

1 Anthony J Badger, *The New Deal* (Cambridge: Cambridge University Press, 1989) p. 7.
2 Phil Melling, 'The Mind of the Mob: Hollywood and the Popular Culture of the 1930s', in *Cinema, Politics and Society*, ed. Brian Neve and Philip Davies (Manchester: Manchester University Press, 1981) p. 21.
3 T. H. Watkins, *The Great Depression: America in the 1930s* (Boston: Little, Brown & Co., 1993) pp. 106–7.
4 Carl N. Degler, *Out of Our Past: The Forces that Shaped Modern America*, 3rd edn (New York: Harper, 1984) p. 450.
5 Brian Neve, *Film and Politics in America: A Social Tradition* (London: Routledge, 1992) pp. 5–14.
6 Colin Shindler, *Hollywood in Crisis: Cinema and American Society 1929–39* (London: Routledge, 1996) pp. 27–8.
7 Ibid. p. 29.
8 Russell Campbell, 'Warners, the Depression, and FDR, Wellman's *Heroes for Sale*', *The Velvet Light Trap Review of Cinema*, no. 4, Spring 1979, pp. 34–9.
9 Ibid. p. 35.
10 Eric Smoodin, 'Compulsory Viewing for Every Citizen: *Mr. Smith* and the Rhetoric of Reception', *Cinema Journal*, vol. 35, no. 2, Winter 1996, pp. 3–23.
11 Peter Roffman and Jim Purdy, *The Hollywood Social Problem Film: Madness, Despair and Politics from the Depression to the Fifties* (Bloomington: Indiana University Press, 1981) p. 84.
12 John Dewey, 'The Public and Its Problems', in *American Political Thought*, ed. Kenneth Dolbeare, 2nd edn (New Jersey: Chatham, 1989) pp. 482–500.

13  Richard Maltby, *Harmless Entertainment: Hollywood and the Ideology of Consensus* (London: Scarecrow Press, 1983) p. 149.

14  Robert Burns's book, on which Mervyn Le Roy's film was based, was entitled *I Am a Fugitive from a Georgia Chain Gang* (1931), and thus any mention of the state in the title or content of the film would have implicitly held up its penal system to scrutiny and brought pressure to bear on the studio.

15  Richard Maltby, *Harmless Entertainment*, pp. 95–6.

16  Ruth Inglis, 'Early Attempts at Control', in *Films of the 1920s*, ed. Richard Dyer McCann (Lanham, MD: Scarecrow Press, 1996) pp. 48–9.

17  Ibid. p. 49.

18  Will Hays, 'The First Years in Hollywood', from *The Memoirs of Will H. Hays* (Garden City, NY: Doubleday, 1955), reproduced in *Films of the 1920s*, ed. Richard Dyer McCann pp. 54–5.

19  For a more detailed account of Upton Sinclair's EPIC campaign of 1934, see Greg Mitchell, *The Campaign of the Century: Upton Sinclair's Race for Governor and the Birth of Media Politics* (New York: Random House, 1992); Fay M. Blake and H. Morton Newman, 'Upton Sinclair's EPIC Campaign', *California History*, Fall 1984, pp. 305–12.

    Sinclair himself, quoting the *New York Times* in his own account of the campaign, displays the extent of Hollywood influence on that election saying: 'Before Louis Mayer, Irving Thalberg, Charlie Pettijohn and Carey Wilson stepped into this political battle here, the whole Republican Party seemed to have been sunk by the insane promises of Mr. Sinclair.' See Upton Sinclair, *I, Candidate for Governor: And how I Got Licked* (Berkeley: University of California Press, first published in 1935, this edition 1994) pp. 168–72.

20  Such was the backlash against Sinclair that no less a person than Irving Thalberg personally oversaw a series of fake newsreels – paid for by the Hearst organisation – distributed free to Californian theatres, and showing respectable people – many of whom worked for the studios – declaring their support for incumbent Governor Frank Merriam, while dishevelled and 'foreign looking' citizens with strong accents pledged their vote to Sinclair offering the thoughts that if his declared policies worked in Russia, they could work in California! See Kevin Starr, *Endangered Dreams: The Great Depression in California* (New York: Oxford University Press, 1996) pp. 142–55.

21  Roffman and Purdy, *The Hollywood Social Problem Film*, p. 11.

22  Review of *Washington Merry-Go-Round* in *Photoplay*, vol. 42, no. 6, 1932, p. 57.

23  Shindler noted that he felt the Hays Office interventions meant this was

a decade of lost opportunities See Shindler, *Hollywood in Crisis*, p. 24 and p. 116.

24  See *Picturegoer* review of *Mad Masquerade* (as the film was called in Britain), 19 November 1932, p. 32. Also review in *Cinema Booking Guide Supplement*, October 1932, p. 10.

25  Review of *Washington Masquerade* in *Variety*, 6 September 1932, quoted in Shindler, *Hollywood in Crisis*, p. 24.

26  Shindler, *Hollywood in Crisis*, p. 23.

27  The bonus army, or 'Bonus Expeditionary Force' as they proclaimed themselves, arrived 20,000 strong in Washington in the summer of 1932 demanding early payment of their 'adjusted compensation' (due in 1945) for service in World War One. Confrontations between protesters and police led to Hoover's order to have the ex-servicemen evacuated by an army led by General Douglas MacArthur and so ensued the 'Battle of Anacostia Flats'. See David M. Kennedy, Thomas A. Bailey, Mel Piehl, *The Brief American Pageant*, 4th edn (Lexington, MA: D. C. Heath, 1996) pp. 504–5.

28  See Review of *Invisible Power* (as the film was called in Europe) in *Cinema Booking Guide Supplement*, January 1933, p. 18. Review of *Washington Merry-Go-Round* in *Photoplay*, vol. 42, no.6, 1932, p. 57.

29  The 'do nothing' approach often defined as Hoover's response to the Depression still remains an unfair representation. It was the case, however, that Hoover lacked real political ability, and he admitted as much himself. 'I have no Wilsonian qualities', he once told friends. But he was an excellent administrator and steadfast in his efforts to solve the Depression. As historian William Leuchtenburg has remarked, it was simply that these efforts did not work. See William Leuchtenburg, *The Perils of Prosperity 1914–32*, 2nd edn (Chicago: University of Chicago Press, 1993) pp. 260–1.

30  In his reading of the film, John Pitney claims that the utopian concepts of world peace that are so carefully positioned in this part of the film were ideas that fascists had no use for in a film that utilises fascist themes all the way through. This seems to me a deliberate ploy to reign in Hammond's wide-eyed dictatorial position to one of global peacemaker, however intimidating his tactics may appear. See John J. Pitney, jun., 'Fascism in *Gabriel over the White House*', in *Reelpolitik: Political Ideologies in '30s and '40s Films*, ed. Beverly Merrill Kelly, John J. Pitney, jun., Craig R. Smith and Herbert E. Gooch III (Westport, CT: Praeger, 1998) p. 56.

31  Glenn Alan Phelps, 'The "Populist" Films of Frank Capra', *Journal of American Studies*, vol. 13, no. 3, 1979, p. 379.

32  The two would later meet during the war also when Capra was second-
    ed into the army but at this time he was outraged by the recent events
    of the Court Packing Plan when Roosevelt had tried to influence the
    composition of the Supreme Court by legislating for more members on
    it, so as to uphold New Deal legislation. He was also distraught at the
    prospect of an unprecedented third term for the President. Nevertheless
    he came away from the press conference that day, having shaken
    Roosevelt's hand, commenting, 'What a voice! What a personality!' See
    Joseph McBride, *Frank Capra: The Catastrophe of Success* (London: Faber
    & Faber, 1992) pp. 408–9.

33  Beverly Merrill Kelley, 'Populism in *Mr Smith Goes to Washington*' in
    *Reelpolitik: Political Ideologies in '30s and '40s Films*, ed. Beverly Merrill
    Kelley with John J. Pitney, jun., Craig R. Smith and Herbert E. Gooch III
    (Westport, CT: Praeger, 1998) p. 13.

34  Thomas Doherty, *Projections of War: Hollywood, American Culture, and
    World War Two* (New York: Columbia University Press, 1993) pp. 70–1.

35  Doherty asserts that 'by the time of *Meet John Doe* the gloomy undertow
    had engulfed the surface optimism'. Ibid. p. 72.

36  Riefenstahl was the subject of a controversial exhibition in 1999 featur-
    ing her life work and the process of rehabilitation had included an invite
    from President Clinton to the 75th birthday party of the magazine *Time*
    (she and Claudia Schiffer have been the only two German women fea-
    tured on the cover) See Paul Myers, 'She was the Genius who Glorified
    Hitler. Can the World Really Forgive Leni Riefenstahl?', *The Guardian*,
    Arts Section, 15 December 1998, pp. 8–9.

37  Frank Capra, *The Name above the Title* (New York: Macmillan, 1971) p.
    328.

38  Ibid. p. 375.

39  McBride noted how the George Bailey/Henry Potter confrontation
    between protagonist and villain reflected on the rhetorical conflicts
    inherent in Populist Party politics at the turn of the century rather less
    than contemporary problems of the 1940s, a reason possibly for its
    enduring, almost timeless feel, as critic James Wolcott observed. See
    McBride, *Frank Capra*, p. 522.

40  Raymond Carney, *American Vision: The Films of Frank Capra* (Cambridge:
    Cambridge University Press, 1986) p. 38.

41  Charles Maland, *Frank Capra* (New York: Twayne, 1995) pp. 89–115.

42  Jeffrey Richards, *Visions of Yesterday* (London: Routledge, 1973) p. 234.

43  Capra has at least an ironic, and taunting, political edge here in devel-
    oping John Doe Clubs around a spiritual philosophy like 'love thy
    neighbour' in the film when they appear quite close in form to the com-

munist-organised John Reed Clubs of the 1930s that promoted class struggle in American society. See Michael E. Parrish, *Anxious Decades: America in Prosperity and Depression, 1920–1941* (New York: Norton, 1992) pp. 423–7.

44 Glenn Alan Phelps, 'Frank Capra and the Political Hero: A New Reading of "Meet John Doe"', *Film Criticism*, Winter 1981, pp. 49–57.

45 McBride, *Frank Capra*, p. 435.

46 Maland quotes a confrontation with a student at a film showing who told Capra that Long John really should have committed suicide and Capra defended this saying he did not really want to display any concerted religious devotion to one creed in his films. See Maland, *Frank Capra*, p. 92.

47 Phelps, 'Frank Capra and the Political Hero', pp. 52–3.

48 Ibid. p. 57.

49 Hedonistic is the word Dudley Andrews uses for the colonel explaining that Capra sees through him the danger of the 'not-normal' in society. Glenn Alan Phelps offers the view that the colonel represents a distrust of human nature and actions reminiscent of the philosophy of Thomas Hobbes. See Dudley Andrew, 'Meet John Doe', *Enclitic*, vol. 5, no. 2, pp. 111–19; Phelps, 'Frank Capra and the Political Hero', p. 52.

50 Phelps, 'The "Populist" Films of Frank Capra', pp. 390–1.

51 Joyce Nelson, 'Capra, Populism, and Comic Strip Art', *Journal of Popular Film*, vol. 3, no. 3, Summer 1974, pp. 245–54.

52 Ibid. p. 254.

53 Saunders is 'repressed by the very language she had hoped to hear spoken', Poague says. Gallagher, meanwhile, suggests that we hear Smith's ideology through Saunders for much of the film. See Leland Poague, *Another Frank Capra* (Cambridge: Cambridge University Press, 1994) pp. 164–5; Brian Gallagher, 'Speech, Identity, and Ideology in "Mr. Smith Goes to Washington"', *Film Criticism*, vol. 5, no. 2, Winter 1981, pp. 12–22.

54 Michael Foley suggests that American liberty and individualism are inextricably linked by the country's need to express salvation in an individual manner which has always led to sects and congregational churches rather than a central spiritual authority See Michael Foley, *American Political Ideas* (Manchester: Manchester University Press, 1991) p. 28.

55 Ibid. p. 43.

56 Eric Johnson, who had become the new head of the Motion Picture Producers Association after the war, saw in Hollywood's recent history the means by which it had become a major influence upon the manners

and morals as well as the economic and political forces of change that had occurred in the country in the previous generation. He therefore saw a critical role for the studios in the coming years. See Lary May, 'Movie Star Politics: The Screen Actors' Guild, Cultural Conversion, and the Hollywood Red Scare', in *Recasting America: Culture and Politics in the Age of the Cold War*, ed. Lary May (Chicago: University of Chicago Press, 1989) pp. 125–53. Eric Johnson's article 'Utopia is Production' appeared in *Screen Actor*, 14, April 1946, p. 7.

57   *The Best Years of Our Lives* took $11.3 million at the box office compared to $3.3 million for *It's a Wonderful Life*. Even in later years Capra had no more than a grudging admiration for the film, 'too downbeat for me' he once said. In the end *Best Years* won Oscars for best picture, director and actor (Frederic March) while Capra could only content himself with the Golden Globe best director award for *Wonderful Life*. See McBride, *Frank Capra*, pp. 515–16 and p. 530.

58   Capra, *The Name above the Title*, pp. 397–8.

59   Poague, *Another Frank Capra*, p. 236.

60   Maland, *Frank Capra*, p. 159.

61   Poague, *Another Frank Capra*, pp. 235–43.

*Chapter 3*

# HOLLYWOOD ON THE
# CAMPAIGN TRAIL

⸺◦⸻

Vote for me and I will bring the values of the common man to bear in
Washington DC.

Bob Roberts in Bob Roberts

As Tim Robbins's character mockingly asserts in his 1992 film, the
Hollywood vision of electoral campaigning shares a common identity
with other political films. Election films seek conformity in the intricate,
complex and unrepresentative world of Washington, and they seek that
conformity through the shared experience of corruptible misanthropes
who are perceived as tearing down the walls of American democracy
through a veil of lies and deceit.

In fact Robbins's bitingly satirical portrait of electioneering in the
1990s stands somewhat detached from the more classical portrayal of
populist idealism set against overzealous demaguery that we have
examined so far in political films. Certainly *Bob Roberts* sets out to chide
the surface acceptability of political candidates as much as other films
mentioned later in this chapter, and in doing so it makes its own claim
for the moral high ground Hollywood has so often coveted. And yet
the spotlight of Robbins is also cast on the sordid and dispiriting process
of forsaking your principles, and even your very soul, for the mere
cause of getting elected. The sycophancy that adorns the film is its
most difficult trick to convince, for it stands out as a condemnatory
discourse against Hollywood itself as much as it is a treatise on the
vagaries of public gullibility in American elections. As Robert Sklar has
noted: '*Bob Roberts* is an entertaining film that may not have much of a
viewpoint at all. Its publicity describes the film as a satire, and the
problem with satire as a form is that it is good at offering targets but
less good at taking positions.'[1]

Sklar highlights a chief dilemma for all political films of course but in this case, with the unfolding of events in the 1990s, and no sign of a let-up for an electoral process that is lacking as much irony as morals, the film's importance as a piece of garrulous muckraking now allows it to stand apart from many contemporary exposés as an even more relevant monument to real-life American politics in the 1990s. The principal legacy of *Bob Roberts*, therefore, is not simply as a satirical lampooning of public life, but as an increasingly enduring testament to Hollywood's prophecy about, and progression towards, late twentieth-century politics in general. At the end of the decade, the film was joined by a companion piece, Warren Beatty's *Bulworth*, that both confirms and elaborates upon many of the satirical notions of electoral politics that have graduated into real campaigns during this era. In short, this chapter will assess the way election films in Hollywood have become imitated as well as imitators of modern electoral campaigning.

The political film examined so far has a set of ideological conventions that subscribe to iconographic symbolism and narrative perspectives while leaving little doubt as to the theoretical countenance they enjoin. Most have forsaken strict partisan ideology for a more apolitical stance based around the values and ideals of religious identity and inclusory democratic participation. Hollywood films that have featured elections are not radically different in this respect; and indeed many of the movies we have begun to talk of, and those still to be discussed later in this book, have a set of narratives driven by a process that utilises electoral subplots as a means of dramatic licence. *Gabriel over the White House*, *Meet John Doe* and *State of the Union* all present electoral campaigns as their narrative undertow without ever displaying the campaigns that brought their characters to the fore. Later films in the action/conspiracy/thriller genre have approached electoral races in much the same way, by using the campaign of a leading character (sometimes indeed, as in Wolfgang Petersen's *In the Line of Fire* (1993), the political figure remains a consciously peripheral character) as a dramatic future obligation to the plot. As the next chapter will illuminate, examples such as Petersen's film, and others like *Absolute Power* (1997), *Jade* (1995), *Storyville* (1992) and *Enemy of the State* exhume controversy in institutional democracy by implicating the invariably honest yet naive political figure in a devious, corrupt and sordid world.

Hollywood films that have *centrally* aligned themselves to the campaign process as narrative, however, are slightly different. By definition films about electoral politics have equated image and personality with electoral viability and campaign success. The investment in character, over and above the relations with party or ideology, is fixed in place here. In Franklin Schaffner's *The Best Man* (1964), for instance, Henry Fonda's character William Russell sacrifices his nomination for president while maintaining a quiet dignity and resolve that suppresses any of the strong political principles he espouses at the beginning (quoting Bertrand Russell and Oliver Cromwell among others). The public's perception of character is everything he tells his wife in conclusion, having facilitated the means to allow the faceless western governor to triumph in the nominating process that climaxes the film. In many of the pictures under discussion here, the safeguarding of institutional doctrines and a resonant iconic purpose, so central to Hollywood's ideological dialogue in other sub-casts of the political genre, are abandoned in favour of resolutions that are meant to demonstrate confrontational ideals and the ethics of smoke-filled rooms. The image of character respectability and public tolerance of personage has thus become a symbolic reference point for Hollywood; it is the scale on which modern-day political success is judged. As Michael Douglas's character, Andrew Shepherd, says in *The American President* (1995) you cannot be elected president today if you sit in a wheelchair (a pointed reference to FDR) and that applies to Hollywood presidents every bit as it does to real ones. The perceptions concerning the institution of the president – as well as that of congress or the Supreme Court – are in this context as vital to Hollywood's ideological conceptions as are the recognisable visions of institutional structures themselves.

Character as politics has therefore allowed Hollywood to regard election films as a perfect construction of battles between good and evil; as a means to investigate, and condemn, theories of political and state power that are antithetical to the prevailing ideals. In election films this is done almost exclusively through the prism of flawed individual personality. Opponents are less nefarious predators than incongruous misfits and thus the narrative tends to present an investigation of what is acceptable as presentation rather than what is inherent in ideological conviction.

And yet it is precisely for this reason, the very simplicity of their nature and grounding in electoral dynamics, that Hollywood election films have had such an impact in the American system since World War Two. Long before image and personality had become the mainstay of real-life electioneering there was Hollywood putting it centrestage in its own portrayal. Its impact has been so considerable that Hollywood's accelerated trend towards media-driven campaigning forced real politicians to address the notion themselves.

It wasn't until Dwight Eisenhower's 1952 campaign for the presidency that television really became a manipulative tool of the candidate. In this time, the 1950s, the infant years of television campaigning provided a cosy, relaxed atmosphere in which candidates could operate. The big three networks – ABC, NBC and CBS – were the mainstays of all American programming and their inquisitiveness remained well checked. However, as Edwin Diamond and Stephen Bates comment in their book *The Spot*: 'The year 1952 transformed the way Americans elected their presidents – a change directly related to the twin developments of television and the TV spot.'[2] The spot was the means by which candidates advertised their manifesto – in reality themselves – on TV and quickly became the propaganda weapon for all media-conscious politicians. Today, with over 400 independent television stations in the United States each vying for coverage and ratings, the political and strategic influence of television seems, despite contradictory evidence, assured.[3] Add to this dedicated news and government stations such as CNN and C-Span together with the expansion of cable services, and TV has led the way in heightening the awareness factor for the American public of politics in general and political campaigning in particular.[4]

Yet, since 1985 political news in all its forms has also become increasingly segmented by the 'cable culture' of single-strand channels concentrating on particular forms of entertainment. The major networks have been accused of 'dumbing down' their political coverage, of realigning their involvement with 'human interest' stories in a bid for better ratings, and of allowing the chat shows to instigate populist social and political debate previously confined to media journalism.[5] Political campaigning has therefore sequentially broadened its means and methods of tactically approaching the electorate, and this new grooming has engendered the criticism of promoting systemic ignorance, or, to put it another way, an increasingly basic level of interpretation about the institutions that guide people's lives.[6] Little wonder therefore that, in the light of this, television and cinema should play a role in the expansion of presentation and image to an electorate cultivated in the significance of this iconography.

In fact the theoretical background to these political advances has a clear delineation. Max Weber was writing about the 'authority of charisma' much earlier in the century and those prophetic thoughts have their realisation in late century American politics.[7] Indeed, Timothy Luke has since elaborated upon Weber's ideas by asserting that: 'Electronic media – and the complex codes of images they generate – have partially displaced large formal bureaucratic institutions as channels of personal identity, cultural communication, political administration, and social organisation.'[8] As Chapter 1 discussed, and these comments confirm, the media is the medium of spectacle, both realised and also claimed for by its own reality and legitimation of human experience. American elections have become a commodification of democracy, as Luke asserts, but the packaging of policy and opinion performed through the media has cinematic presentation as one of its sources.[9]

Despite a long history of the importance of political character to national politicians – reverberating all the way back to Washington and Jefferson – and in spite of the way that Franklin Roosevelt in the 1930s utilised the medium of radio especially, it was not really until the rise of television then, and following this the groundbreaking campaign and style on the stump of John F. Kennedy, that serious empirical scholarship was first drawn to the cult of personality and character in electoral politics.[10] Influential writers like Kennedy's own adviser, Richard Neustadt, and later James David Barber began to theorise that image, rhetoric and character had become vital ingredients of a politician's make-up.[11] 'The Washingtonians who watch a President have more to think about than his professional reputation', said Neustadt. 'They also have to think about his standing with the public outside Washington. They have to gauge his popular prestige.'[12]

Yet Hollywood campaigns, I would argue, had already begun to address these particular issues of prestige and reputation in the late 1940s, and their accelerated trend towards the blurring of real and constructed imagery has reached its apotheosis in the contemporary post-*Bob Roberts* era: the late 1990s' manifestations that see films like *Primary Colors* and *Bulworth* as the simulacra of real campaigns, an extension of reality fictionalised for an alternative form of presentation.

Thus at the end of the 1940s, for example, Spencer Tracy as Grant Matthews in Frank Capra's *State of the Union* was already making a striking public declaration for accountability and honesty in the face of television cameras that pointed the way towards the future of modern-day campaigning. Matthews' closing speech, in which he refuted any ambition he had to run for president, was less a valediction than a prophetic warning of the trials and tribulations to come for the seekers of public office, and Capra deliberately made this long final scene a more awkward experience for his protagonist by having the emerging medium situated in his own front room. A year later Robert Rossen's *All the King's Men* even more blatantly exposed the notion that verbiage was about to be consigned to history in light of the new media.

Come the 1960s and 1970s, Hollywood was engaged in reproducing the classic Kennedy/Nixon debates of the 1960 campaign through the eyes of a synthetic media showdown (in *The Best Man* for example); a real-life construct of disparate political wills that for Hollywood's liberal establishment could not be bettered for its good versus evil match-up. In the 1980s and 1990s the distinctions between real and fabricated campaigns had finally become so stretched by the interchange of personnel in each profession, that it was at times difficult to tell who were the screenwriters plying their trade in Washington and who had been real political speech gurus giving advice in Hollywood.

Michael Ritchie, the director of *The Candidate* (1972), and his screen-writer Jeremy Larner, for instance, both worked on political campaigns in the 1960s – Larner wrote speeches for presidential candidate Eugene McCarthy in 1968 – while Marty Kaplan had been engaged by Walter Mondale before working on *The Distinguished Gentleman* (1992), and Gary Ross, the writer of the Kevin Kline vehicle *Dave* (1993), penned speeches for Gary Hart among others.[13] Such has been the composite set of circumstances being thrown up by Hollywood portrayals that real and imaginary discourse has become too blurred a distinction adequately to surmise its roots with any confidence. Consequently the central notion of a character's trust, reliability and honesty has not simply been a defining issue for Hollywood politicians but a truism of real electoral politics that the voters have suspiciously come to accept, and it has been garnered by Hollywood from the experiences of real campaign veterans that have given a pseudo-authenticity to the presentation.

Where this did not work, as we will examine below, was when Hollywood found itself playing catch-up to a set of perceived notions that were simply no longer a revelation. Sidney Lumet's long neglected 1986 film *Power* is a perfect example of this. The narrative sets Richard Gere up not as a candidate but as a manipulative spin doctor for a New

Mexico governorship election, but it fails to persuade the audience of its subversive pretensions with the premise that technology is being used as a tool of contorted image-making. The public had already seen this done by Hollywood and its basis in real campaigning had become a given of the American political landscape. Hardly surprising therefore that the film's denouement, which attempts to shake Gere's moral conscience, is too shallow an offering in what the film determines is clearly a cynical profession.

Hollywood's output has thus reflected a trend whereby the political and sociological pretext involves not an examination of elections *per se*, which Gere's character in *Power* was the cipher for in many ways, but a rites-of-passage trail that follows the candidates, the heroes, through a series of examinations; examinations almost solely to do with personality, with the inbuilt dimensions of personal trust and moral fibre, rather than the ideological substance that governs policy ideas and formulation. In films such as *The Best Man*, and *The Candidate*, there is the adoption of a broadly similar strategy that pits a righteous, dignified, principled campaigner against a ruthless, ambitious career hack, backed by an unscrupulous political machine.

Each film asks its audience to regard values, truth and the American way as the principal battlegrounds rather than the mundanities of jobs, welfare and balanced budgets. Robert Redford's character in *The Candidate*, Bill McKay, is in fact driven so far down the road of sound-bite politics – forsaking his earlier intellectual liberalism – that by election day, director Ritchie has him on the verge of political meltdown, spouting gobbledygook in the back seat of a car on the way to another public rally.[14]

There are, however, ideological difficulties here with Hollywood's appraisal of politics that is distracted by charismatic star status. As Richard Maltby has remarked in relation to *The Candidate*: 'The movie asserts that politics has no place for sincerity, but it relies on the sincerity of Redford's performance to convey its theme.'[15] Maltby is entirely accurate about the proclivity of Hollywood to allow star billing to dictate the agenda, to engage with the image-conscious demands of its stars, and at the same time dilute its message. But *The Candidate* is as much about a false sincerity borne out of resentment as it is a naive tumble into political cynicism. There is a degree of irony in McKay that possibly emanates from Redford's persona, but is nevertheless sure not to mix sincerity with falsehood. Redford, Ritchie and Larner,

for example, admitted to many discussions that toyed with a similarity
to the earnest Bobby Kennedy in McKay but the director concluded:'If
we had anyone in mind, it was someone like Ralph Nader or Jerry
Brown, the kind of guy who hates politics, then gets involved with it.'[16]
From that perspective, the film concentrates on a false idealism under-
pinned by a lack of personal honesty as a focus for *all* politics; politicians are by nature rhetoricists – the anti-politics message of the film
cannot help but become *the* message of electoral and therefore political
success – and they fashion their wares accordingly.

The construction of the Hollywood election film has therefore par-
alleled the growth in image and personality that has developed significantly over time, but particularly since 1975. This has in addition made
politicians conscious of a cultural generation tutored in the mythology
of cinematic and televisual composition. As Philip Davies has observed,
'campaign advertising has continued to look towards cinema and
television for technique and inspiration'.[17] The politics of American
campaigns has been waged in these mediums almost entirely since the
end of the 1960s and the power of elections to sublimate the message
of democracy, for allegedly libertarian instincts, is inherent in both real-
life and Hollywood characters that inhabit these electoral landscapes.
Each decade has therefore produced a comparable set of candidates
dictated by the pattern of change in America; from the anti-communist
crusade and Kennedy homages of the 1950s and 1960s, to the developments in the public consciousness following the dysfunctional
breakdowns of the 1970s, and the anti-establishment, anti-incumbency,
anti-Washington backlash of the later 1980s and 1990s. Hollywood has
shadowed these developments, mimicking the moves and thought
processes, but it has also become a party to the virtual ideologies that
reside in real modern campaigns; a player and authority in the subor-
dinated discourse, not merely a watcher and recorder.

## HOLLYWOOD AND EARLY ELECTION CAMPAIGNS

In the 1930s and early 1940s, the Hollywood politician was either
about to survive, or had already survived, the rigours of an election
campaign. We never see Jefferson Keane's electoral experience in
*Washington Masquerade*, and the first time we meet B. G. Brown in
*Washington Merry-Go-Round* is on a train making his way to the capital.
Likewise the beginning of *Gabriel over the White House* reveals to its

audience a scene showing Judson Hammond's inauguration and White House reception which only alludes to the new president's tactics on the stump, while Jefferson Smith never reaches the position of having to be elected in Capra's film. Although, as we have just identified, *State of the Union* signposted the way ahead for election films in 1948, by giving its audience at least a taste of the 'behind closed doors' manœuvrings that dominate races, an earlier Hollywood example of the election milieu is perhaps best represented in Orson Welles's classic *Citizen Kane* (1941).

In a film that, as Joseph McBride commented, attempts to examine the notions of truth and objectivity, Kane's campaign to get himself elected to congress by his fabled 'Declaration of Principles' document perfectly encompasses later debates here about the manipulation of ideals and values.[18] Welles's sense of style and perception in his portrayal of the nominating process and campaign rhetoric was as entirely plausible as, say, Henry King's re-creation of Woodrow Wilson's 1912 presidential race in his own self-titled biopic released only a couple of years later (see Chapter 5).[19]

Robert Rossen's award-winning adaptation of Robert Penn Warren's Pulitzer Prize book *All the King's Men* (1949) followed on from Welles's portraiture of a biographical rise and fall in a similar manner though from the perspective of strictly political, rather than business ambition. Broderick Crawford plays Willie Stark, a small-town representative with high hopes for advanced public office. The extended narrative course of the 'rags to political riches' Hollywood film had been rich pickings for classic screwball directors like Preston Sturges, whose early offerings – *The Great McGinty* (1940) and *Hail the Conquering Hero* (1944) – both played with the notion of publicly misguided adulation for apparently battle-scared heroes, and the subsequent demands for grassroots political leadership. Rossen's story offered up this scenario in a far more melodramatic fashion. The film, like the book, only moderately concealed its references to inspiration, and legendary Louisana politician Huey Long, but the story was similarly dictated by the documenting of a public life – here using a contemporary time voice-over rather than one in retrospect – by a newspaperman: in *Kane* the reporter is Thompson, while in Rossen's film it is the idealist Jack Burden, played by John Ireland.

Moreover, Burden becomes an integral rather than detached figure to the Stark story. He meets Stark while he battles against small-town graft in Kanoma, champions his hopeless cause to get elected the first time, but is then brought back into the fold four years on when Stark has 'learned how to win' and has bought Burden's closest friends, the Stantons, into his court in order to achieve victory. The judge becomes Attorney-General, Adam accepts a post as head of a new hospital and even Burden's romance with Ann sours as Stark takes her as his mistress. The film was subject to exhaustive editing as Rossen attempted to pack all of the issues of Warren's book into the film. As Brian Neve points out, the picture connects the audience to the possibilities of democratic authority – in the first instance the early days of the administration appear to fire a warning shot across the bows of New Dealism as Stark embarks on an ambitious public works programme – and the need to control its excesses, but from the perspective of the time its themes bespoke of nothing so vital as totalitarian will.[20] Visually Rossen utilises the clearest symbols of historically recent fascist dictatorship with flaming torches, blown-up images of Stark adorning his rallies, and his protagonist placed on a podium high above the audience during speeches in the later half of the film. In addition, at all points in the movie practically every character is disillusioned and yet won back to the Stark cause, all unable or unwilling to break the shackles of power until the wily Attorney-General resigns. The director, however, had conventional narrative devices, rather than strict idealistic principles, in hand to explain Stark's taste for power, and seeming ignorance at the authoritarian machinery he sets in motion, the most revealing of which is his conversion to liquor from abstinence as an explanation for his increasingly heated diatribes on the stump.

Against the backdrop of the production Rossen was being hounded by the investigations that devoured Hollywood in the late 1940s, and he only just managed to complete work on the picture. Released at the conclusion of one set of HUAC hearings he was named for his subversive beliefs and only just persuaded the head of Columbia pictures, Harry Cohn, to let him keep working on the film which he was vindicated for by eventually winning the 1949 Best Picture Academy Award. Rossen made only one more film though in the next five years, *The Brave Bulls*, after he was named by the House Un-American Activities Committee when the committee returned to Hollywood in March 1951, and his individual, social and political style never resurfaced after this.[21] *All the King's Men*, however, has been paid an enormous debt over the following decades for its influence upon other election films, and that investment began within a short time after Rossen had accepted the plaudits for his picture.

In the anti-communist 1950s, films that looked at the American political process in any depth were anathema to Hollywood. The black-list, and publications like *Red Channels* that 'outed' supposed commu-nists working in the film industry, made any possible examination of democracy in America a superfluous and wasted exercise for Hollywood filmmakers. Commentators like Robert Toplin have also pointed to the economic necessities of the time in downplaying political storylines, and he cites Leonard Quart and Albert Auster as scholars who identified Hollywood's first priority of the time as the need to 'recapture its audience' now that the threat of television was looming on the hori-zon.[22] In addition to the moderate financial potential of films about politics Quart and Auster themselves point to a political culture in America that, certainly after McCarthy, was reinforced by a political consensus and, as Daniel Bell would have it, an end to ideology.[23] Jackson Lears notes that by mid-century America had turned from 'a vague populism to an equally murky notion of free enterprise', and that the monolithic tendencies in society blindly ignored crucial power relations.[24]

Henry Levin's *The President's Lady* (1953) was the only conspicuous exception to the moratorium on Hollywood political biographies pro-viding, in any case, a fairly triumphant historical assessment of Andrew Jackson, discussed in Chapter 5. But only Raoul Walsh's *A Lion Is in the Streets* (1953) and Elia Kazan's *A Face in the Crowd* (1957) released later in the decade really dared to challenge the political uniformity of the 1950s and put electoral politics into any context during this period. In the former film, an adaptation of Adria Locke Langley's novel, James Cagney plays a lowly southern politician, Hank Martin, seeking to ride into the governor's mansion of a poor cotton-picking state at the election by exploiting the support of the menial sharecropping community.[25] Similar in tone and message, and surely with at least a nod to Rossen's film, in which Stark directly appeals to the 'hick' vote, the chief twist was that the film stuck to the novel's depression-era setting, giving it a historical context. But this structure, with a graphic portrayal of recent poverty and subsistence, and even with Cagney as its star, ultimately proved its undoing and the picture's appeal remained slight. The latter film, Kazan's *A Face in the Crowd*, was a very different proposition, locating itself in the developing cultural environs of the 1950s. As with his earlier *On the Waterfront* (1954), the film felt obliged to disguise its intentions, and thus heighten the director's apologist tone for his disclosures to HUAC, in the still simmeringly raw atmosphere of the tail-end of the McCarthy era.

Kazan and scriptwriter Bud Schulberg saw the potential to exploit the new influential power of television with the story of a down-on-his-luck hobo who becomes an entertainment sensation first on radio and then TV before joining forces with a hopelessly inadequate Senatorial figure. Drawing upon similar narrative strands again from Capra and Sturges, it is also no coincidence that in calling up references for *A Face in the Crowd* both writer and director speculated once again about the reach of a politician like Huey Long had TV come along sooner. Ironically enough, *A Lion Is in the Streets* clearly had pretensions to be a roughly hewn Long biography also, although *Variety*, in its own review, attempted to distance this connection by pointing to a number of structural changes between the film and novel.[26] Nevertheless, the two pictures clearly helped further to elaborate many of the same ideals incorporated from Rossen's *All the King's Men.* 'We talked of how much more powerful Huey Long would have been if he had had TV at his disposal', said Kazan of his story.[27]

In an article devoted to the film, John Yates assesses the concentration on image and the portrayal of that image to the people. His critical assessment is of a hollowed-out democracy that embarrasses the people and indeed the filmmakers. Eighteen years on, Yates sees the same prophecy incorporated into Robert Altman's *Nashville* as a disparate group of rednecks feel the blast of political exploitation by a campaigning zealot (Hal Phillip Walker). He lambastes both directors for making the 'common folk' in their movies just plain dumb and giving them no credit for their cultural receptiveness.[28]

Karel Reisz's review of *A Face in the Crowd*, written at the time of its release, in *Sight and Sound*, picks up on this theme with similar criticisms: 'They display the same sort of contempt for the audience that Kazan and Schulberg showed for the silent dockers in *Waterfront*, and imply that the crowd will follow whatever the cleverest entertainers and politicians have to offer.'[29] *Films in Review* was even more scathing at the time, perhaps not untypically accusing the film of 'a synthetic truth, reminiscent of the Marxist delusions of the '30s'.[30] But, like *All the King's Men*, the film offers a prophetic statement about the coming influence of TV and the changing nature of electoral races. The fact that all three films closely echoed real campaigns, and provided subtle touches of southern political tradition, partly contradicts this simplistic lowly impression of the voters, but perhaps it also reflects on the need to explain and at once disassociate the pictures from a threatening patronage that was the reality of American politics for so long, an alternative view to the urban machine politics on offer in films like *State of the Union*.

Writing about his own film for instance, Kazan, possibly in a further effort to depoliticise his contribution, liked to emphasise the human angle of Pat Neal's loyalty to 'Lonesome' Rhodes in *A Face in the Crowd*, of the nature of women as moral consciences to men, and in this way somehow dilute the political treatment.[31] The critical perceptions of the era, of the notion that talent could only be drawn out, that the public would spot frauds and charlatans, that the elite would never open their doors to some 'shyster' figure of media construction, were being severely challenged by progressive directors like Rossen and Kazan in these pictures, and proved an early indication of how exploitative and seismic the new medium of television was proving to be. Perhaps most poignant though was a review French director François Truffaut wrote when *A Face in the Crowd* was released in Europe. 'In America', he simply professed, 'politics always overlaps with show business.'[32]

Both Rossen and Kazan established a tone and character reference that tilts us towards later Hollywood narratives of media infiltration, and stories where innocent idealism is perceived as being politically manhandled in films such as *Being There* (1979) with Peter Sellers and *Forrest Gump* (1994) with Tom Hanks.

The media explosion in America during the 1950s thus provided a stick to beat the public consciousness about its commitment to the democratic process, and further accelerated the race towards a consensus that President Eisenhower appeared to represent. As Stephen Whitfield has observed, 'the sanctions for political dissidence were capricious'.[33] The result was that the growing awareness of paranoia fixated upon Cold War ideology, and the fears over nuclear annihilation, extended the reach of Hollywood election films into overt global scenarios at the end of the decade and the beginning of the 1960s, classically represented in John Frankenheimer's ubiquitous *The Manchurian Candidate* (1962).

The film manages to include just about every policy crisis or social issue going from the era. It is ostensibly about the rumours of brain-washing among American GIs during the Korean War, but it is again also about the seductive qualities of TV presentation, the passage, declaration and freedom of information, and most clearly of all it is about McCarthyism. As Andrew Sarris has pointed out, the story is quick-witted enough to mock the Senator from Wisconsin while dis-engaging itself from any underlining criticism of other interested parties of the period, such as FBI director J. Edgar Hoover, or indeed of attempting to present any challenge to the 'system' in its own right.[34] The film is able to do this by contrasting rationality with lunacy and plain stupidity in the guise of John and Eleanor Iselin (John Gregory and Angela Lansbury respectively). The electoral story, which is actually incredibly central to the plot, appears at times to be superfluous to Frankenheimer's existentialist meanderings about psychoanalysis and philosophical self-fulfilment. It is finally coalesced, however, into attempts by the scheming, communist-infiltrated and hyper-intelligent wife (brilliantly played by Lansbury) to get her slow-witted Senator husband into the White House using TV propaganda and allegations of communist subversives in government organisations.

The many layered complexities of Washington life are given a darker and more conspiratorial feel by Frankenheimer in the movie and it bears comparison in this respect with Otto Preminger's *Advise and Consent* in the same year (see Chapter 4). Preminger too was interested in showing the power structures – or breakdowns – in the Washington hierarchy and touches upon similar Cold War themes of infiltration in a manner reminiscent of, and borrowed from, Frankenheimer himself who picks up on these structures with his following film, *Seven Days in May*, in 1964.[35]

In that same year, Hollywood returned to the electoral arena as pure subject-matter with an adaptation of the Gore Vidal play *The Best Man* (1964). With the benefit of hindsight and the 1960 campaign fresh in the memory, Vidal produced a screenplay of condensed tension that focused the action into a few days of the nomination convention in Los Angeles for 'the party' (we may speculate that it is almost certainly the Democrats though the villain of the piece, Joe Cantwell, is ambivalent enough to reside in either party). The story pits the scholarly, intellec-tual, William Russell (Henry Fonda with more than a little reference to Adlai Stevenson, Democrat candidate in both the 1952 and 1956 presidential elections) against McCarthyite impersonator and anti-communist rabble-rouser Joe Cantwell (Cliff Robertson), thus managing to carve out black and white lines of confrontation even in the same party.

Hollywood has often been good at engaging its dynasty of political players to occupy positions and play with an ideological discourse the audience thought it was sure about before it came into the theatre. In *The Best Man*, director Franklin Schaffner, with one eye on the politics of the era, cast his players with the subtle skill that reflects this tradition. Fonda, a man who had of course played Abraham Lincoln for John Ford, is perfectly cast as the aspiring, bookish, liberal candidate, while Robertson gives rival Cantwell a hyper-ambitious zeal (cleverly given the villainous role here in contrast to having already played JFK in *PT 109* (1963)); but it is Lee Tracy as ex-President Art Hockstader who steals the film by performing as the wise old sage who offers meretricious advice, as only a politician who has reached the top can, while devilishly trying to play each candidate off against the other, and cynically downplaying the merits of political idealism. Tracy, remember, played B. G. Brown thirty years beforehand in *Washington Merry-Go-Round* precisely against this type. His performance was criticised by Henry Hart in *Films in Review* for playing Hockstader without any of the dignity that comes from statesmanship.[36] But it is precisely his deviousness and obsession with the roots of power and control (hence the cleverly wrought confrontations with Russell – too lightweight, too forgiving, too dignified! – and Cantwell – too manipulative, too extreme, too much like the President himself) that make the contrasts between his public endorsements and private criticisms so overbearing but true to his character. This contrast between the public and private realms of political figures was an enduring constant about the increasingly revelatory nature of public life in the 1960s and one that writer Vidal might have been thinking of in conditioning Hockstader towards the personality of Lyndon Johnson.[37]

It is also this mixture of convention arena activity and press conference aphorisms, juxtaposed by double-dealing and backstage arrangements, that gives the film an edgy alternative slant to the usual trials and tribulations of getting elected that Hollywood had not really attempted before. Much more condensed than its later companion films, *The Candidate* or *Bob Roberts*, and thus closer to Warren Beatty's *Bulworth*, the action takes on a 'real time' feel as the Los Angeles convention builds towards its climax. In addition, Schaffner adds this vivid new stylistic treatment of the action by alternating between set-piece scenes of discussion amongst confrontational protagonists and hand-held representations of convention floor debates among the delegates, a technique subsequently adopted and developed in later films.[38] Vidal's presentation of what is, in effect, a traditional old style party convention also gives a historical counterpoint to the action. The days when the chief combatants were already preordained and the 'also rans' were the usual suspects of unelectable southern mayors and faceless western governors (wherein the lesson of the film lies), resulting in lengthy party conflagration, was a scenario whose heyday was already drawing to a close by 1964 and would be well on the way out by the turn of the 1970s as the primary system of elections began to tie up nominations far earlier.[39]

But from this setting, Vidal and Schaffner wring a conventional moral dilemma out of political infighting. Will Russell play equally dirty tricks on the dangerous Cantwell – who is willing to get endorsed at virtually any cost – or wash his hands of the whole process and keep his principles intact? Vidal offers us mental instability (in Russell's case) and homosexuality (in Cantwell's, interestingly never the other way around as one review observed) as the skeletons that the public would never accept in their future president.[40] The undercurrent of 'new right' battlegrounds, so pertinent to the times, is never far away but the acute reflections on political personality make it remarkably prescient today. Vidal's story is complex enough to impress upon us that there is truth and lies in both claims that hang over each candidate, and only Shelley Berman's rather idiosyncratic portrayal of whistle-blowing stooge Sheldon Bascombe deflects from the desperation of both men in their cause as they attempt to do a deal for the cost of silence.

The denouement returns to what Maltby describes as the film's interest in 'content, spectacle, message, and neutrality'.[41] Image, in both its literal and metaphorical form, is its guiding doctrine. Russell relinquishes his claims on the nomination pledging his delegates to the faceless Governor Merwin. He contends that this will put a stop to Cantwell, which, as his primary aim, it indeed does. But it is also an endorsement of idealess politics as he informs his wife in the concluding moments of the film. Russell states that the public prefer safety, someone they (think?) they can trust, who will do a steady job, just like the previous incumbent, ironically a man whose endorsement Russell started off so badly wanting.

Rather like the convention itself then, this view of patronage as presidential leadership potential was losing its theoretical credibility by the 1960s. The pattern of selectivity and a somewhat archaic view of the presidency as some grand office of state rather dates the ideals inherent in the picture. In that very same year, 1964, Lyndon Johnson was already setting about destroying the credibility of his opponent, Barry Goldwater, with the damming and infamous 'Daisy' campaign spot indicating that statesmanship was rather less impressive a tactic than hardball politics by the mid-1960s.

The TV ad, featuring a little girl picking the petals off a flower as the countdown to nuclear war booms all around her, was shown only once in that campaign, on 7 September 1964 on CBS. Yet its impact sent reverberations all around America and signalled how instructive the negative and powerfully constructed image could be.[42] Johnson did use positive ads of his record in the campaign but 'Daisy' cast a shadow over virtually all of them.

*The Best Man* does give some credence to this notion of a changing order in the 1960s but its references again deal with the acceptance of persona rather than ideological conversion or the structural alterations to political campaigning. When, at the pre-convention dinner, Hockstader contemporaneously observes that the bastions of political prejudice are coming down, as seen by a Catholic reaching the White House, he is touching upon a real-life scenario exploited by the devotion to image and style itself. At the same time, however, Hockstader's comments are surreptitiously revealing Schaffner and Vidal's limitations in tackling the bigotry of candidate selection. None of the films discussed here even entertain the notion that religion, as one instance, is a defining trait of political character let alone a source of friction for American politics in general, and Hollywood presentation has consistently been unable adequately to tackle this area of American public life.

## THE BOYS ON THE BUS:
## HOLLYWOOD CAMPAIGN FILMS FROM THE 1970s

By 1972, Hollywood had become the talk of the actual Republican convention that came together in Miami to endorse Richard Nixon for a second term, and the conversation was drawn to Michael Ritchie's film *The Candidate*. Well immersed into dirty tricks campaigns by now, the Nixon White House actually tried to get the film banned during the election race. The film's protagonist Bill McKay (Robert Redford) was clearly identified as being a Democrat even though once again no party labels were attached to the candidates in the film. Nixon failed to stop the film and ultimately it did not have a great impact on the contest as he romped home to victory against George McGovern in any case.

As a film, *The Candidate* shied away from the 'big politics' of *The Best Man*, choosing instead to focus on the nuts and bolts of a senate campaign in California allied to behind-the-scenes arguments and tensions that unravelled the organisation and monotony of modern electioneering. Ritchie did this by adopting a pure form of documentary style, *cinéma vérité*, and thanks to technological advances was able to make much greater use of hand-held cameras for the location shooting that dominates most of the film. In effect then Hollywood in the 1970s jumped on the campaign bus and created for itself a style of semi-real detached observation. This cinematic development took up where Schaffner's film had tentatively left off and quickly went on to establish itself as the defining style of Hollywood election films; to such an extent that Tim Robbins's later so-called 'mockumentary' approach in *Bob Roberts* spends a great deal of the picture self-parodying the whole style. What critic Robert Sklar identifies as Robbins's historical reference point for his film is equally as relevant, if not more so, for Ritchie in *The Candidate*; that is, its indebtedness to the Drew Associates' 1960 film *Primary*, which followed Democrat hopefuls Kennedy and Hubert Humphrey around on the campaign trail in Wisconsin.[43]

Ritchie mimicked this realist style by filming hours of footage of Redford shaking hands with ordinary Californians – one key scene taking place outside the Long Beach shipyards – making his character McKay ad-lib introductions to various meetings, and shooting head and shoulders shots of the general public giving their 'off the cuff' endorsements. Director of photography on the film, Victor Kemper, made use of as many 'public' events as possible to get Redford immersed into naturally enthusiastic crowds; the ticker-tape open-top car scene in San Francisco, for example, taking place on New Year's Eve 1971 during shooting when employees in the city's financial district traditionally tear up their old year calendars and toss them to the street below.[44]

As many reviewers of the film pointed out, this commitment to 'realism' only partly works. The narrative is at pains to point out the way McKay's early idealism is slowly drained away amid the campaign machine that freewheels towards election day at his expense – literally as we are never given any indication of costs in this race, a point starkly made by Sarris in his criticism – yet McKay's timidity and innocence at the process revealing itself to him grates when we know that his father is the legendary governor John McKay (played with some relish by Melvyn Douglas, Hollywood campaigner himself and husband of Helen Gahagan Douglas who ran against Richard Nixon for the Senate in 1950).[45] Even more than this, the early scenes hint that McKay's existence as a small-town civil liberties lawyer, who is not even registered to vote in his own town, is a signal of his disenchantment with politics, his father's past actions, and is indicative of his own political mentality. Yet this naivety and public uncertainty, demonstrated by his early embarrassing speech at a fund-raising dinner, is given no examination by Ritchie. Instead the director's realism of political campaigning is stretched to there being no Hollywood constructed climax as McKay takes the election by a comfortable margin. It suggests that Marvin Lucas (Peter Boyle) is the real power behind his protégé and that his Faustian pact with McKay at the beginning of the film, that whatever he says he will lose, is just that; a contract with the devil designed to tempt McKay back to what we the audience are led to believe is his natural environment. Lucas has no intention of seeing McKay lose and if the election was so comfortable, and McKay so able, as Lucas's talent-spotting of him at the beginning of the film implies, then how can we expect to react to his apparent shock at the conclusion?

McKay's mouthing of the phrase 'What do we do now?' to Lucas as well-wishers crowd into the hotel suite at the end of the film is certainly meant to be symbolic, and could simply be read as a condemnatory exposé of candidates who like the thrill of the race in politics but have no care for the aftermath. It might also be read as a commentary on amateur politicians who, as in McKay's case, capitalise on their good looks if not their innocence, only to find that they have little in the way of plans once they reach office.

It is certainly true, as one reviewer noted, that Ritchie's style allows his characters to maintain a certain ambiguity in their relationship to the audience and this may be seen as crucial in the concluding moments.[46] The amateur as political host to the hopes and fears of the watching audience also has a strong tradition in Hollywood. Jefferson

Fig. 4 *Robert Redford as Bill McKay in* The Candidate, *addressing matters of style, image and perception in the 1970s (BFI Films: Stills, posters and designs).* The Candidate © *1972 Warner Bros Inc., All Rights Reserved.*

Smith is often viewed as the archetypal example of this character but director Frank Capra revealed more about his own position again in the later *State of the Union*, when political boss Jim Conover exclaims to Kay Thorndyke that he has never liked amateurs and never will, a pointed remark about the kind of opponents Franklin Roosevelt faced in his time – Grant Matthews being a representation of FDR's 1940 presidential opponent Wendell Willkie – but also reflective in the film's need to establish control of the political message. In this respect Lucas is just like Thorndyke and Conover who also want a malleable candidate, a blank canvas on which to construct heavy image but light politics.

Ritchie's conclusion in his film appears to have dubious intent but the message in electoral terms is arguably consistent: that political campaigning by the 1970s had become a business, running for office was a separate world from being in office. As one reviewer commented, McKay's 'street politics' style is clearly a vote winner but the realities of electoral politics in this modern age see him chewed up and spat out with little regard for the problems he knows are befalling society at the time.[47] The dilemma for the director was to answer these charges of media power and soundbite manipulation, not simply pointedly to allow campaign guru Lucas to fly off to his next candidate as if going to a sales meeting in the final scene of the picture. The more recent *Primary Colors* (1998) arrived at a time when the scope for a presentation of internal campaign relations has been given greater credence, and Mike Nicholls's film delves into the world of the campaign manager in greater depth, allowing a more significant investigation of these issues and questioning not only candidate assumptions but those of the whole campaign team as well. Although not as well plotted as Joe Klein's descriptions in his novel, the presidential candidate Jack Stanton becomes Lucas and the campaign aide Henry Burton assumes the guise of McKay, as Nicholls plays with this role reversal and extends a similar feel for the construction and temporal nature of relationships and business in electoral campaigns.

Win Sharples' concluding ideas – that Bill McKay refuses to compromise his vision in *The Candidate* and that the film only leaves us wondering whether his idealistic notions of politics can be implemented in the harsh world of Washington – are too expectant a reading of Redford's supposedly brave, upstanding portrayal.[48] Penelope Houston's assertion that Redford carries McKay off without too much sycophancy or imitation of the Kennedy style is more accurate and, given the time and context, the openness of the options left vacant at the end is perhaps understandable.[49] Hollywood was in the process of working out its new role in the political world, the Camelot era was over, and cynicism was being associated with political action in a growing sense of disenchantment about to be manifest in Watergate. As the next chapter demonstrates, Hollywood was getting ready to associate politics and politicians with things far worse than loose morals. The dislocation of the complete political process, as conspiracy thrillers like *Executive Action* (1974), *The Parallax View* and the copycat documentary style of *All the President's Men* displayed, was being embedded with the 1970s' vogue for democratic deviancy.

In the immediate aftermath of the Nixon fall from grace, the summary of political intent that Hollywood offered in electoral terms still remained impressively prescient while generating a recurrent downbeat tone in Robert Altman's *Nashville* (1975). If not the doyen of the style then Altman has long been one of the chief archivists in the *cinéma vérité* format. Paring down the script and set-piece scenes in this picture, he filmed it as a series of episodic engagements between twenty-four characters – a precursor to his more ambitious piece, *Short Cuts* (1993) – giving screenwriter Joan Tewkesbury only the barest of details from which to fashion improvised scenes.[50] Filming in Tennessee itself, Altman concocted a semi-realist election campaign, complete with baton twirlers and majorettes, that the population of Nashville took to be a real political rally.[51] The irregular structure of the piece and Altman's relentless fashioning of a corporate capitalist ethos, separated by Hal Philip Walker's dismembered voice campaigning for office around the city, has often been portrayed as its defining emblem. Robert Self has argued that the notions of politics and capitalism are in addition shaped by the religious treatment in the film and that the central part of the five-day narrative is the Sunday, thus allowing Altman to emphasise his sense of 'value displacement'.[52] The film's 'cultural dislocation' is what further oppresses human emotions, according to Michael Klein, and the mad spectacle of country festival, political campaign and bicentennial celebrations, juxtaposed against each other, is a bleak landscape that appears to give Altman some considerable satisfaction, as Leonard Quart surmises.[53] Certainly the depressingly allegorical feel in *Nashville* for the laziness and despondency in the 1970s was summed up at the Washington premiere by one of that decade's victims, former presidential candidate George McGovern. 'I can't say it left me in high spirits', he said. 'It had the combination of tragedy and comedy which characterises both good drama and the poignant condition of our lives in the seventies. It looked into the soul of the country and it ended without any answers.'[54]

At the tail-end of the 1970s Hollywood returned to Washington politics again slightly redirecting the genre and attempting to point its way out of the decade-long malaise but on into an almost more false period of harmonised manipulation and concentrated spin doctoring. Alan Alda (who wrote the screenplay) and Jeffrey Schatzberg (director) made *The Seduction of Joe Tynan* (1979); a trawl through the media-driven world of a popular, good-looking liberal senator, involved with another woman (Meryl Streep), and riding to the ultimate election success on the back of his effervescent style and personality.

Alda's vision of Washington seemed centred upon sexual proclivity and a 1970s' moral tone for therapy and self-analysis, but its reflections on presentation are quite acute for the era to follow. What at first appears a conventional play for dignified political representation is partly redirected by Alda's portrayal and the underrated pretensions of the film that push the ambiguous motives of its characters even further into a parallel political world than happens in *The Candidate*. Prophetically, in a somewhat Clintonesque style, you are never sure about Tynan as a person although you cannot help but be impressed by his performance as a media politician.[55] Just like Grant Matthews forty years earlier Tynan is always seeking office without ever running for it. His timing and position on the Senate recommendation of a racist judge to the Supreme Court also helps to tackle that other perennial Hollywood question of generational change. Tynan's friend, the ageing Senator Birney (played again by Melvyn Douglas), is facing up to the fact that his time is about to pass if the judge is not confirmed and he cannot subsequently win re-election, leaving Tynan with the simple dilemma of friendship or career to make in exposing – through an old film – the reality of the judge's bigotry. On the cusp of an era that would attempt to destroy the progressive liberal politics on offer here, and shove the moral conscience of America to the forefront of a Reaganite Republican agenda, *Joe Tynan* appears somewhat at odds with its times, and that may account for its limited success. Also, implicit in the title, and contradictory given his pointed objections to his wife's revelatory declaration to a reporter of her breakdown, the expectation that Tynan's affair would never be revealed is doubtful given the events about to unfold in the 1980s. However, its separation of private activity and job responsibility is what real political discourse in the 1990s has been debating, and this statement of intent gives the picture an insight that was less obvious at the time.

   The Reagan era itself, by contrast, saw Hollywood increasingly shy away from virtually any kind of political discourse. It was almost as if the 1950s were being revisited. Apart from *Power* by Sidney Lumet, which was a box-office disaster, few other films tackled American politics let alone elections during the decade. For Lumet this film was something of a nadir in his career. Having been responsible for some of the most hard-hitting social commentaries of the previous few decades (*Fail Safe* (1964), *Network* (1976), *The Verdict* (1981)) *Power* tries, and fails, to instigate Hollywood moral redemption into a story of campaign image-making. Pete St John (Gere) is a high-flying spin guru who we meet while taking the expensive fees and going through the motions of campaigns he doesn't believe in. Ex-wife, Julie Christie (rather embarrassingly unconvincing), and former mentor, now turned alcoholic, Wilfred Buckley (Gene Hackman) attempt to find the young kid's heart and convince him that ideals and belief in the system do matter. The trouble is Gere still thinks he's in *American Gigolo* (1980) and there, where he successfully asserted that his was a character with low esteem in a society where any morals had already been exorcised, his detached aloofness worked fine. In *Power* his performance finds sympathy difficult to come by. Added to this, the image pyrotechnics on display are already weak and facile for 1980s' politics and Lumet, unlike Ritchie at least, doesn't even attempt to go behind the rationale of political advertising and engage in much dialogue between client and hired hand. Neither satirical nor worthy, the film was quickly lost in a decade where the triumphalist call in politics was that 'It's morning again in America'. *Power* tried to enlighten a generation of Americans into thinking that this kind of manipulation was eating away at their democracy when in fact the above phrase, from Reagan's most famous 'Spot' of the 1984 campaign, had already convinced the populace that economic depression and the Vietnam syndrome were over, while the Los Angeles Olympic Games of the same year had returned the United States to greatness.

## RECASTING THE POLITICAL CANDIDATE: ELECTION FILMS IN THE 1990s

By 1992, Hollywood was so well attuned to the over-inflated bombast that had become American politics, that it could finally shake off its own excesses of the individualistic 1980s and accommodate a no-holds barred satire for the 1990s. Recasting the realist style to create a 'mockumentary' approach allied to the film's episodic structure – borrowing heavily from his mentor, Robert Altman – Tim Robbins crafted a modern morality tale for grown-ups with *Bob Roberts* (1992), a movie only overwrought in its rather obvious contemporary references to the Gulf War, periodically shown on TV screens that adorn most scenes in the picture.

What at first sight appears a heavy-handed duty being paid particularly to the impact of TV in 1990s' campaign politics becomes, with repeated viewing, a subliminal endorsement of Marshall McCluhan's tribal culture in the hands of Robbins. Those in the beginning who are Roberts' handlers such as Lucas Hart III (Alan Rickman) are entirely plausible until the second half of the picture when the faintly ridiculous madness of their persona begins to catch up with the viewer. The 'Bob disciples' who religiously follow his every move are not the watchers to identify with, it is the background crowds, the onlookers who Robbins cleverly weaves into the most witty, and often most denigrating scenes in the film – the beauty pageant or the visit to the orphanage being excellent examples – that need to be regarded more intently. The satirical message is thus achingly relevant but one senses throughout that Robbins is laughing *at*, as much as *with*, his audience, and 1990s' political films have repeatedly had to contend with treading this fine line in declaring their propositions.

The film, perhaps unsurprisingly, was still a pretty outstanding failure at the American box office taking only $4 million. Although generally praised in many reviews the irony that Robbins employed – its mid-Atlantic humour endorsed by the use of a deadpan British documentary team following Bob around – came across in American eyes as vacuous. Applauding Robbins's performance and the accuracy of his mannerisms, for instance, Todd McCarthy nevertheless wondered why anyone would want to spend time in the company of such an odious personality.[56] More than this, the right-wing reaction against *Bob Roberts* killed any potential it had at the box office. Yet the film is not about right- or left-wing politics and deliberately so in Robbins's eyes. Although party labels are once again absent from the candidates, the film is at pains openly to reveal its political heritage. Rather than conceal its identity, therefore, as *The Best Man, The Candidate* and, to an extent, *Joe Tynan* do, Robbins juxtaposes his ideological metaphors in the film to produce a truly translucent political framework. Thus the Dylan motive of album references ('The Times They Are a Changing Back', 'Bob on Bob') and original songs (a brilliantly conceived homage (!) to D. A. Pennebaker's 'Subterranean Homesick Blues' sequence from *Don't Look Back*), together with Bob's parents being interviewed by documentarist Terry Manchester, is as equal a low blow to 1960s' chic radicalism and hippy communitarianism, as is the coded Republican terrorist connections of Lucas Hart – to Iran-Contra – and the obsession with money-making – that is, read campaign finance in general – observed by the campaign bus having a Wall Street stock market area on it. Robbins likened the film to current-day politicians and their obsession with appearance and he consciously drags conflicting imagery into this recurring motif of the film. Crucially, all this baggage places *Bob Roberts* in a provocatively ambivalent ideological position, as Robbins commented:'He's [Roberts] representative of a lot of political figures, not only from the Republican right wing, but from the Democrats.'[57]

Cleverly constructing a parable between the past and present in American elections, and tying up a link to generational change about to be thrust on real American politics in the 1992 and 1994 campaigns, Bob gets to run for the Pennsylvania Senate seat against an ageing intellectual patrician incumbent, Brickley Paiste, played with world-weary ease by Gore Vidal. Paiste stands as the most discernible malcontent that the picture offers. He is the film's political epicentre, its moral conscience as one review noted, because in his confrontations with Roberts – most effectively the pastiche of a campaign debate – the film sets out to offend not only real politicians but Hollywood sensibilities as well.[58] This is because it takes issue with the 'mom-and-apple pie' righteousness of earlier cinematic political heroes – Jeff Smith, Judson Hammond, Bill McKay, Joe Tynan – and sets out to make a mockery of their goodness and morality. Bob is a good guy on camera because he stands up for the causes of American democracy, and pleads with his potential constituents, 'What happened to your American Dream?' Yet Robbins viciously contrasts this with an off-screen character who is, to all intents and purposes, a racist, misogynist, power-hungry mega-lomaniac. As doomed reporter Bugs Raplin (Giancarlo Esposito) observes, 'there are no Mr Smiths in Washington', and the film is a wake-up call to any in the audience who think there might be, as much as it is a savage indictment on the duplicity of contemporary American politics.

In its musical vein, Robbins echoes Kazan's *A Face in the Crowd*, and *Nashville* of course, by the use of songs as both texture and ideology: in its soft-soap construction of candidate image-making, it has clear references to *The Candidate*, and in its treatment of women especially, both the latter film and *Joe Tynan* have clearly made impressions on Robbins. The peripheral nature of women and gender politics in general (McKay's references to the contemporary debate on abortion are made increasingly ambivalent in Ritchie's film) strike at the heart of the debates on public acceptance and nuclear family structures over the last generation of Hollywood history.

*Bob Roberts* further plays with the audience's emotions by fashioning a heavily stylised assassination scene – itself a planned stylised con-struction in the narrative and thus again pushing back the limits of image and reality – reminiscent of the Robert Kennedy shooting in 1968, but with cinematic comparisons dating back to *All the King's Men*. In Rossen's film, the closure is based on an analogy with Huey Long's assassination in 1936, though it has remarkably strong visual connotations with especially the later public slaying of Lee Harvey Oswald in a Dallas jail in 1963. Stark's death, and the frenzy of faithful supporters outside the state legislature, provides the film with an uncomfortable finale that, as Burden reminds Ann, leaves them having to convince the people of Stark's greed and manipulation of power in office. Robbins leaves the paralysed Roberts in a similar position with the disciples still believing and the election of a martyr now imminent. Rather like other films, however, it is in the manner of casting where once again important political signposts in *Bob Roberts* have been erected.

Comparable only to Altman's film – and there are significant differences here in any case – *Bob Roberts* deliberately revaluates the 'star vehicle' theory of election films that Maltby complains of in the manipulation of image. For Robbins this film appeared before his mainstream breakthrough as a leading man in *The Shawshank Redemption* (1994), and his own highly praised *Dead Man Walking* (1995), and so he was hardly a star himself when the film was released. Using this to his advantage he turns the tables on the traditional dichotomy of good and bad personality by having as his opponent the real 'star', Gore Vidal. He plays Roberts' erstwhile opponent Paiste as a liberal intellectual grandee, the progressive chronicler of the nation's problems, but is importantly recast as the anachronistic figure here, a politician who has lost touch, partly with the people, but more or less with the modern-day modus operandi of electoral politics.

In his review, John Harkness compared the film to the upcoming 1992 presidential election, partly in the attendant rise of Ross Perot's independent Reform Party, but most particularly in its spooky mirroring of Democratic candidate Bill Clinton's appearance on chat show host Arsenio Hall's show, complete with saxophone. For Harkness, winning is the message of *Bob Roberts* and that message is carried through television so effectively – most particularly the daytime chat shows of Oprah, Ricki, Jenny Jones and Jerry Springer – because for the medium of TV winning is the simple explainable principle behind elections.[59] In this respect Robbins's political *mise en scène* for the 1990s is as well attuned to the cultural landscape as the vision Altman created for not only politics but modern day life in the 1970s. *Bob Roberts* does though have to answer the same charge as *Nashville* in many ways, and that is what Stephen Abrahams wrote of the former film declaring: 'Altman presents a commercial art which is more self-expressive than product-related and a political campaign which is more commonsensical than issue-orientated.'[60] Ideology is difficult for Robbins, as he admitted to, and the more so for a film that is a self-styled parody. But because it is so closely associated with campaigning rather than society and culture it bypasses these elements of life in a way wholly consistent with political goals and candidate behaviour in elections. The picture makes the world of Bob Roberts a parochial endorsement of every one of its candidate's beliefs. Add the Perot phenomenon in and Robbins offers many of the same allegories of political campaigns that *The Candidate* touched upon historically in 1972 and *The Best Man* alluded to in 1964. But the film in general and Vidal's character in particular are not projections of the state of politics in 1992. What they really demonstrate is Robbins's prophetic allusion to 1994, to the Republican take-over of congress, to the dismissal of so many liberal patrician Democrats, and to the attempted construction of a new defining ideology for right-wing politics in the United States, the Contract With America. Brickley Paiste is thus Tom Foley or Dan Rostenkowski and Robbins presented a collage of imagery and idealistic notions that really articulate the new post-structuralism at the heart of American politics.

Returning these themes to the mainstream, Mike Nicholls's *Primary Colors* in 1998 draws upon real political history for its narrative – on film even more than on the page it is clearly Clinton's 1992 campaign – but at the same time acknowledges the film's debt to previous electoral movies. Its appearance in 1998, slap bang in the midst of the Lewinsky controversy, seemingly confirms its, and Hollywood's, status as concurrent storytellers of the age. But if we assume for a moment that sex and concealment is what the Clinton White House has always been about anyway, the film really belongs in its true moment: the 1992 campaign. Both John Travolta and Emma Thompson play the ambitious couple, Jack and Susan Stanton, as rather desperate politicos, out to impress, clever, knowledgeable but with a naivety of presidential campaigning and Washington's ways that could pass muster only in an initial campaign for the White House.

This is really what gives the film its slant towards Clinton. Reports were widely circulated before its release in America that the film had lost some of the satirical and calculating edge directed at the President in Klein's book.[61] The second half of the picture is in somewhat of a hurry to get the scandals of adultery out of the way and it finds it difficult to engage with Jack Stanton as Southern governor on his way to the White House when the innocent idealism of Henry Burton (Adrian Lester) as his aide – through whose eyes the audience perceive the campaign – is often diminishing the scale of the crisis surrounding the candidate.

Where Nicholls's film does perform well, as Eric Pooley has commented upon, is in its refusal to tie up narrative loose ends or to give any hints to the audience about the nature of Stanton's marital infidelities, in short: 'unresolved questions and muddied waters are hallmarks of the Clinton presidency, glossing the indiscretions and lingering over the cover-up feels just right.'[62] But Pooley also realises that such analysis treads on thin ice as a critique of modern-day presidential politics. The film's simplistic and one-dimensional conclusion tempts Henry with the opportunity of making history, a history that Stanton asserts is just the same as Abraham Lincoln or any other of the great leaders who were flawed by power and responsibility laid claim to. With this tempting scenario Nicholls offers us nothing more than a parting shot that is a direct take from *The Candidate*, even though, as the director admitted, it was audience test screenings that forced his hand towards a less ambiguous ending.[63] The concluding scene is the inauguration ball at the White House where Henry congratulates the now Chief Executive mouthing the words 'thank you Mr President', leaving us in no doubt as to his compromised choice back on the campaign. Henry has lost his voice just like Bill McKay in the earlier film, and has instead given himself over to the manipulation of success and the temptation of victory, but it is a private sacrifice rather than a national indiscretion and Nicholls's film leaves the ideological questions inconclusive, a fair enough comment on Clinton but rather a safe observation for the future of the office.

One is left to wonder, as reflected upon earlier, whether this simulacra of political events is closer to the truth than the speculative 'real' news stories emanating from the White House. Does Travolta as Clinton perform better than Clinton himself, did the director as friend of the President know more about the administration than the expert watchers of Washington events? Travolta was open enough in interviews about Clinton turning up on the set in Washington, but the temptation to regard the film fan Chief Executive as a man who would never pass up

Fig. 5 *John Travolta as Jack Stanton on the campaign trail in* Primary Colors. *Copyright © 2000 by Universal City Studios, Inc. Courtesy of Universal Studios Publishing Rights. All Rights Reserved.*

an opportunity to make political capital seems strong for a picture that still pulls apart the character of a sitting president more than any other mainstream Hollywood production has ever done.[64]

What *Primary Colors* really adds to the collection of Hollywood election movies is an issue largely ignored until now: obliqueness. In the 1990s evasion is the cruise missile of tactical weaponry in political campaigns and its only target is victory. What the film endorses about late twentieth-century American politics is not that rules can be bent, or that the cover-up of one's illicit activities is a serious and professional arm of campaigning when we are aware of this already, but that television and Hollywood have shown the way in adjusting visual composition by refocusing public perceptions of morality and satire to produce political debate out of any issue, be it topical or trivial.[65]

This is especially pertinent with the final political election film of the century, for in Warren Beatty's satire on the democratic system, *Bulworth* (1998), the attack on deceit, rhetorical vagaries, on obliqueness itself, is what remains fixed in Beatty's mind for his own analysis of American politics. Early impressions compared the mood to Capra and an idealism that strove for a revisionist critique of black politics not entertained in mainstream Hollywood for some while.[66] Such determinism at a new liberal, racially inclusive consensus does not weigh as heavily in the film as that. Its didactic attention may be directed towards a Chomskian model of multinational capital in politics and society, as reviewer Linda Holt noted, but it's not as though other films with far less ideological intent than Beatty's have not hinted at the same claim.[67] Although *Bulworth* serves as both rejoinder and a companion piece to *Bob Roberts*, its own satirical swipe really concentrates on cutting a swathe across the landscape of relations between Hollywood and politics in the United States. As a result the picture crucially rewrites some of the rules for election films.

Jay Bulworth is a California senator only a few days away from the primary election that is meant to confirm his bid for renomination by the Democrat Party. Polls suggest he is about to lose, a victim of public dissatisfaction at political graft in Washington and a waning appeal for what we are invited to believe was once a charismatic political image. Returning home to California with arrangements made for his own assassination, Bulworth begins to realise there is an alternative way: tell the people the truth, and do it appropriating the language of the 'street', rap music.

To begin with, in stylistic terms and cinematic technique Beatty as director shied away from the *cinéma vérité* genre used by other directors as a means to guide the narrative, and indeed went in totally the opposite direction by fashioning a far more glossy and urbane visual presentation. Once more utilising the expertise of Oscar-winning cinematographer Vittorio Storaro – who had previously worked with Beatty on *Reds* (1981) and *Dick Tracy* (1991) and whose work with Bernardo Bertolucci earned him an Academy Award for *The Last Emperor* (1987) – Beatty positions his character against the backdrop of textured interiors and unitary lighting, most effectively in the TV debate scene when Bulworth is cast into shadow by assistant Murphy turning the lights off on the studio floor but is left in profile set against the definitive backdrop of the Stars and Stripes, while other, hostile characters (cleverly prefacing the narrative) are painted in an alien green hue.

Lighting and texture are also complicit in Beatty's often haggard and whitened features being contrasted with Halle Berry's Nina as a young, lean and aspiring personality. The sucking of lollipops and faintly revealed virginal white underwear have Lolita-like tendencies for the relationship but politically she is in touch with Bulworth's ideological spirit (she grew up with his black heroes) and her character is also the critical macguffin for the plot.

From an additional ideological point of view, the film, unlike almost all other election movies, also has a designated political time and place. It is no coincidence that Jay Bulworth is a Californian senator, or that he should be fighting the 1996 primary in the state, with a cast list of candidates from that year tying up Hollywood to a campaign process that included figures like publisher Steve Forbes, Lamar Alexander, Colin Powell and Ross Perot. Beatty is even careful to infer that Barbara Boxer remains as the state's other 'real' representative – an overtly liberal senator herself – while remaining Californian senator Dianne Feinstein is presumably excluded by the presence of his Bulworth character. The film touches base with virtually all recent political and cultural events and people emanating out of the state, from O. J. Simpson, via Rodney King, through Arsenio Hall, to the virtually ubiquitous appearance of Larry King – he makes cameos in *Dave* and *Primary Colors* also – and sets up its intentions quite firmly from the first scene of the senator in his Congressional office repeating a campaign speech on the video ('we stand at the doorstep of a new millennium') before flicking his remote through a host of iconic cultural/television references (WWF wrestling, the shopping channel, and *The Simpsons* among others).

Beatty is actually transferring the direction of political character by inclusion of all these elements. Bulworth is an incumbent representative and, although it is never made completely clear, the inference is that he is a well-established political animal who has served in office for many years. This opening scene of mental and political breakdown even allows Beatty a little ironic symbolism by glancing around his office at old pictures including ones that in reality do actually come from his own work on the campaign trail, for Bobby Kennedy in 1968 and George McGovern in 1972.[68]

Contrast this experience then with a number of other characters including Eddie Bracken's discharged 'war hero' Woodrow in *Hail the Conquering Hero* (1944), Robert Redford's character of Bill McKay in *The Candidate*, Bob Roberts himself in Tim Robbins's film. The line of electoral thinking in these movies pitches characters into campaigns with nothing to offer at first but raw personality. Jay Bulworth, by contrast, has used up that originality earlier in his career and is therefore searching for identity in a modern age where campaign speeches are old hat and where unique and niche personification is what sells. The premise of the film, its most controversial element, is not that Bulworth wants to be seen as making a white man's stab at comprehending black culture – through rap music and the garb of 'street' clothes – but that he is a confused, parochial driven public servant who sees modern culture as communication and the message of communication, even political communication, comes at the end of the twentieth century through entertainment. Rap music culture and its dysfunctional reputation amongst the white middle classes become the 'radical wisdom' that leads Bulworth to try political incorrectness allied to 'truth' as his strategy.[69] A key scene for the film's closure is the reappearance of Bulworth in Nina's house with requisite suit and tie – he goes to sleep for nearly two days having been permanently awake since before the film's narrative opens – only for his campaign manager Dennis (Oliver Platt) to arrive persuading him to go back to 'the other clothes' he has been wearing, at first to remain incognito, but later turning up in them for an outrageous but obviously successful TV interview. All parties in the room realise that his streetwise attire has quickly become an accessory to a newly created image for the senator that the media has already defined for the watching public, as the reporters and cameras crowding into the South-Central street outside are testimony to. This scene critically tests the cynical nature of the audience in accepting Bulworth's mental incapacity for what it is (was!) rather than as a manipulative tool of electioneering. Thus Bulworth's character, as well as his politics, reside in a delicate state of sympathy on the one hand, but derision on the other, demanding approval for his bravery, but questioning the extent of his ethical sentiment.

The role of the media in general, projecting alternate shadows on the senator's persona, is one area that *Bulworth* actually recasts in quite a familiar light. For example, the tactic of having C-Span (the congres-sional news channel) follow the senator round on his final week of campaigning is a cinematic device directly taken from *Bob Roberts*. The middle part of the film has a TV campaign debate repeated in virtually any election film you care to name, and the intrusion of songs as com-mentary has already been documented from Kazan through Altman to Robbins again.[70] Even Beatty's witty repetition of his 'doorstep of the millennium' speech at every rally has a heritage as part of Bill McKay's breakdown in *The Candidate* ('We can no longer play off the young against the old, the black against the white') and has been adapted quite recently by Jack Lemmon's character, former President Russell Kramer, in *My Fellow Americans* (1997) ('our dreams are our children').

Appropriately perhaps, considering it is a film that arrived (in Britain at least) in the final year of the millennium, Hollywood notions of conservatism, liberalism and communitarianism – indeed the role and future of political ideas and values in any sense – are questioned incessantly. As Angie Errigo opined, the collapse of party politics in America is a given here but hope springs from the plea for recognition that people can save themselves if they face up to the fact that society is failing them.[71] Beatty pointedly throws in the 's' word, socialism, into his brunch speech rap during one scene, and Nina's back seat polemical confession about materialism, the degeneration of the urban working class and her knowledge and respect for the ideas of former Black Panther Huey Newton are indeed comments few other film-makers would dare to ascribe to their stories. The film tries hard to make politics realise its legacy and promulgate the notion of class being equally as important as race for the great divisions in American society. But ultimately it does remain satirical, and satire needs persistently clichéd characters in order to make its point. In this sense the reporters in the film talk of having to do their jobs and report the 'facts', the LAPD are gun-toting racists, and the black women are 'home girls', while a character like 'D' (Don Cheadle) gets to find out about the possibilities of life beyond his drug business and the confines of the South-Central ghetto.

All of these stereotypical cultural references become recognisable tools of conflict, resolution and renewal. Like all election films as distinct from other political movies, there is always a final lesson to be learnt because any soliloquy involves the representation of victory and defeat. No election film in Hollywood's history has followed a protagonist

where defeat is the only closure on offer. Each victory has consequences and involves the pretext of sacrifices; that public life and
American politics are a game of truth and consequences and that
happy endings are all relative. Hollywood has arguably never instilled
a truly idealised, hopeful redemption for American elections because,
of all the sub-genres on offer here, it has remained the closest to real
tangible cinematic influence over the means and manner of process.
American elections have thus not simply become the spectacle of
image over content, style over substance, but the transformation of
symbolic language and rhetorical excess from a mythologised fantasy
existence into a mythologised reality at the heart of modern media politics in America.

## NOTES

1  Robert Sklar, 'Bob Roberts', *Cineaste*, March 1993, p. 78.
2  Edwin Diamond and Stephen Bates, *The Spot*, 3rd edn (Cambridge, MA:
   MIT Press, 1992) p. 37.
3  Diamond and Bates quote famous political consultant Roger Ailes as
   saying: 'You can present all the issues you want on the air, and if at the
   end the audience doesn't like the guy, they're not going to vote for him.'
   As spots have become more technologically and 'artistically' creative,
   voters also become inured to the spectacle and imagery rather than the
   message, an argument important to the Hollywood influence on electoral campaigns. Ibid. pp. 381–3.
4  Tim Hames, 'The Changing Media', in *Developments in American Politics
   2*, ed. Gillian Peele, Christopher J. Bailey and B. Guy Peters (London:
   Macmillan, 1994) pp. 336–8.
5  Philip John Davies, 'The Media and US Politics', in *Developments in
   American Politics 3*, ed. Gillian Peele, Christopher J. Bailey, Bruce Cain
   and B. Guy Peters (London: Macmillan, 1998) pp. 343–6.
6  Dan Schiller, 'Transformations of News in the US Information Market',
   in *Communicating Politics: Mass Communications and the Political Process*,
   ed. Peter Golding, Graham Murdock and Philip Schlesinger (Leicester:
   Leicester University Press, 1986) p. 21.
       One of the most influential pollsters in America, Frank Luntz – who
   helped to develop a strategy for Newt Gingrich's 'Contract With
   America' in 1994 – found that mid-1990s' American popular opinion
   believed unemployment was running at New Deal levels of 25 per cent
   when it was only 6 per cent for instance, the budget deficit was rising

when it was actually falling and, most spectacular of all, the United States had some form of high-tech defence shield along the lines of the Strategic Defence Initiative or 'Star Wars' system that would automatically protect Americans from any attack. See Gavin Esler, *The United States of Anger* (London: Penguin, 1998) pp. 249–53.

7 Max Weber, 'The Nature of Charismatic Domination', in *Weber: Selections in Translation*, ed. W. G. Runciman (Cambridge: Cambridge University Press, 1978) pp. 226–50.

8 Timothy W. Luke, *Screens of Power: Ideology, Domination, and Resistance in Informational Society* (Urbana: University of Illinois Press, 1989) p. 130.

9 Ibid. p. 132.

10 As Theodore White reminds us, following on from campaigning, Kennedy went even further by becoming the first president to have his press conferences televised live and thus give even greater emphasis to the needs of presentation and image. See Theodore White, *America in Search of Itself: The Making of the President 1956–1980* (London: Jonathan Cape, 1983) p. 183.

11 See Richard Neustadt, *Presidential Power and the Modern Presidents: The Politics of Leadership from Roosevelt to Reagan* (New York: Free Press, 1990); James David Barber, *Presidential Character* (Englewood Cliffs, NJ: Prentice Hall, 1972).

12 Neustadt, *Presidential Power*, p. 73.

13 It would be wrong to assume that these people could immediately churn out scripts as if they had been doing it all their lives. Larner, for one, was heavily mentored by none other than Robert Towne, who went on to win an Oscar for his screenplay of *Chinatown* in 1974. See Peter Biskind, *Easy Riders, Raging Bulls* (London: Bloomsbury, 1998) p. 50.

14 The scene in the back of the car where McKay begins spouting gobbledygook was almost left out by Ritchie and Larner who felt that the script account of the scene just would not fit in with their tone. See James Spada, *The Films of Robert Redford* (New York: Gilded Press, 1977) p. 162.

15 Richard Maltby, *Hollywood Cinema* (Oxford: Blackwell, 1995) p. 380.

16 Spada, *The Films of Robert Redford*, p. 157.

17 Davies, 'The Media and US Politics', p. 339.

18 Joseph McBride, *Orson Welles* (New York: De Capo, 1996) p. 40.

19 King was praised by a number of critics for his re-creation of the 1912 Democratic convention where Wilson captured the party nomination for president on the forty-sixth ballot See Alton Cook, 'Wilson Offers Colorful Panorama of War Era', *New York World*, 2 August 1944. Reproduced for the *New York Motion Picture Critics Reviews*, 7 August 1944, p. 285.

20  Brian Neve, *Film and Politics in America: A Social Tradition* (London: Routledge, 1992) pp. 142–4.

21  Neve describes briefly how, after HUAC returned in 1951, Rossen was named as a communist by a number of separate witnesses and, although he had a separate production company, his contract with Columbia was terminated and he was cast out of the Hollywood community. Ibid. p. 144.

22  Daniel J. Leab, 'Hollywood and the Cold War 1945–61', in *Hollywood as Mirror: Changing Views of 'Outsiders' and 'Enemies' in American Movies*, ed. Robert Brent Toplin (Westport, CT: Greenwood Press, 1993) pp. 129–30 See also Leonard Quart and Albert Auster, *American Film and Society since 1945* (New York: Praeger, 1991) p. 52.

23  Ibid. p. 50.

24  Jackson Lears, 'A Matter of Taste: Corporate Cultural Hegemony in a Mass Consumption Society', in *Recasting America: Culture and Politics in the Age of Cold War*, ed. Lary May (Chicago: University of Chicago Press, 1989) pp. 38–57.

25  The Cagneys (James and wife Jeanne who also appears in the film) brought the novel before the war but it remained unfilmed for a considerable time. Its feel for time and place, nominally the Depression, is offset by the fact that the central character's success is not allowed to be as assured as it is in the book, and thus the dramatic edge of exploitative political gain is never quite carried off.

26  In the film, Cagney is struck down by an assassin's bullet before he can ever win office, and the storyline gives little scope for the dalliance between Hank and Flamingo (Anne Francis) which is a central element of the Langley book. See review of *A Lion Is in the Streets* in *Variety Film Review*, 9 September 1953, p. 6.

27  The introduction to Schulberg's published script of *A Face in the Crowd* is quoted in John Yates, 'Smart Man's Burden: *Nashville, A Face in the Crowd*, and Popular Culture', *Journal of Popular Film*, vol. 5, no. 1, 1976, p. 19.

28  Yates claims the two films are joined as critiques that 'are produced by people who don't have, and don't really want an understanding of the lives of common people'. Ibid. p. 27.

29  Karel Reisz, 'A Face in the Crowd', *Sight and Sound*, October 1957, p. 89.

30  Review of *A Face in the Crowd* in *Films in Review*, vol. 8, no. 7, Aug.–Sept. 1957, pp. 350–1.

31  Kazan said that in this way the story 'has little to do with American politics . . . It is more fundamental and intimate'. However, in describing how proud he was of *A Face in the Crowd* he also cannot help but talk of

it as a 'hard-hitting exposé'. See Elia Kazan, *Elia Kazan: A Life* (New York: Alfred A. Knopf, 1988) pp. 566–9.

32  Truffaut's comment is referred to in a discussion speculating on the influence of Rhodes' character concluding that Louisiana Governor Jimmy Davis, Texan W. Lee 'Pappy' O'Daniel, and none other than Ronald Reagan himself all had some claim to Kazan's hillbilly singer. See Stephen J. Whitfield, *The Culture of the Cold War* (London: Johns Hopkins University Press, 1991) p. 117.

33  Ibid. p. 16.

34  Andrew Sarris, 'Film Fantasies, Left and Right', *Film Culture*, no. 34, Autumn 1964, p. 33.

35  Ibid. p. 32.

36  Henry Hart, 'The Best Man', *Films in Review*, vol. 15, no. 5, May 1964, pp. 301–3.

37  In reviewing Lyndon Johnson's book *My Hope for America* during the mid-1960s, Norman Mailer interestingly saw the President as a character in private much closer to Broderick Crawford's Willie Stark in *All the King's Men* as a tactile, wildly fluctuating emotive man. See Norman Mailer, 'My Hope for America: A Review of a Book by Lyndon B. Johnson', reproduced in his *The Time of Our Time* (London: Little, Brown, 1998) pp. 540–5.

38  Although not an election film in itself, Penelope Houston had observed a similar kind of style for Preminger's *Advise and Consent*. She described it thus: 'The film has a documentary surface calculated to imply that he [Preminger] knows everything worth knowing about his location.' See Penelope Houston, review of *Advise and Consent* in *Sight and Sound*, vol. 31, no. 4, Autumn 1962, p. 194.

39  See Tim Hames and Nicol Rae, *Governing America* (Manchester: Manchester University Press, 1996) pp. 243–8.

40  In retrospect it is easy to see how Russell and Cantwell are composites of many political figures. For Russell it is Kennedy, Adlai Stevenson and Nelson Rockefeller; for Cantwell, McCarthy, Nixon and Barry Goldwater. (Cliff Robertson was actually asked about his opinion and character link to Goldwater as the film's release coincided with the 1964 primaries.) It is also possible to see the way blackmail and undesirable character traits became fixed in the public mind by Hollywood, and homosexuality on the right – rather than the left – was one such area. See Francis Wyndham, 'The Best Man', *Sight and Sound*, vol. 33, no. 4, Autumn 1964, p. 185.

41  Maltby, *Hollywood Cinema*, p. 379.

42  The creator of the Daisy ad, Tony Schwartz, later recalled how certain

people forgot or misplaced some of the imagery and even that it condemned Goldwater himself when he is not even mentioned in the thirty-second ad. See Diamond and Bates, *The Spot*, pp. 122–8.

43 Sklar, 'Bob Roberts', p. 77.

44 For an in-depth discussion of the *cinéma vérité* style that Kemper and Ritchie employed on the film, consigned as they were to a production budget of $15 million, see Rand Layton, 'Filming "The Candidate" on Location Calls for Some Fast "Natural Habitat" Decisions', *American Cinematographer*, September 1972, pp. 1022–3 and 1048.

45 Andrew Sarris, *Politics and Cinema* (New York: Columbia University Press, 1978) p. 19.

46 Win Sharples, jun., 'Depth of Field: Michael Ritchie's *The Candidate*', *Filmmakers Newsletter*, vol. 6, no. 2, December 1972, pp. 55–6.

47 See review of *The Candidate* in *Sight and Sound*, vol. 44, no. 3, Summer 1975, pp. 146–8.

48 Win Sharples, jun., 'Depth of Field', p. 55.

49 Penelope Houston, 'The Candidate', *Sight and Sound*, vol. 42, no. 1, Winter 1972–3, p. 49.

50 Many years later, being interviewed about her experience with *Nashville*, Tewkesbury commented that few really knew what Nashville was like until her trip which inspired the characters, and even then she engaged in rewriting scenes from actors' suggestions while on set See Damian Kostik, 'Creation, Content & Context', *Creative Screenwriting*, vol. 4, no. 3, Fall 1997, pp. 18–23.

51 Louis Giannetti, 'The Thrill of Discovery: The Cinema of Robert Altman', in his *Masters of American Cinema* (Englewoods, NJ: Prentice Hall, 1981) pp. 426–9.

52 Robert T. Self, 'Invention and Death: The Commodities of Media in Robert Altman's *Nashville*', *Journal of Popular Film*, vol. V, nos. 3 and 4, 1976, pp. 273–88.

53 Michael Klein, 'Nashville and the American Dream', *Jump Cut*, no. 9, October–December 1975, pp. 6–7; Leonard Quart, 'Altman's Metaphoric America', *Film and History*, vol. 7, no. 3, September 1977, pp. 59–63.

54 Giannetti, 'The Thrill of Discovery', p. 428.

55 In an article written about the 1992 campaign and related to *Bob Roberts*, John Harkness makes a similar claim for Clinton to be the true heir of Alan Alda's character in Joe Tynan, a real-life workaholic, with a professional wife who he cheated on. See John Harkness, 'Hall of Mirrors', *Sight and Sound*, September 1992, p. 5.

56 Todd McCarthy, 'Review of Bob Roberts', *Variety*, 18 May 1992, p. 43.

57 Colin Brown, 'Notes on the Film *Bob Roberts* and Comments from Its

Director and Star, Tim Robbins', *Screen International*, no. 855, 1 May 1992, p. 14.

58  Rita Kempley, 'Review of Bob Roberts', *Washington Post*, 4 September 1992.

59  Harkness, 'Hall of Mirrors', p. 5.

60  Stephen Abrahams, 'Buying Nashville', *Jump Cut*, no. 9, October–December 1975, pp. 7–8.

61  Travolta in an interview went as far as to say: 'You have to be dead not to see that the film favours Clinton. I've always said that I think he'll be pleased with it, because more than anything it promotes what a decent fellow he is.' See Tony Allen-Mills, 'United Colours of Clinton', *The Sunday Times*, News Review, 1 March 1998, p. 9.

62  Eric Pooley, 'Tale of Two Bills', *Time Magazine*, US edn, vol. 151, no. 10, 16 March 1998, p. 34.

63  Nicholls felt the conclusion, with Stanton trying to convince Henry of his need for him to stay on the campaign team, was just too inconclusive, and so he shot a revised finale with and without the Henry Burton character at the inauguration ball. See Peter Biskind, 'Compromising Positions', *Premiere*, vol. 11, no. 8, April 1998, pp. 96–101.

64  Travolta noted how gracious Clinton had been on set and remarked that he promised to help with the matter of recognition for Travolta's religious sect, Scientology, in Germany, where allegations have remained strong that it is a radical group looking to cheat people out of their lifesavings. See Roald Rynning, 'All the President's Women', *Film Review*, October 1998, pp. 40–5.

65  Political morality and social satire is what Peter Biskind feels the film is all about. See Biskind, 'Compromising Positions', p. 99.

66  One review asserted that the movie was left-wing and 1990s' populism, when many of its harmonised racial epithets – amid the political incorrectness is this call for unity among *class* as well as racial groups – are subjects already tackled, albeit in a more sanitised way, by Lawrence Kasdan's *Grand Canyon* and Joel Schumacher's *Falling Down*. See Peter W. Kaplan, 'Red, White and True', *The Guardian*, Review, 12 May 1998, pp. 2–3.

67  Linda Holt, 'Is this how White People Rap?', *The Times Literary Supplement*, 29 January 1999, p. 23.

68  In 1972, Beatty had one of his extended spells away from Hollywood working full-time as national vice-chairman of fund-raising on George McGovern's presidential campaign. 'He has the instincts of a man who has spent a lifetime in politics and a political maturity astounding in one so inexperienced', said McGovern at the time. See Gary Younge, 'Rebel

with a Cause', *The Guardian*, Review, 23 January 1999, pp. 6–7.

69  As Richard Kelley's review observes, the underlying ethos of the film is that Bulworth is a product of the bipartisan, New Democrat, Clintonian third way and that he is only reduced to muttering a 'stream of "incautious" remarks'. See Richard Kelley's review of *Bulworth* in *Sight and Sound*, vol. 9, no. 2, February 1999, pp. 41–2.

70  Holt makes a similar point, observing that popular songs play a far greater role in real *and* Hollywood elections than they have ever done in British ones for example. Note Sam Brownback's victory in Kansas at the recent mid-term elections of 1998 strumming his guitar with a rendition of 'This Land Is Our Land'. See Holt 'Is this how White People Rap?', p. 23.

71  Angie Errigo's review of *Bulworth* in *Premiere over Here*, UK section, vol. 12, no. 3, November 1998, p. UK6.

*Chapter 4*

# ACTION, ADVENTURE AND CONSPIRACY IN HOLLYWOOD POLITICAL FILM

In the post-Cold War world of Hollywood films, a strange 1990s' phenomenon has slowly grown in intensity and provoked a stream of imitators that can lead us to only one conclusion: paranoia is truly back in vogue. The cult TV series of the 1990s, *The X-Files*, finally came of age in 1998 by spawning its own movie, *X-Files: Fight the Future*, in which our intrepid heroes, Mulder and Scully, come at last to the dawning realisation that society, government, even history, has been withered by conspiracy, corruption and manipulation. Of all the TV series that took advantage of the public appetite for the unexplainable in this decade, *The X-Files* has proved to be the one true runaway success, integrating real historical puzzles into its storylines, while the grafting of recurrent alleged government cover-ups (Roswell being the most prominent though not the only one) has remained as its underlying leitmotif.

The desire to see our complex world and its institutional structures decoded through the ideological timeframe of the millennium, used as a watermark for the upheavals of history, has not actually been the all-encompassing phenomenon of the last decade that some might have us believe. Other television series, like *Dark Skies* for example, were less successful at targeting audiences with their blend of alien-dominated historical revisionism, and institutional corruption, spread over the last thirty years. With many films failing to receive similar box-office approval (Robert Zemeckis' follow-up to *Forrest Gump*, *Contact*, starring Jodie Foster, was one picture that had poor returns) this should at least place a question mark on the public's universal acceptance of a digest of conspiracy and paranoia at century's end.

But in divesting film scholars of an important alternate theory of political economy, paranoia and the paranormal have continued to be true observants of movie cult status in film lore, 'sleeper' films (word of

102

mouth pictures slowly accumulating gross revenue over a period of time) on the edge of mainstream production that have acquired a select but dedicated following. Indeed action thrillers in the 1990s have often made cultdom a defining motive of the newly revived *noir* thriller, regardless of any film's overwhelming mainstream popularity, as 'cult' offerings like *Pulp Fiction* (1994), *Fargo* (1996), *The Usual Suspects* (1995) and *LA Confidential* (1997) have displayed. What is clear though is that many of the imitators of the genre in this decade reflect on, and borrow from, what has been in actual fact a long tradition of political thrillers in Hollywood, dating back at least as far as the hard-boiled detective *film noirs* of the late 1940s and 1950s, and with an ideological bent welded onto their plots by the fallout from the Nixon, Reagan and now Clinton eras.

Recent commentators have even gone as far as to assert that the 1990s are in actual fact a natural successor to the great paranoid movie period of the 1970s. The leap forward in technology, further discussed below, and the extension of an observable culture that can perpetrate all our lives have been important motivating factors argue critics like Jonathan Romney and Adam Barker. In this decade, however, Hollywood has produced a more disparate collection of films that, as Romney says, 'is rather abstract, less about real-world skullduggery than about the power of media imagery and, ultimately, about film itself'.[1] His examples, from *The Truman Show*, through David Mamet's *The Spanish Prisoner* (1998), to *LA Confidential* and David Fincher's *The Game* (1997), certainly reflect a rather amorphous collection of contemporary Hollywood genres, and seem representative of the current state of postmodern culture and society which accepts the compression of composite ideologies and values into a medium accelerating the rapidity of change as the twenty-first century approaches.

In Barker's discussion of paranoia movies, which is centred on the many and varied reactions to *JFK*, he argues that in Stone's story – and we could add some of the more recent offerings from the likes of Richard Donner (*Conspiracy Theory* (1997)) and Clint Eastwood (*Absolute Power*) here too – there is the construction of what he describes as a 'heroic quest' model of conspiracy thriller.[2] In other words, the moral fortitude of the chasing protagonist seeking to uncover the secret plots and deception cannot ever be halted by inner doubt or a subversion to the conspiracist's cause. It is arguably part of the success of a series/film like *The X-Files* that it can torment the audience with just such a recurring possibility for the driven Mulder and the sceptical but scientifically investigative Scully; that they could be tempted by the forces of darkness lined up against them.

What Barker suggests is that with the exception of the reconstructed personalities for Bob Woodward and Carl Bernstein in *All the President's Men* (1976) (director Alan J. Pakula following a similar character vein as that employed by Stone's recalculating of Jim Garrison into a personality with heroic moral gravitas in *JFK*) 1970s' paranoia films also truly left their audience gasping at the collapsing moral certainties surrounding the protagonists of these films, and added to this their narrative closures offered a better-than-even possibility of fifth column takeovers.[3] The singularly isolationist world of bugging and wiretapping, for example, is left unhinged by the apparent mental collapse of Gene Hackman at the conclusion of Francis Ford Coppola's *The Conversation* (1974). A rogue CIA band of operatives escapes justice in the dead-end narrative closure of Sidney Pollack's *Three Days of the Condor* (1975), and Warren Beatty becomes trapped by the enveloping political assassination *coup d'état* in Alan J. Pakula's earlier *The Parallax View* (1974).

The last film offers us the most enticing connection to the 'politics in film' nature of the thriller genre. Pakula's double-header in the 1970s made him the Oliver Stone of his times; the chronicler of political breakdown and subservient democratic discourse being used for elitist, hidden aims. *JFK* (1991) becomes almost a homage in this context parading, as it does, a mixture of both assassination theory and investigative journalism pioneered in Pakula's work with both *The Parallax View* and *All the President's Men*. Talking about the former film, the director asserted that: 'Although I do myths, I am interested in exploring some views of the world as it is seen through a distorting glass which may point out more intensely certain realities.'[4] Stone's didactic agenda similarly utilises real historical discourse and analysis for his own myths, forces a reassessment of government accountability and proselytises a whole iconic vision of idealised political power and character. And, as this chapter further investigates, both *The Parallax View* and *JFK* made claims and forcibly thrust agendas onto an institutional establishment having to contend with mutually dependent conspiracy scenarios (Hollywood narratives as well as journalistic exposés) as an explanation for the death of President John F. Kennedy in Dallas in November 1963.

J. Hoberman even goes as far as to suggest that in stimulating the paranoia style for the 1970s, Kennedy was an instrumental figure in creating the Cold War thriller out of the mass culture fascination for his life and political legacy. The classic ideological conspiracy films of the early 1960s, he argues, were the product of Kennedy-inspired scenarios, as *The Manchurian Candidate* (1962), *Dr Strangelove* (1964), *Fail Safe* (1964) and *Seven Days in May* (1964) all aptly testify to.[5]

Following Kennedy's death, Hollywood was left to speculate on the nature of his demise, and on the forces that apparently had lined up against him. Little wonder therefore that it should move on from the images and global crisis that dominated his presidency, in the above films, to a presentation of the theses that purported to explain his death. In this regard it is often forgotten that both in style and temperament neither Stone nor even Pakula was the first filmmaker to make Hollywood the bulwark of an ulterior conspiracy plot in the Kennedy assassination. David Miller's *Executive Action* (1973) made use of, in a more basic fashion, Stone's cinematic forte of contrasting and suggestive imagery using colour footage laced with black and white 'reconstruction' to posit its own alternative theory to the Warren Commission's report on the events in Dallas. Miller's film equally tapped into a mentality of 'lost generation' theory – the optimism and shining beacon of Camelot destroyed in a few seconds by an 'arranged' assassination – that the exciting but dangerous narratives of the 1960s helped to exacerbate in the conspiracist's Kennedy argument, and which provided the roots of a successful 1970s' paranoia that Hollywood was to become sensitive to.

It also seems useful to observe that by the 1990s, while accepting the skill and legacy of the 1970s era for the breathtaking panorama of conspiracy that was on offer in *JFK*, Hollywood was also by now pointing to nostalgia culture as historical reflection initiating a means to ingratiate its latest assassination thrillers with some sort of ideological perspective. While *Executive Action* might have been dull and plodding as a narrative, it did at least peddle theories of institutional action that questioned societal wisdom. Wolfgang Petersen's *In the Line of Fire* (1993), by contrast, became an incorporation of the Kennedy myth wholly sanitised for the video generation. Petersen's film somewhat served to define the action/conspiracy thriller for this decade with its morphing of Clint Eastwood's character, Frank Horrigan, into a semi-legendary piece of assassination history.[6] In other words, 1990s'

Hollywood went to the heart of the institutional fabric of American
society in a series of thrillers raging from this one, Eastwood's own
*Absolute Power* (1996), through *Murder at 1600* (1997) and *Shadow
Conspiracy* (1997), to Petersen's own more recent *Air Force One* (1997)
and Tony Scott's *Enemy of the State* (1998); but it has done this almost
entirely by substituting themes of state power and public accountability for iconic reference points the audience seem willing to take on
board without any semblance of ambiguity. In examining the rationale
for Hollywood's latent output in this area, and detailing its historical
development, a number of issues seem apparent.

First of all the political thriller – in whatever guise we choose to
adopt here – has increasingly moved towards the heart of institutional
power in America as a plot device, but has done so without any hint of
what critic Jim White calls a 'coherent ideological perspective'.[7] For
White's contention is that, when subjecting Stone and British director
Ken Loach's film *Hidden Agenda* (1990) to analysis, the conclusion is
that politics in these stories has no political, social or historical analysis
attached to it. The central influence upon his theory is Guy Hennebelle's
reading of 'Z Movies'; in other words, those political thrillers influenced
by Constantin Costa Gavras's contemporary account of a right-wing
political assassination set in Greece, coded by its one letter title, *Z*
(1969). Hennebelle makes the critical distinction that these types of
films are often playing with politics, only using it as an illusory device
to give weight to what are, in effect, conventional detective stories.[8] In
contemporary Hollywood conspiracy thrillers, that political prefix of
'motif theorising' seems especially prescient, but arguably Stone, far
from being a subservient practioner of the art, is more likely, in the
contemporary Hollywood era at least, the sole guardian of Hollywood
ideological sensibilities by comparison. Who else is even considering
attacking the social, economic and political foundations of American
society in modern Hollywood without the facade of an alternate genre
approach, whatever the flaws of his ideological outlook?

The second point is that the political thriller has become ever more
conscious of its own historical countenance. The Clinton administration
has developed into a better story than any Hollywood movie could be
given credit for, but fact and fiction, the crucial distinction between
truthful account and clumsy supposition, have become its defining
symbol. Yet how feasible is it to speculate that these traits arrived
before or since the release of a number of films that uncannily

resembled the activities of the President? All of them were written and/or filmed before the events of the Lewinsky scandal at the beginning of 1998 took over – *Absolute Power, Wag the Dog* and *Murder at 1600* were already available long before sex in the White House or further foreign policy intervention in Iraq and Yugoslavia were on the real agenda – but undoubtedly the increased Hollywood fascination in the Executive, and its considerably more absent moral tone in the thriller genre, have at least contributed to a wider re-evaluation of the office and the man. As Mark Lawson's critique of 1990s' Hollywood presidential roles has observed: 'Where once movie presidents tended to be Solomon-like figures played by Henry Fonda, Jason Robards or Hume Cronyn, the fictional leaders of the last five years have predominantly been liars, cheats and even murderers.'[9]

Lawson's character-driven assessment of politics serves the conspiracy/thriller realm of political films very well when the moral cause is often centred upon a purge of the current order – very much a generic western motif within Hollywood – while running into problems in the revived screwball comedy genre that Hollywood has re-created in the 1990s – discussed in the final chapter – and which is fixed around the construction of redemptive leadership while in office.[10]

American cinema has, in effect, redirected the audience towards personal style and honesty as a calculation of capability in the 1990s' political thriller, much as the previous chapter asserted similar ideals in the area of election films. The crisis of institutional government, or the failure of particular democratic theories within the polity, is less apparent, if not totally absent, in these modern-day paradigms. It seems reasonable to contend here, as in other chapters, that far from just dumbing down the wider populace's appreciation of political discourse under its own terms, Hollywood has in fact been an observable participant in a much broader, contemporary media personification of American politics in general. A character witness but not a wholly compliant accessory because, as this chapter is at pains to point out, Hollywood has in the past engaged with the democratic legacy of the nation much more pro-actively as opposed to now simply co-opting its rhetorical myths. Analysis by Ryan and Kellner, for example, maintains that 1970s' conspiracy thrillers had both progressed as a genre and also incorporated a more robust examination of political theory.

First of all they argue that the narrative premise of films in this era suggested that institutional power was a source of danger in American

society where previously thrillers of the 1930s, or the immediate post-
war years, had rarely criticised the structural foundations of the polity.
Secondly, they assert that 1970s' thrillers underwrote the declining liberal consensus that saw individual critiques of anti-statism under-
mined by a commitment to large-scale welfare provision and bureau-
cratical assistance. In other words, Hollywood's liberal establishment
protested vigorously about the safeguarding of the New Deal and
Great Society programmes while their films attacked this very same
concept of big government as conspiratorial and dangerous to a free
and libertarian community.[11]

The paradox of a declining political liberal establishment in the
1970s being condemned by an artistic liberal establishment should not
be lost either, and two decades on it comes as no surprise perhaps to
learn that while Hollywood is ready and willing to engage in critiques
surrounding the deviancy of sexual politics, for example – made recognisable in the Clinton era by an administration that has seemed
especially capable at establishing White House secrets and deception
in this area – it has tended to rely, in more contemporary narratives, on
a more vague pursuit of political accountability and only carefully
embellished calls for future democratic resurgence.

In addition, Hollywood has further manufactured its post-structural
links to establishment orthodoxy by making increasing use of particularly the presidency as an iconic institution in itself, fighting injustice
and world domination in the cause of freedom and democracy enshrined
in the office. In a comedic sense this notion is perhaps best used in *My
Fellow Americans* (1997) for not one but two ex-presidents, played by
Jack Lemmon and James Garner, teaming up to honour the office, oust
the current incumbent, Dan Ackroyd, and thus save the union by
revealing the fraudulent activities going on in the White House. The
force of presidential imagery has been most carefully and interestingly
adopted, however, in Roland Emmerich's *Independence Day* (1996)
and the previously cited *Air Force One* for the creation of 'all-action'
presidents – in the guise of Bill Pullman and Harrison Ford – from a
seemingly previous can-do generation.

The final point to make in examining the history of political thrillers
is to acknowledge the critical function of high-tech advancement as a
means to unpeel the secrets that lie at the heart of all our lives. As
the final section in this chapter deciphers, Tony Scott's reworking of the
paranoia tradition with *Enemy of the State* is also an updating of the

surveillance culture that permeates modern society. The film follows a dual path which alludes to both an uncertain collection of rogue individuals in government agencies as well as pointing out the possibilities of mistakes and factual inaccuracy within this technology-driven world of modern spying. Certainly in the contemporary era then technology has played an important part in redefining an 'enemy' within Hollywood narratives, never mind how passive that entity may be in other films, as Peter Weir's *The Truman Show* (1998) revealed in its small-town, communitarian tale of trapped TV star Truman Burbank (Jim Carrey); and adaptations of Michael Crichton's works (*Jurassic Park* (1993), *Rising Sun* (1993), *Disclosure* (1994)) and vehicles for Michael Douglas (*The Game* (1997)) and Sandra Bullock (*The Net* 1995)) revealed in their more conventional thriller settings involving political or, more often, economic global supremacy.

But while genres like the recently revived science-fiction have also accumulated the critical and commercial plaudits for identifying paranoia and the state of human control in, amongst other features, the *Alien* quartet, *Blade Runner* (1982) – whose Tyrell Corporation became a futuristic equivalent to the Parallax Corporation in Pakula's film – and more recently *Event Horizon* (1997), *Dark City* (1998) and *Gattaca* (1998), little attention has been paid in critical circles to this succession of 1990s' thrillers and political conspiracy movies that have partly drawn upon the classic 1960s' and 1970s' ideological tone, while redirecting the conspiratorial agenda less towards unseen and shadowery 'fifth column' forces in society, and more particularly towards the heart of a concocted power elite, most directly in the 'White House trilogy' of B-thrillers in 1996–7 mentioned above.[12]

Undoubtedly, if Hollywood is at least a reflection on the concerns and stimuli for society then it has picked up on the misapprehensions and anger that has emanated from a populace tired of being politically and socially manhandled. Politics has had an enormously bad press in the 1990s, arguably worse than in the 1970s, and yet Hollywood has shied away from any contemporary critical observations of its procedure and inner workings – with the relative exception of the nostalgia-driven comedies of *Dave* and *The American President* elaborated upon in Chapter 6 – in favour of revealing a corrupted system serviced by the usual concoction of sex, blackmail and murder. Just how reliable, truthful or stereotypical the politicians and political institutions that inherit these films are is a key element as worthy of attention in the

1990s as more conventional films about politics, examined in other eras. Indeed action/conspiracy thrillers from Hollywood have often been more successful at establishing a definitive political character (if presidents are not heroic, that is if they are not Harrison Ford, then they are usually gutless and hopelessly indecisive) allied to at least a passable imitation of institutional decision-making in action, than many other genres. More than this, the action/conspiracy thriller has often been accurate in its reflection of the political times and of the forces of ideological influence at work in America, not least because the forces of perception and judgement that were operating, as we are about to examine, invariably involved Hollywood itself.

## THE PRE-COLD WAR THRILLER FILMS

However one might wish to define the collection of films on offer here the roots of their development are clear enough in the Hollywood tradition. The political backdrop to action films/thrillers emerged out of the 1930s' gangster motif that incorporated corruption and the scandal of public officials into the sub-text of films like *Little Caesar* (1931), *Angels with Dirty Faces* (1938) and *The Public Defender* (1931). Mervyn Le Roy, who made the first of these films, and William Wellman, who made the last, mixed stories of small-time hoodlums into the wider cultural reference point of their discovery, manipulation and rise to the top in 'the city' (nominally Chicago) set against the backdrop of crime, corruption, bribery and scandal.

By this time, the early 1930s, the question of whether Hollywood had the wherewithal to be a purveyor of 'social-problem' films was being explored by the establishment of a succession of legal/courtroom dramas trumpeted at the mainstream Warner Bros studios. One of the most famous of these was *The Mouthpiece* (1932), a loosely based interpretation of the life of unethical criminal lawyer William J. Fallon. Reflecting again a rough amalgam of criminals, crooked businessmen and shady politicians, it had a slight institutional edge that was quickly translated into films like *State's Attorney* in 1932 and the aforementioned *Public Defender*.

As we saw with 1930s' political films like *Washington Merry-Go-Round* and *Gabriel over the White House*, Hollywood could make use of the gangster narrative and one-man vigilante crusade to give an authenticism to stories of political intrigue (bootleg gangster Nick Diamond is hunted down in La Cava's story and the violent justice imposed on him defines the'gritty realism'at the heart of the gangster genre's social commentary) that added pace and structure to a story apparently straight off the pages of the previous day's newspapers. Yet Hollywood found few other ways to explore contemporary political ideologies like communism, fascism or nationalism, and even if it could investigate these ideas, the widespread control of the Hays Office still remained as a prohibitive barrier to radical topics, as Walter Wanger found out with his Spanish Civil War film *Blockade* in 1938. It was not that Americans had forgotten about nationalism in particular during this decade, but that the Depression, foreign policy isolationism, and the ideological debates over modernism, including the role of Darwinian thought in American society, had muddied the waters for a country hellbent on national self-determination but having to come to terms with international economic competition and military threats. As Michael Foley notes, the influence of a progressive writer like Herbert Croly (whose book *The Promise of American Life* (1909) earlier in the century had a profound effect on the likes of Teddy Roosevelt and Woodrow Wilson) tended to promote a philosophical idealism reminiscent of Hegel – national citizenship as a communal obligation – which Hollywood's political ethos appeared to baulk at as the ferment of fascism and communism came to a head in 1939.[13]

It was only with World War Two that Hollywood began to look outwards to other political landscapes, most famously in their Russian collection of films such as *North Star* (1943), *Song of Russia* (1944) and in particular *Mission to Moscow*. Made in 1943, Michael Curtiz's film stood out as one willing, for the sake of wartime allegiance, virtually to condone the Stalinist purges of 1937–8, and its production crew were rewarded with anti-communist witch-hunts against them less than a decade later.[14]

## POST-1945 AND THE ANTI-COMMUNIST THREAT

In the immediate post-war era it appeared that social consciousness or social problem cinema would maintain the strong cultural and political settings of the pre-war era. The success of films like *The Best Years of Our Lives* (1946), *Crossfire* (1947) and *Home of the Brave* (1949) was complemented by a series of so-called semi-documentary features based on real-life events, the most important and characteristic of

which were arguably Elia Kazan's *Boomerang!* (1947) and Henry
Hathaway's *Call Northside 777* (1948).[15] For David Cook, this heady
period before the anti-communist witch-hunts was Hollywood imbib-
ing the influence of European neo-realist auteurs such as writer Cesare
Zavattini and directors Jean Renoir, Luchino Visconti and Roberto
Rossellini.[16] However, with the genre that served to define the modern
conspiracy thriller, *film noir*, Hollywood slowly began to give an
American spin to revenge stories challenging moral convention and at
the same time increasingly distanced itself from the French and Italian
avant-garde.[17]

Beginning more or less with *The Maltese Falcon* (1941) and *Double
Indemnity* (1944), Hollywood created a cinematically challenging series
of angular pictures that included *The Killers* (1946), *They Live by Night*
(1949), *The Big Clock* (1948), *D.O.A.* (1949) and *The Big Heat* (1953). As
Cook recalls there was more than a hint of German expressionism also
in the composition and settings of such pictures, and little wonder
given the influential reach of a director like Fritz Lang, who made the
last of these films.[18] Including Billy Wilder, Nicholas Ray and John
Farrow, Hollywood introduced to its audience an ensemble of artists
that would influence its style thereafter, and in a filmmaker like Otto
Preminger, an important protégé for the later development of the
political thriller.

This sense of progression in content was important for all the above
pictures, regardless of their visual sensibilities, because they had little
in the way of political or institutional discourse to speak of. Billy
Wilder's *Double Indemnity* is ostensibly about money, sex and revenge,
a commentary itself on the *noir* tradition emanating out of the post-war
instincts of Los Angeles society – the setting for the film – but barely a
reflection on the political aspirations of the era. What these films did
incorporate though was a psycho-analytical framework from which to
begin to examine individual consciousness and reactions to power and
control, an area exploited later in 1960s' conspiracy films. At this time
though the accent was on an imagery of loss, anger and isolation, but
the desperation and fragmentation conveyed by characters at odds with
their landscape was also an important signal of post-war disenchantment
that allowed for a quizzical social agenda to be incorporated more
forcefully into later material.

Once these themes had been joined by the emerging threats of
the Cold War, rather than just domestic angst, Hollywood could look

further afield towards the threat of infiltration and was able to incorporate darker ideologically un-American characters into its pictures. Carol Reed's *The Third Man* in 1949 was one such film that famously incorporated Hollywood *noir*, together with European expressionism and neo-realism, to create a shadowy world of espionage and double agents in post-war Vienna. With the McCarthy era finally over and HUAC on the retreat from Hollywood, the kinds of themes that Reed specialised in at the onset of the Cold War became standard fare by the early 1960s; and John Frankenheimer's *The Manchurian Candidate* established itself as the definitive Cold War conspiracy thriller of the Kennedy era.

Often cited, by Quart and Auster amongst others, as a neat balancing act for a liberal elite critical, but too frightened, to challenge the conventional orthodoxy of control freaks like J. Edgar Hoover, Frankenheimer's McCarthyite agenda – involving communist takeover and brainwashing, interspersed by a collection of misfit characters that only former Korean war veteran and now military press officer Major Ben Marco (Frank Sinatra) can, and is supposed to, make any sense of – sometimes deflects from the film's strong condemnatory charges against the power of television and the insular parochial world that Washington was already becoming by the 1960s.[19]

In fact this representation of a tight-knit, closeted community, all manners and officialdom, was a viewpoint that Otto Preminger developed in the same year for his adaptation of Allen Drury's Pulitzer prizewinning novel *Advise and Consent* (1962). In some senses Preminger's film acts as a better conduit to *The Manchurian Candidate* than Frankenheimer's own *Seven Days in May* two years later. This is because, with both films adapted from political novels by commentators well versed in institutional procedure, there is a recognition and acceptance of the conventions of language and the motivations behind the most subtle of political actions. Preminger surmised that the mere demonisation of political characters, a familiar Hollywood trait, involved too clean-cut a distinction between the scheming and the sincere. Political decisions involved surreptitious glances and hushed conversations, dramatic entrances or exits, and the support or otherwise of a myriad of alternate political characters and fringe observers.

This determination to extend the bounds of realism stretched to the cast as well. In addition to giving President Kennedy's brother-in-law, Peter Lawford, a role as a rather cantankerous representative,

Preminger made a much publicised request for Martin Luther King to play the small but crucial role of a Georgia senator.[20] King took some good advice and rejected the advances citing the fact that his public role as a black representative from the South might inflame the delicate state of the civil rights movement at the time.[21] In an amazing about-face, given the director's intentions with King – whose participation was meant to be a message of unity for political advancement of the black cause in the 1960s – the part of the honourable member from Georgia eventually went to Charles Laughton playing Senator Seab Cooley as a kind of patrician aristocratic grandee straight off the plantation estate.

If Preminger's left-wing philosophy appeared unsure of itself on the issue of race in the film, then he was certainly alive to the fact that the recent political climate was ripe for satirical criticism. The in-fighting among politicians in *Advise and Consent* could easily lead one to forget that these were members of the same party; and as such Preminger tapped into a consensus that saw political ideology in Hollywood as a manipulative tool of revenge on the extremism of the previous decade. Indeed, as Penelope Houston's review asserted, Preminger manages also to convey a lasting impression of facade and virtuosity in politics, its larger-than-life semantics personified by Cooley's final act of rhetorical posturing at the film's close.[22]

*The Manchurian Candidate* affected a similar position but its making was directly afflicted by just the same sort of opposing factions that both films were attempting to expose in their respective narratives. As Frankenheimer observed, one day on the set the production crew were due to be picketed by both the American Legion *and* the Communist Party, each protesting about the film from their polarised positions, and each displaying to the director the absurdity, as he described it, of such extremism.[23]

Character as well as casting was also critical to these films. Not unlike Senator John Iselin in Frankenheimer's story, the chief character in *Advise and Consent*, Secretary of State designate Robert Leffingwell (Henry Fonda), is actually a strangely peripheral figure in the narrative, and the two films are further joined in this respect by a groundswell of opinion in Hollywood at this time towards a more considered appreciation of congress in operation. This makes for quite an under-stated piece, and the more so considering there is nothing as dramatic as an assassination plot like that included in *The Manchurian Candidate*.

But again appearance and preconceptions are everything and Preminger steered the film around to a conclusion that subtly creeps up on the audience by suggesting that Leffingwell may fail in his pursuit of political office by having to accept rejection by the Senate (the 'advise and consent' of the title), but the real scapegoat is ambitious Senator Brig Anderson (Don Murray), tarnished by a past that his present occupation has no control over. The film's second half descent into a more sordid and murky underworld of blackmail emphasises the anomaly between appearance and reality in public figures but its tone is less mocking and more condemnatory of the Senate as an institution and the processes by which it is governed.[24] This view of public figures clearly made an impression because the film was heavily criticised for its appraisal of political character, and for not presenting favourable images of Americans to foreign audiences, by none other than Edward R. Murrow, the media scourge of Joseph McCarthy in the 1950s but a government official by the early sixties.[25]

In *The Manchurian Candidate*, people and actions are also meant to be deceptive, though here they are encompassed more by reflexive notions of brainwashing and Oedipal fixations. As Hoberman observes, the film not only offered a portrait of America that appeared sick beyond belief, but its imagery, narrative concoction and characters themselves colluded in making the mood of the film appear sick to begin with.[26] It brought a surreal as well as satirical angle to conspiracy thrillers and its, at times, deliberate and knowing claustrophobia is consciously meant to taunt the restrictive conventions of 1950s' society – where nominally the film is set. The brainwashing scenes in particular have been the subject of much speculation but the director took it upon himself directly to address issues that, at the time, appeared far-fetched and belonging in a more rigid Cold War mentality compared to a society still basking in the innocence of the emerging New Frontier.

As Susan Carruthers has argued, the return of POWs from Korea after the war gave an authenticism to the film at the beginning of the 1960s that proved both a turn-off for its audience, yet also helped to establish it as cult viewing, and as a precursor to the paranoia tradition emerging in Hollywood as the decade wore on. Returning prisoners were extensively analysed in the 1950s and pointedly, also infamously at the time, twenty-one Americans refused to go back to the USA in the voluntary repatriation programme that was worked out at the Geneva Convention of 1954.[27]

All the pre-publicity the film received as a consequence of these scenarios resulted only in controversy; the film had a very mixed reception in the USA, but its reputation, as Frankenheimer himself has commented on, was made by the acclaim it received in Britain.[28] Author Richard Condon – who had written the novel *The Manchurian Candidate* in 1958 – continued the assassination theme for a later book, *Winter Kills* (1979), but that too failed to pull in audiences when it was filmed in the late 1970s despite receiving even more substantial critical acclaim than Frankenheimer's effort.[29]

In fact *The Manchurian Candidate* would never have been made at all, according to Frankenheimer, but for the involvement of Frank Sinatra with finance and production duties. Sinatra's links to the film only adds to the mystique surrounding its making. Almost exactly a year after its official release the Kennedy assassination is most often cited as the reason why Sinatra, who had a degree of copyright control, had the film shelved. Yet he also appears to have been deeply affected by the fact that in a doubly prophetic manœuvre, he had not long ago starred in another low-budget assassination plot thriller, *Suddenly* (1954), directly involving the death of a president, in this case, rather than just a candidate.

In *Suddenly* Sinatra played John Barron, an ex-war hero but with an unstable past and an unsavoury taste for killing. He and a couple of cronies con their way into a house overlooking the railway station in the small town of Suddenly (literal and metaphoric connotations to the title) the intention being to assassinate the president when his train stops and he takes a car on to a desert location where he is vacationing. The action all takes place in the afternoon leading up to the five o'clock deadline with the film focusing on the tensions between John and the hostages he takes in the house. Given the time and setting of the film one would imagine that it would make a strong case for communist subversion, but Barron, far from being brainwashed with Marxist doctrine, is only really concerned, in his own unhinged state (we learn he had a mental discharge from the army), with making history. The place and perception of history becomes the crucial theoretical lesson of the movie because the town sheriff and the ex-Secret Service agent who owns the place remind him that nobody in history has ever got away with presidential assassination – reciting the fate of those who killed Lincoln, Garfield and McKinley – and as the time moves towards the fateful hour, the masterplan becomes fatally flawed, not because Johnny has not thought everything out, but because history and his degenerative state are conspiring against him.

Ten years on Sinatra appears to have been badly shaken by the experience of life coming to imitate art, particularly as Marina Oswald commented that her husband had actually watched *Suddenly* prior to the Kennedy assassination in Dallas.[30] As Art Simon recounts, this fact has also entered into the mythology of the JFK plot, endorsed by Don DeLillo's use of the tale in his late 1980s' book *Libra*. The conspiracists hit back, to compound the debate further, by establishing that although *Suddenly* had been broadcast on 19 October 1963 around the United States, it had not been shown in the Dallas area where the Oswalds were residing at the time.[31] Whatever the reality of each claim, the cataclysmic events in Texas certainly contributed to the removal of *The Manchurian Candidate* from general release although its twenty-five-year wait for re-emergence leading to its 1988 re-issue, as the publicity trumpeted on its return to cinemas, is not quite the whole story. As Michael Scheinfeld explains, *The Manchurian Candidate* was actually aired on CBS in 1965, less than two years after the assassination, again in 1966, and was then sold on to NBC in the 1970s where it was shown once more on American TV.[32] The notion of cultdom was therefore a prescient selling point for a film that seemed, inadvertently as it happens, to have direct and pre-emptory links to the Kennedy affair. As French journal *Positif* concluded in its assessment of the film, there may also be significance in interpreting Sinatra's turn to the right and supporting of both Reagan and Nixon in the 1970s as a statement about the tearing down of the sacred cows of liberalism.[33]

Frankenheimer persisted with the Cold War themes for his next picture, *Seven Days in May*. Just as *The Manchurian Candidate* and *Advise and Consent* had grown out of a burgeoning market in Cold War thriller novels, so too *Seven Days in May*, and its companion cinematic piece, Sidney Lumet's *Fail Safe*, had both been best-sellers before being committed to celluloid, written by pairings Fletcher Knebel and Charles N. Bailey, and Eugene Burdick and Harvey Wheeler respectively. Frankenheimer's film chose a more precipitous ideological route by having a gung-ho air-force general (Burt Lancaster) seek to promulgate nuclear war as a retaliation for what he perceives is American appeasement of the Soviets. Thus the debates about retaliation and the contingencies engendered by the MAD (Mutually Assured Destruction) scenario continued to be played out in the public realm, both films being given authentic credence by the activities of the Kennedys. The President offered the White House itself for Franken-heimer to film in, while Bobby Kennedy's publication of his events surrounding the Cuban Missile Crisis (*Thirteen Days*) and a claim that one of the air force chiefs of staff had advocated a military strike against Russia at the height of the stand-off appeared to indicate that both Frankenheimer and Lumet had the inside track on discussions at the highest levels of government.

In fact the critical distinction that drove these early 1960s' narratives into the conscience of watching Americans was their ability to trans-late cultural icons, and semi-authentic events, into a *mise-en-scène* of absurdity, while giving an almost breathtaking sweep of assumptions and misnomers about American power and politics through its history. In *The Manchurian Candidate*, for instance, a costume party is filled with Abraham Lincoln lookalikes while a number of other scenes involving John Iselin feature Lincoln's picture or bust in the background. In *Fail Safe*, Henry Fonda is finally a president on film, but one who ironically enough has to destroy New York by nuclear annihilation, while Burt Lancaster's role as General Scott in *Seven Days in May* appears to have uncanny resemblances to the actions engendered by the said Air Force Chief of Staff, Curtis LeMay, at the height of the Cuban Missile Crisis.

More critically Charles Maland has argued how this series of films, most especially focusing on Stanley Kubrick's *Dr Strangelove*, both defined and in turn sought a new, alternative cultural consciousness in America during the 1960s challenging the conformity of Cold War tenets.[34] All this points to the fact that as well as teasing the audience with familiar iconographic symbols left unhinged, the Cold War con-spiracy/political thriller also emerged in the early 1960s with a mandate to throw out the established rules on Hollywood political opinion. These films did not directly rebuke the political establishment for its endangerment of human kind, but pointed out that in having the mushroom cloud as your shadow for future existence, then the cer-tainties of traditional values, replete with iconic references, becomes vaguely absurd. As Susan Sontag commented at the time in reviewing Kubrick's *Dr Strangelove*, no one was picketing the theatre or raging about the imminent collapse of democracy as if Hollywood had broken some sacred taboo about American life; in fact the kids who were queuing up to see the film understood the virtues of it far better than the intellectuals who surmised a radical change of direction for

Hollywood cinema in the 1960s as a result.[35] Kubrick was able to level off the playing field in this manner by parodying that which was most terrifying in real life, while at the same time having a dig at audiences taken in by Hollywood's heightened sense of the dramatic in their climaxes to possible real-life scenarios. Originally intending to make a straightforward adaptation of Peter George's nuclear pulp thriller *Red Alert* (1958), the treatment kept drifting into farce and Kubrick redirected the whole venture towards a stinging indictment of the ideology of consensus.[36] The multiple roles of Peter Sellers (including that of liberal President Merkin Muffley) and Sterling Hayden (no pretence of literal subtlety with General Jack D. Ripper) are played as formal parts in a series of unfolding events at once farcical and yet recognisable as well. This was Cold War domino politics with tongue firmly in cheek, and Kubrick was quick to defend himself against the literalists who thought it a celebration of nuclear holocaust.[37]

Paranoia had therefore not reached the audience yet in these pictures – either the watching public in the theatre or the dormant citizens in the films – it merely resided in the minds of those disturbed by the responsibility of control in the thrillers themselves. But Hollywood did begin to translate the mood of deception emerging in the 1970s when audiences took on paranoia as an emblem of the misguided forces that ruled their lives. In this following decade, politics was a source of control and conspiracy but it was not the only institution Hollywood opened up to investigation.

## HOLLYWOOD AND THE PARANOIA STYLE

If the 1960s presented nuclear war and political assassination as a satirical game of chance, in *Dr Strangelove* and *The Manchurian Candidate* at least, the 1970s treated subversion in a much more po-faced manner. It was not simply the flotsam left by Watergate and the disintegration of Vietnam, whose wounds had been opened for the American public by the unveiling of the Pentagon Papers at the beginning of the decade – itself a perfect conspiratorial story – that left a sour aftertaste, but the sense that cohesion in society and a belief in progression and maturity had been stunted by the experiences of the past few years.

In actual fact, from a historical perspective, the rise of paranoia discourse in the 1970s was more the re-emergence of a recurrent theme, as Richard Hofstadter had pointed out only a few years before. He argued that America's past was littered with the debris of conspiracy scenarios, all intent on subverting the progressive course of the nation, be it the masons or the Communist Party. Given the disintegration of ideological strategy and the breakdown in progressive social programmes during the previous decade, it was hardly surprising that a 'preternaturally effective international conspiratorial network' should spring up in response within a few years.[38] What is critical about this, as Simon persuasively points out, is that once again real and mythological analysis became subverted by the frame of reference: paranoia in the Hollywood style made paranoia in the real world a selection of clichéd images, from lone gunmen to seedy politicians, by way of dark and shadowy urban scenes.[39] Paranoia could be seen to be a real explanation of the current predicament of society and yet at the same time be written off as nothing more than Hollywood fantasy.

With Hollywood now trying to broaden the path of these elaborate themes, and presenting a well-rounded collusion of political and economic power, Ryan and Kellner point to a series of conspiracy thrillers in the 1970s centred on economic or corporate power elites, and their legacy of the appropriation of the public interest for selfish, antithetical means, that neatly complemented the political genre.[40] Beginning with *Network* in 1976, and continuing on through *Coma* (1977), *The China Syndrome* (1979), and stretching into the 1980s with *Silkwood* (1982), Hollywood explored the context of global multi-national dominance in an increasingly transnational cultural environment with this series of semi-realist narratives. Ryan and Kellner describe these films as pointing to a mode of populist tragedy where individuals are left ostracised and disillusioned by the corporate elite but through which a kind of affirmation of resolute individual action can be asserted.[41]

A film like *Network* also established many parallels with earlier Hollywood narratives, most prominent of which being Kazan's *A Face in the Crowd*, and in this manner served to update the notion of economic capitalism at the heart of media power. More than ever in Lumet's 1976 film, the technological control that rocks the cradle of human existence is much in evidence in the almost tele-evangelical prophecies of Peter Finch. But this collection of films was also matched in its endorsement of isolationist discourse by the paranoia government conspiracy movies of *Executive Action*, *Three Days of the Condor* and *The Parallax View*.

In each of these films, government is revealed as being the perpe-
trator behind a series of events related to assassination, institutional
infiltration or Cold War secret operations. *Executive Action* posits an
even more clear delineation of a rationale for the Kennedy killing than
*JFK* by bringing to realisation story writer Mark Lane's belief that the
underlying establishment conspiracy in Dallas was based on evidence
that Kennedy was about to relinquish all US responsibility in Vietnam.[42]
*The Parallax View* and *Three Days of the Condor* further reinforced the
sense of institutional control and the downbeat narratives collapse in
on themselves as conventional escapism or explanation for the series
of events is seen as irrational and undesirable. Even though, as Ryan
and Kellner assert, Robert Redford's character in *Three Days*, Joe
Turner, is as stereotypically homespun as you are likely to get, his own
extrication from a seemingly impenetrable web of evidence – and that
is the point – is anything but certain. The final scene in the film has
him making a phone call indicating that he has firewalled himself by
sending all his evidence – of a rogue CIA band of operatives out to
maintain oil supplies in the Middle East by subversive tactics, again
tapping into very contemporary recognisable subjects – to the *New York
Times*, but the audience are left with a closure that is nothing more
than the disembodied voice on the other end simply asking how do
you know they will publish it?[43]

Turner, like Joe Frady (Warren Beatty) in *The Parallax View*, is deliberately constructed as a rather offbeat character – he is only a CIA
researcher rather than agent – whose machismo is sadly lacking and
therefore unlikely to win the day. Pakula's film offers elements of
Frankenheimer's psychological mind games in *The Manchurian
Candidate* with the Parallax Corporation acting as an underworld force
who are responsible for the mysterious deaths of a group of people
who witness the assassination of a senator at the top of the Space
Needle in Seattle, not a million miles away from Miller's conclusive
voice-over in *Executive Action* that details the fate of eighteen material
witnesses to the Kennedy slaying. It turns the tables on its audience in
a way reminiscent also of Coppola's *The Conversation* (1974) by never
being sure who the good guys are or providing any explanation as to
why they are involved in the plot as it unwinds. Frady is a journalist
attending the function who cannot be persuaded in conspiracy until he
finds out the truth about the Parallax Corporation at which point his

character becomes decidedly unreliable and ambiguously converted to the cause.

Writing a critique of both *Executive Action* and *The Parallax View* at the time of their release, Fred Kaplan was drawn to conclude that each film's closure was actually a travesty of conspiracy, that the unexplainable nature of their endings, the lack of motivation for actions, and the global perception of 'organisations' that seemed to be biding their time in the takeover of the world when it was well within their capability, was paradoxical paranoia. 'This neither necessitates nor logically implies the notion, or even the efficacy, of conspiratorial assassination as a means of domination', he said.[44]

Kaplan further expounded that Hollywood was engaged in one-dimensional political theory. That in an age where historical reactionism could easily conclude that the hegemony of the power elite was under threat, the logical conclusion in these narratives was assassination of the chief executive to solve the problem, when even the simplest

Fig. 6 *Conspiracy and political assassination on top of the Space Needle in Seattle in Pakula's* The Parallax View *(BFI Films: Stills, posters and designs).*
*Courtesy of Paramount Pictures.* The Parallax View © *1974 by Paramount Pictures. All rights reserved.*

reading of C. Wright Mills would lead one to understand that power and elitism is a mixture of many sources and usage rather than that vested in one office.[45] Joan Mellen's criticism of *Executive Action* follows similar lines to Kaplan's though she seems intent on berating Lane and Miller for not quantitatively detailing the blatantly obvious elements of the Kennedy conspiracy in favour of crudely driven newsreel imagery and roughly hewn characterisation.[46]

Hollywood at the time, and still today, had no real answer to such contentions as these. But of course neither should it have necessarily. As Kaplan raised at the time, and Mellen seemed perfectly ameliorative to, America had become awash in the 1970s with not even half-baked conspiracy stories almost all having at least something to do with Kennedy and Dallas. The trauma of Vietnam was a stark reality, urban unrest had shocked the population, insecurity, cynicism and the oil crisis were all hitting home, long before one even begins to analyse Watergate. Paranoia and conspiracy, political assassination and economic hegemony, were the realities of a sort for Americans in the 1970s, and if the cultural personifications did not always feel the need to explain themselves, neither did the politicians and leaders around them. But some stories unfolded that did attempt to bring gravity and answers to the unravelling of society as the decade progressed.

Attempting to make some sense of this 1970s' dislocation and reveal the methods as well as the means of uncovering conspiracy, Pakula and the *Parallax* team joined with Robert Redford to make the adaptation of Woodward and Bernstein's exposé of Watergate with *All the President's Men* in 1976. Redford's interest in a picture of this kind dated back to his involvement on *The Candidate* and he observed the reporters work in the *Washington Post* as each new revelation of the Watergate scandal surfaced through 1973. Indeed Bob Woodward – who was portrayed by Redford in the film – came to acknowledge that while screen rights were being negotiated before the book was completed, the actor was actually a big factor in the way the structure took shape.[47]

Because of its relativity to the subject-matter, *All the President's Men* courted controversy and praise with equal measure. Woodward and Bernstein acquired a much more heroic poise for Hollywood purposes and the 'detective plot' involving the shadowy meetings with 'Deep Throat' was resented in some journalistic and critical circles. But the film made documentary political filmmaking respectable and its unveiling of the depth of malfeasance in the Nixon administration brought political as well as cinematic plaudits. *All the President's Men* joined *One Flew over the Cuckoo's Nest* as the top two grossing films of 1976, reflecting a mood of anti-authoritarianism that would dissipate from Hollywood within a year. As Ryan and Kellner observed, in 1977 the two biggest box-office films were *Rocky*, starring Sylvester Stallone, and a science-fiction epic by a still developing filmmaker in Hollywood whose only previous minor success had been *American Graffiti* in 1973: the director was George Lucas and the film, *Star Wars*. Escapism was returning to the screens and the political conspiracy film would wait a decade before re-emergence.

## POLITICAL CONSPIRACY IN THE 1980s AND 1990s

Nothing could really shape the future direction of political thrillers more in Hollywood than the collapse of the Soviet empire at the end of the 1980s. Everything that suggested certainty about spying, nuclear annihilation and the battle for liberal democratic capitalism was embellished by any recourse to the Cold War and the conflict with what Ronald Reagan described during the decade as the 'evil empire'. By 1990, following violent reactions in Romania, eastern Germany, and the yielding of the Communist Party in Poland, Bulgaria and Hungary, all this was swept away. The White House, the Pentagon, CIA and FBI no longer had a clear enemy, and neither did Hollywood.

Following on from the paranoia style of the 1970s, studio productions in the 1980s embarked on an almost cartoon-like caricature of the bi-polar battles for supremacy. Movies like *Red Dawn* (1984, featuring a young Patrick Swayze) had high school children battling a Red Army invasion in mid-western Kansas, and the fourth instalment of the *Rocky* series saw Sylvester Stallone make his way to Moscow to take on a 'part man/part machine' automaton, Dolph Lungren. Most ludicrous of all, Gregory Hines and Mikail Barysnikov attempted a partial imitation of the Nureyev break from the Soviets by escaping the clutches of communist artistic enforcement in Taylor Hackford's *White Nights* (1986).

By the close of the decade Hollywood was already conditioning itself to accept the Cold War as a piece of history by giving a retrospective narrative to the first cinematic instalment of Tom Clancy's Jack Ryan series of novels in *The Hunt for Red October* (1990). Most interesting was the last breath of Cold War ideology, released in the year Reagan and

Gorbachev signed the INF (Intermediate Nuclear Forces) Treaty, that Hollywood could transplant into Roger Donaldson's *No Way Out* (1987), a loose adaptation of Farrow's *The Big Clock* (1948), but here set in the corridors – quite literally and officially for the first time on film – of the Pentagon.

Kevin Costner plays Tom Farrell, a marine officer who is also the mysterious, legendary deep-cover Soviet mole Yuri. Farrell has to pass on secrets to the Soviets and the plot implicates a defence secretary, Gene Hackman, in a murder of a society girl, Sean Young. Its themes of sex and blackmail – Hackman's private secretary (Will Patton) has a sexual obsession with him that allows for an all too convenient descent into psychotic megalomania to the extent that he is prepared to murder just about anyone to keep his boss's secret covered – became the sobriquet for a succession of 1990s' political stories. In Cold War terms Yuri is not quite the compliant spy he might be, demonstrated by his pointed remarks about his love for dissident – at the time – writer Alexander Solzhenitsyn. More consciously than most other films had done for a long time, *No Way Out* also reorientated the audience back to the parochial corridors of power in Washington, by virtue of its clever chase sequences through miles of corridor in the Pentagon.

As the Cold War era further dissipated, however, Hollywood had to look for other enemies and forms of threatening discourse, and the continuing Ryan series, *Patriot Games* (1992) and *Clear and Present Danger* (1994), opted for Irish terrorism and Columbian drug cartels while *Lethal Weapon 2* (1989) saw Riggs and Murtagh (Mel Gibson and Danny Glover respectively) battle South African terrorists before Nelson Mandela made a play for newly revived status. Conspiracy and the blurring of acceptable principles as well as resolute closures became far too complex a theoretical undertaking for 'by-the-numbers' mainstream Hollywood productions, largely constructed off the story-board rather than any definitive script.

One American director specifically ran against the tide of endless chase sequences, explosions, and soundbite Reaganist politics to create a whole different kind of visceral depiction of American power relations in his films. Oliver Stone's critique of American actions in Central America won critical plaudits for his first real breakthrough film as a director, *Salvador* (1986), after which *Platoon* (1986), *Wall Street* (1987), and *Born on the Fourth of July* (1989) all attracted mainstream audiences towards the director's very particular brand of social and cultural

Fig. 7  *Oliver Stone invokes the iconography of power relations in* JFK *as Garrison
(Kevin Costner) and X (Donald Sutherland) surround themselves in
Washington's symbolic edifices.*
JFK © 1991 Warner Bros Inc., Regency Enterprises V.O.F. and Le Studio Canal +.
*All Rights Reserved.*

polemics winning accolades along the way in equal measure. In 1991,
though, Stone embarked on his most ambitious project, a reassessment
of the Kennedy assassination through the eyes of one participant in the
story who had influenced earlier screenwriters, namely New Orleans
District Attorney Jim Garrison. Garrison was the only man who had
brought any sort of a trial to the American courts in relation to
Kennedy's death, and his most recent book at the time, *On the Trail of
the Assassins* (1988), became, with Jim Marrs's much debated, but
heavily controversial *Crossfire: The Plot that Killed Kennedy* (1989), the
chief influence upon Stone's cinematic re-creation of the events.

   Although certainly revelling in an acquired status as America's most
significant modern filmmaker, even Stone was probably not prepared
for the kind of backdraft that was to accompany his most visually
brilliant cinematic piece, but also his most tortured and tortuous ideological narrative. Clocking in at just over three hours and including a
documented 'book of the film' that incorporated ninety-seven pieces

about the film from reporters, scholars and academics, *JFK* became, quite simply, the most talked-about and controversial film of the decade.

So all-encompassing are its themes and presentation that *JFK* is more than simply an heir to the genre style of *Suddenly*, *The Manchurian Candidate* or *Executive Action*. It involves, in addition, a whole gamut of ideas that have infused this book and are relevant to large sections of the Hollywood tradition, putting *JFK* at the heart of the brutal cutting edge of paranoia in Hollywood films. As Norman Mailer and others have commented, it is not only Kevin Costner's portrayal of Jim Garrison, imbibed as it is with the values of a Mr Deeds or Mr Smith from Capra's 1930s' films, but also partly the ability of the film to relocate the searing memory of John F. Kennedy and his wife Jackie, dressed in pink, and of the motorcade drifting through Dealey Plaza, and the mythological imprints of the Zapruder film itself, that connect the audience to the notion that the film in its own right is an iconic reference point for the history it traces.[48] Geoff Stokes persuasively observes that the enduring legacy of *JFK* remains its conscious aggrandisement of the public memory of John Kennedy.[49] The administration was 'saturated with evocative imagery' he says, and the spectacle of Dealey Plaza is the dramatic epilogue to a life of visual representation.[50]

It became crucial for Stone to re-create that sense of mythologised historical imagery, to show the car, the dress, Governor Connolly's hat, the secret service agent jumping onto the boot, all the minute pieces of the visual jigsaw in independent and conflicting positions jumbled up in the conscience of the viewer just as they have been in the public's psyche for thirty years. As Norman Kagan has observed, the film went to extraordinary lengths to reflect on the literature of the event, and made extensive use of official files kept by most particularly the Assassination Archive and the Center for Defense Information in Washington DC.[51] All apparel needed for the re-creation of the Dealey Plaza scenes for example had to be painstakingly reassembled. Structurally Stone attempts to sign-post fact and dramatisation by the interjection of black-and-white footage where appropriate but even at the outset, when he commissioned co-writer Zachary Sklar to the project, he had a very clear picture in his mind of the ways to construct and reconstruct the assassination.[52]

The film has been constantly re-examined as a counter-myth to the Warren Commission, to the Kennedy administration, and even to our notion of what history is or what it represents. All of these debates continue to rage. *JFK* is action/political/conspiracy/thriller filmmaking at its most thrilling but on the edge of that dangerous precipice of being also most propagandist. As David Ansen, a defender of the film commented: 'Movies are by definition a demagogic art form; they can persuade you of almost anything.'[53]

But what Stone persuades us most of is that Hollywood political films are in essence visual spectacles personifying elitist aims through institutional domination. Much as Stone draws us again and again to Dealey Plaza, it is the scene between Garrison and Colonel X (Donald Sutherland) among the political environs of Washington's symbolic edifices where the film's most steadfast tenets are presented to the audience. X makes the play for endemic conspiracy not only in the elite but in the fascination of a society bred on a media age, an audience only able to glance at the most symbolic and definable moment of the twentieth century. He urges Garrison not to think of the who and the how's, that's just scenery, but the why.

Robert Toplin's broadly objective opinion of the film remains one of the most recent but striking observations of this line of thinking. *JFK* did not reveal the answers to any number of the theories it was advancing beyond what had already been promulgated by other scholars and commentators since the 1960s. What is remarkable is the firestorm of commentary the film received and the impact it made, leading to a number of tangible debates and results.[54] *JFK* created discussion by making conspiracy and paranoia a part of genuine historical debate in Hollywood's eyes. The 'why did Kennedy get murdered in Dallas' question that Colonel X so forcefully espouses is easily answered in *JFK*: by Castro, the Mafia, by Lyndon Johnson indeed! But the more complete legacy of emotive imagery and iconic representation of a slain king is what remains most impressive and tangible for an audience tutored in political media. This sense of the cultural ramifications rather than the practical historicism has carried over into other 1990s' political outings that seek to include the Kennedy legend as appropriate background to the context of any given film. John Mackenzie's *Ruby*, released less than a year after *JFK*, suffered as a result of the latter film's towering shadow over the subject-matter, but one should not dismiss the inability of the audience to fixate its attention on the actions of one of the key players (night-club owner Jack Ruby and his deeply disturbing shooting of Lee Harvey Oswald in the basement of the Dallas County Jail three days after the President's own death) when Kennedy remains the iconic focus. Even Stone himself only briefly features Ruby, in the partly reshot killing of Oswald, and a scene where he appears to be prompting Oswald in a press briefing. Ultimately, X states to Garrison on The Mall, people are suckers for the truth, and truth is Stone's greatest ideological weapon in the movie, but also the most damning enactment of his vision.

The situation is very different, however, for the use of Kennedy as symbolic reference point in Wolfgang Petersen's *In the Line of Fire*. For a film that encompasses nothing so much as a 'buddy cop movie' with a romantic interest, Petersen's film makes history and political assassination a historical continuum. The selling of the film was based on the premise that it is now (on release) 1993 rather than 1963, and thus a thirtieth anniversary of the Kennedy slaying. Frank Horrigan (Clint Eastwood) finds that he is reliving that moment in Dallas all over again when the current incumbent is threatened by assassination himself. The film's brief flashbacks unveil a younger Horrigan protecting JFK and Jackie (thanks to modern cinematic morphing techniques), and revealing him as the man closest to the President when the shooting started but who didn't react. As well as defiantly assuming Oswald to be the sole assassin, the film also builds on the earlier historical contentions of *Suddenly* by having prospective shootist Leary (John Malkovich) assume the title Booth – Lincoln's assassin – and invoke the traditions of past killers as well as recount the mythological poetry of the Camelot years describing Horrigan with the Kennedys in old photos – from *Life* Magazine – as 'radiant and able'.

By contrast it is Horrigan who embodies the mantle of political greatness by virtue of standing next to the great man, and it is his history and thoughts – and philosophy since – that litter the film throughout while the current president remains a background, peripheral figure. Horrigan thus transposes the receptacle of political history as a patron to its most defining moment.

Petersen enlarges on this sense of spectacle and mythmaking by converting his president, James Marshall, into an all-action superhero in *Air Force One* (1997). Marshall (Harrison Ford) is confronted by Russian terrorists on his own plane and Petersen largely resorts to an airborne-confined chase sequence with claustrophobia abound, somewhat akin to his most critically acclaimed film, *Das Boot* (1980). As Geoffrey Macnab's review noted, Ford plays Marshall as a cross between Henry Fonda and James Stewart, and although he allows a degree of angst and conflict to be aroused in his cabinet, the political anomaly of having Glenn Close play a vice-president, Kathryn Bennett, is never developed.[55] While Petersen is aware of the gender politics at work in Bennett – and Rene Russo's Secret Service agent from *In the Line of Fire* – he is less than sure how to approach the sensibilities of those gung-ho commanders who are now faced with taking orders from a woman.

Hollywood has become progressively more enamoured by the breakdown of accountability and political fallaciousness in its treatment of politicians and institutional life. In Eastwood's own film, *Absolute Power*, the later 1990s' dimension of open personal fallibility becomes predominant in a story where a cat burglar witnesses the president assault a woman who he is having an affair with, resulting in her death by secret service detail. The sex and blackmail agenda is further built upon in *Murder at 1600* with Wesley Snipes as a DC cop, Harlan Regis, called to investigate the murder of a young White House intern. Dwight Little's film is probably as close to replicating Hennebelle's detective political narratives as any of the recent attempts. Set against the predictable backdrop of military hostages in Korea forcing a foreign policy crisis for the president, Jack Neil, National Security Adviser Alvin Jordan (Alan Alda) confronts Regis at one point on the banks of the Potomac with the Jefferson Memorial and Washington Monument on prominent display in the background. Jordan pointedly reminds him there is more at stake than a girl, to which Regis replies that it is all about a dead girl in the White House, and no more. The bigger picture is constantly refuted by the down-at-heel cop just doing his job. *Shadow Conspiracy* (1997), in a somewhat overinflated manner, looks to uncover a similar extensive conspiracy of murder and blackmail where the president is about to announce dramatic defence cuts much to the consternation of members of his cabinet. Special adviser to the president, Bobby Bishop (Charlie Sheen) uncovers a government traitor in their midst, linking a mysterious 'agent' into a convoluted plot to assassinate the president. All three films are perfectly attuned to late 1990s' cynicism over the conduct, performance and perceived betrayal of politicians to the people. All also have their svengali-like brokers of power behind the scenes (Dean Stockwell's hawkish Defence Secretary in *Air Force One*, Alan Alda's National Security Adviser in *Murder at 1600*, and Donald Sutherland's Chief of Staff in *Shadow Conspiracy*) and perpetuate a critical endorsement of the decision-making capacity of the chief executive as breaking down.

Reinforced by a number of mainstream thrillers that have all inculcated politicians in economic, legal or sexual malfeasance, the 1990s' Hollywood vehicle for insinuating political criticism has been this genre more readily than any other area. Mark Frost's *Storyville* locates itself in Southern political machinations, starring James Spader; William Friedkin's *Jade* has David Carusso on the trail of murder and sexual liaison in San Francisco; while James Cameron's *True Lies* is a suitably Bond-like jaunt around Washington and its trendy suburbs – mainly Georgetown.

These films certainly do entertain the notions of Romney and Barker that heroic resolution by the chief protagonist is never far away, and that their institutional settings act as no more than deeper portentous camouflage for what are in effect chase-and-cop movies. As was noted of *Air Force One*, security surrounding the most important aircraft in the world is all too easily breached by a rather obvious collection of Russian thugs.[56] Likewise in *Murder at 1600*, personnel stream in and out of the White House with barely an afterthought for the amount of Secret Service and FBI detail that nowadays surround the building.

In addition, the films' visual presentation opts more and more for recognisable cinematic motifs that align themselves and pay homage to – or is that blatantly steal? – moments from Hollywood history. Philip Kemp's review of *Shadow Conspiracy* begins by noting that the picture is an anthology of scenes and/or themes lifted from, amongst other films, *Three Days of the Condor*, *North by Northwest* (1959) and *No Way Out* (1987).[57] Although this might tend to emphasise for us the tiredness of the genre by the end of the 1990s, it is also a lack of societal or political revelation, in Hollywood as much as anywhere else, only broken by attempts to enliven the cultural milieu with bouts of technological wizardry. *Shadow Conspiracy*, for example, conveys a very like-minded vision of satellite visual monitoring and infra-red scanning that Tony Scott makes such great use of for *Enemy of the State*. Indeed these are movies that are more definable as action thrillers mimicking the paranoia tradition, and in the 1990s finding politics ripe for tongue-in-cheek ribbing more than the 1970s' seriousness of political breakdown. In *Absolute Power*, Clint Eastwood and Gene Hackman appear unsure of the weight of their many laboured thoughts about political concealment and the trust and aptitude of leaders, while appearing to send up previous incarnations of their characters in other films.[58]

Ultimately the vicarious nature of power relations and the wider disillusionment in political processes and figures of authority have become less satirised than sanitised by real-life contemporaries. We understand concealment and deception to be a given of American public life, along with money, reciprocity and self-aggrandisement. But politics has also been given a gloss and acceptability in recent political thrillers that connect the detached disillusionment of the 'beltway mentality' to the consensual nature of modern-day political ideas. Nuclear war may no longer be a threat but rogue values continue to possess the power of paranoia.

## NOTES

1 Jonathan Romney, 'They're Out to Get You', *The Guardian*, Media Section, 19 October 1998, pp. 6–7.

2 Adam Barker, 'Cries and Whispers' *Sight and Sound*, vol. 1, no. 10, February 1992, pp. 10–11.

3 Ibid.

4 Andrew C. Bobrow, 'The Parallax View: An Interview with Alan J. Pakula', *Filmmakers Newsletter*, vol. 7, no. 11, September 1974, p. 20.

5 J Hoberman, 'When Dr. No Met Dr. Strangelove', *Sight and Sound*, vol. 3, no. 12, December 1993, pp. 16–21.

6 Thanks to modern cinematic techniques, Petersen could achieve the technological feat of morphing a 'young' Frank Horrigan into the actual footage from Dallas and at the same time offer the merely impression-istic notion that Horrigan was closest to Kennedy when the bullets started flying but he didn't react and thus was 'responsible' for the president's assassination.

7 Jim White, '*Hidden Agenda* and *JFK* Conspiracy Thrillers', *Jump Cut*, no. 38, June 1993, pp. 14–16.

8 Guy Hennebelle, 'Z Movies or What Hath Costa-Gavras Wrought?', *Cineaste*, vol. 6, no. 2, 1979, pp. 28–31.

9 Mark Lawson, 'The President's Other Star Report', *The Guardian*, Media Section, 23 September 1998, p. 6.

10 Films like *Independence Day* and *Air Force One* are part of the 'Counter-Clinton' collection for Lawson but this is a rather unhelpful and slight analysis of their worth to the Hollywood presidency realisation Ibid. p. 6.

11 Michael Ryan and Douglas Kellner, *Camera Politica: The Politics and*

*Ideology of Contemporary Hollywood Film* (Bloomington: Indiana University Press, 1988) pp. 95–7.

12  In his work on the JFK assassination theories, Art Simon concludes that science fiction has been important in creating the visual dynamics for technological subversion and conspiracy paranoia, suggesting William Burroughs as a critical inspiration. The notion is important though one might be tempted to promote a writer like Philip K. Dick as an even bigger inspiration on the genre. See Art Simon, *Dangerous Knowledge – The J.F.K. Assassination in Art and Film* (Philadelphia: Temple University Press, 1996) p. 167.

13  Michael Foley, *American Political Ideas* (Manchester: Manchester University Press, 1991) pp. 180–1.

14  See Daniel Leab, 'Hollywood and the Cold War, 1945–1961', in *Hollywood as Mirror: Changing Views of 'Outsiders' and 'Enemies' in American Movies*, ed. Robert Brent Toplin (Westport, CT: Greenwood Press, 1993) pp. 116–37; also Siegfried Kracauer, 'Buffoons and Bravehearts: Hollywood Portrays the Russians 1939–44', *California Historical Society Quarterly*, Winter 1973, pp. 326–37.

15  Both these films centred around police procedure and the 'real-life' scenarios of dealing with a criminal case. Kazan's film takes place in a small American town (actually Stamford in Connecticut) where local enforcement officials are attempting to uncover a murder, and is a rough selection of events based on the early life of Attorney-General Homer Cummings. Hathaway's *Call Northside 777* (1948) meanwhile is set in Chicago with a reporter (James Stewart) looking to discover the truth behind what was in fact a real eleven-year-old murder case. See Brian Neve, *Film and Politics in America: A Social Tradition* (London: Routledge, 1992) pp. 105–6.

16  In Cook's analysis, the extremities of neo-realism – 'a cinema of poverty and pessimism' he calls it – could never outlast the growing prosperity of the 1950s and could never be wholly 'combatable with American sensibilities either. Nevertheless its enduring legacy in stylistic and structural terms is enormous and lives on. See David A. Cook, *A History of Narrative Film*, 3rd edn (London: Norton, 1996) pp. 424–38.

17  What was also interesting about *film noir* was that, unlike the pre-war gangster genre – and James Cain's novels *The Postman Always Rings Twice* and *Double Indemnity* are classic early examples of how Hollywood tapped into this growing field of writers – *noir* was increasingly set in the west, especially California, and most particularly Los Angeles. The hard-boiled writing coming from there in the 1940s, Raymond Chandler etc., emphasised a rotten core at the heart of the facade that was the

American, and particularly Californian, dream. In doing this it attempted to deconstruct the 'boosterism' that had been so endemic to
Californian and Hollywood development, and impinge on the narrow-
minded optimism that had reigned for so long. Thus an important
development was being forged in Hollywood moves towards a more
critical institutional agenda. See Mike Davis, *City of Quartz* (London:
Vintage Edition, 1992) pp. 36–46.
18  Ibid. p. 451.
19  Leonard Quart and Albert Auster, *American Film and Society since 1945*
(New York: Peager, 1991) pp. 79–80.
20  Preminger took it that the presence of Lawford was a kind of tacit
endorsement by President Kennedy that he approved of the film. See
Willi Frischauer, *Behind the Scenes of Otto Preminger* (London: Michael
Joseph, 1973) p. 202.
21  Ibid. p. 201.
22  Penelope Houston, review of *Advise and Consent* in *Sight and Sound*, vol.
31, no. 4, Autumn 1962, pp. 194–5.
23  Stephen J. Whitfield, *The Culture of the Cold War* (Baltimore, MD: The
Johns Hopkins University, 1991) p. 213.
24  In his analysis of this film and *The Manchurian Candidate*, Andrew Sarris
is virulently critical of writers Alan Drury and Richard Condon for their
characterisation of politicians. This, he regards, as 'political audacity'. He
has little more time for director Preminger in *Advise and Consent* either,
who he in effect accuses of both convenient Hollywood 'objectivity' in
trying to play both ideological ends against the middle, and for being
weakest when attempting partisan arguments. See Andrew Sarris, 'Film
Fantasies, Left and Right', *Film Culture*, no. 34, Autumn 1964, pp. 28–34.
25  Frischauer, *Behind the Scenes of Otto Preminger*, p. 204.
26  Andrew Sarris commented that the film reflected 'a new conception of
America as dangerously "sick".' See Hoberman, 'When Dr. No Met Dr.
Strangelove', p. 19.
27  Susan Carruthers, 'The Manchurian Candidate (1962) and the Cold War
Brainwashing Scare', *Historical Journal of Film, Radio and Television*, vol.
18, no. 1, 1998, p. 76.
28  Frankenheimer has personally commented that the only reason *The
Manchurian Candidate* is revered is because of the reviews it received in
England See John Frankenheimer, 'My not so Brilliant Career', *The
Guardian*, Review, 20 November 1998, p. 11.
29  Condon described *Winter Kills* as getting 'absolutely electrifying reviews,
the like of which you cannot imagine'. See Nigel Fountain, 'Candidate
for Survival', *City Limits*, 18–25 August 1988, p. 22.

30  Michael Scheinfeld, 'The Manchurian Candidate', *Films in Review*, vol. 39, no. 11, November 1988, pp. 539–46.

31  Simon, *Dangerous Knowledge*, p. 161.

32  Scheinfeld, 'The Manchurian Candidate', p. 545.

33  'The Manchurian Candidate', *Positif*, no. 335, January 1989, pp. 68–70.

34  Kubrick foresaw that the film of Peter George's book *Red Alert* (1958) he was trying to make merely confirmed the grim but terrifying reality of Cold War politics. It was close in tone to Lumet's *Fail Safe*, and Kubrick wanted to implant black humour into the piece, and show the absurdity of the nuclear strategy. See Charles Maland, '*Dr Strangelove* (1964): Nightmare Comedy and the Ideology of Liberal Consensus' in *Hollywood as Historian*, ed. Peter Rollins (Lexington: University Press of Kentucky, 1983) pp. 190–210.

35  See J. Hoberman, 'When Dr. No Met Dr. Strangelove', p. 20.

36  Maland posits the connection between the film and the influential Geoffrey Hodgson book *America in Our Time* written in the 1970s. It was Hodgson who used the term 'ideology of liberal consensus' and went on to determine the dilemma at the heart of American Cold War policy. Maland, '*Dr. Strangelove* (1964)', pp. 190–1.
   'Confident to the verge of complacency about the perfectibility of American society, anxious to the point of paranoia about the threat of Communism – those were the two faces of the mood', commented Hodgson. See Geoffrey Hodgson, *America in Our Time* (New York: Doubleday, 1976) pp. 75–6.

37  Kubrick commented that just because he recognised insanity, played out with relish by Sellers in the role of the physically afflicted Doctor of the title, that did not mean he celebrated it. See Louis Giannetti, *Masters of American Cinema* (Englewood, NJ: Prentice Hall, 1981) pp. 401–4.

38  Richard Hofstadter, *The Paranoid Style in American Politics and Other Essays* (New York: Vintage Books, 1976) p. 14.

39  Simon, *Dangerous Knowledge*, pp. 167–9.

40  Ryan and Kellner, *Camera Politica*, pp. 101–5.

41  Ibid. p. 101.

42  Lane wrote a book and produced a documentary with Emilo de Antonio in 1967 called *Rush to Judgment*. It asserted that had Kennedy won the 1964 election he would have certainly pulled US forces out of Vietnam.

43  Ryan and Kellner, *Camera Politica*, p. 100.

44  Fred Kaplan, 'Parallax View, Political Paranoia', *Jump Cut*, no. 3, September/October 1974, p. 5.

45  Kaplan cites C. Wright Mills's classic *The Power Elite* as the most significant rejoinder to the regiment of conspiracists that had built up since

Kennedy, the most prominent in his time being Thomas Buchanan (*Who Killed Kennedy?*), Mark Lane (*Rush to Judgment*) and Jim Garrison (*A Heritage of Stone* and later to publish *On the Trail of the Assassins* in the 1980s). Ibid. p. 4.

46 Mellen's argument is that while inserting real images of Kennedy and Martin Luther King may on the surface give an authentic documentary feel to the narrative, the establishment of characters like Foster (Robert Ryan in his final role) and Farrington (Burt Lancaster) offers only pretence and caricatured cranks rather than a 'coherent political force'. The silencing of eighteen material witnesses to the assassination is where the real story lies she claims. See Joan Mellen, 'Executive Action: The Politics of Distortion', *Cineaste*, vol. VI, no. 2, 1974, pp. 8–12.

47 Redford tried a number of times to call the reporters, finally getting a brief meeting with Woodward in the spring of 1973 just as the resignations of Bob Haldeman and John Erlichman were taking place and the firing of president's counsel John Dean. See Robert Brent Toplin, *History by Hollywood: The Use and Abuse of the American Past* (Chicago: University of Illinois Press, 1996) p. 183.

48 Robert Toplin describes Garrison in the film as looking like Jimmy Stewart straight out of *Mr Smith Goes to Washington*. Ibid. p. 54.

Norman Mailer's original article 'Footfalls in the Crypt', *Vanity Fair*, February 1992, is reproduced in: *JFK: The Book of the Film*, ed. Oliver Stone and Zachary Sklar (New York: Applause, 1992) pp. 438–48.

49 Geoff Stoakes, 'JFK, Vietnam and the Public Mind', *Representing and Imagining America*, ed. Philip John Davies (Keele: Keele University Press, 1996) pp. 200–9.

50 Ibid. p. 200.

51 Norman Kagan, *The Cinema of Oliver Stone* (New York: Continuum, 1995) pp. 183–4.

52 In a number of interviews Stone compared the film to Kurasawa's *Rashomon* and in particular Costa-Gavras's Z. He basically envisioned seeing the event time and time again until the final reel opened up the events to show the full picture. He was also attracted to the notion of codification for the title hence *JFK* and not *J.F.K.* as a means to signify an operational directive. See Kagan, *The Cinema of Oliver Stone*, p. 185.

53 Norman Kagan quotes David Ansen in his chapter on *JFK*, ibid. p. 203.

54 See Toplin, *History by Hollywood*, pp. 58–9. Academically the film had an *American Historical Review* symposium dedicated all to itself, and politically calls emerged early in the film's release for fuller disclosure of material pertaining to the assassination. See *American Historical Review*, vol. 97, no. 2, April 1993, pp. 487–511.

55  Geoffrey Macnab, review of *Air Force One* in *Sight and Sound*, vol. 7, no. 10, October 1997, pp. 42–3.
56  Ian Freer, review of *Air Force One* in *Empire*, no. 100, October 1997, pp. 40–1.
57  Philip Kemp, review of *Shadow Conspiracy* in *Sight and Sound*, vol. 7, no. 10, October 1997, pp. 53–4.
58  Angie Errigo, review of *Absolute Power* in *Empire*, no. 96, June 1997, p. 40.

*Chapter 5*

# POLITICAL BIOGRAPHY IN FILM

⸺⊃⊂⸺

· The life of a man and his significance in history cannot be described
with clear and judicious definition in broadly pictorial terms – especially
when the subject is one of great depth and scope.

Bosley Crowther review of *Wilson, New York Times*, 2. Aug. 1944[1]

Commenting on reaction to his work around the time of the release of
the film *Nixon*, director Oliver Stone remarked:

I really believed in what I said in *JFK* and *Nixon*. But I think I made
mistakes in details. People have nailed me for it . . . Every movie
has an interpretation. Historians throw facts at me all the time.
Facts are very precious things. Facts are sometimes erroneous.
Sometimes the facts have been badly reported. It would be great
to know everything.[2]

Stone echoes that which is most treacherous for the biographer and
potentially catastrophic for any film biographer like himself. The road
towards creating the story of a factual life on screen is filled with traps
and always judged by that impossible constraint identified by Bosley
Crowther. It would be easy to surmise that a filmmaker like Oliver
Stone has, throughout his career, created a number of problems for
himself in the area of historical re-enactment, being one renowned for
his own individualistic and visually challenging style. He is also very
well known for his politics and it has suffused all his pictures, but never
more so than in his dramatic and original portraits of Kennedy and
Nixon.

Richard Reeves, a vocal critic of Stone's work, has realigned many
of the same arguments that might be applied to other directors in the
genre, but does admit to a 'dangerous cinematic brilliance' at the heart
of Stone's work that is additionally the central feature of political

biography in film history.[3] He further owns up to the fact that a movie like *JFK* has continued to haunt the imagination; a scenario important, typical and gratifying for any director with an illusion of social polemics, but troublesome for the conventional historian attempting to make words an enforceable treatise over visual histrionics in the modern age. It is also the heart of any debate over cinematic, and especially political, biography. This genre lays its own claim to history and allegorises for us, the audience, a set of signifiers that resonate beyond the story or portrayal or re-enactment of a life. The problem in this area of film is not what the politics is, or where the history is located, but why and how it is said in a particular way. In other words, these films allow for what Allan Lloyd Smith has called the circumvention of rhetoric through society.[4]

By any account Stone was not the first, and certainly will not be the last, director to feel the icy blast of definitive history chasing after new and alternative visions of political leaders and the events that surrounded them. It is an issue as old as cinema itself. As far back as 1915, the incumbent President Woodrow Wilson had one of his very first cinematic experiences watching D. W. Griffith's *The Birth of a Nation* and afterwards commented that it was like 'writing history with lightning'.[5]

Like the President, other budding filmmakers were similarly awe-struck by the scale and breadth of Griffith's work, and by the sweeping ideological reconstruction of the Civil War all contained within a few thousand feet of celluloid. But, like all historical judgements in Hollywood, history also got to it eventually, and the racist overtones of a hugely rewritten southern history provided the film, in retrospect, with a particular notoriety as well as its own place in historical revisionism. The film, adapted from Thomas Dixon's 1905 novel *The Clansman* (which was to be Griffith's original title), even offers an early, indelible portrait of political character, casting northern, abolitionist Republican Thaddeus Stevens as a hardened, capitalist villain.[6]

All political history and certainly all biography is of course open to similar charges of misrepresentation. Recounts by individuals concerned are often hazy, interpretations can be wildly conjectural, and portraits are apt to give distorted accounts of real character and individual actions or intentions. Even the most faithful of reproductions cannot help but become a victim of happenstance and overtly critical or hagiographic subjectivity.

Griffith himself returned to the historical scenes of his greatest triumph in 1930 by staging what turned out to be a revisionist re-creation
of the life of the Civil War president in *Abraham Lincoln*, starring Walter
Huston. This film was Griffith's first talking picture but it was not only
that technological innovation of dialogue cinema that made the movie
a more reserved piece than his silent work. Griffith forsook most of
the tracking shots and mounted camera positions that had made his
reputation and concentrated on small intimate scenes between his
players with subtle reflections allowing us, as John Door says, 'to observe
the psychological depths to which these characters are realised'.[7] It
resulted in a particular stylised setting for the picture but one that
exacerbated the concept of figurative and lyrical destiny.[8] Perhaps the
more static narrative convention was less coincidental considering that
Lincoln had already become a popular theatrical character in later
nineteenth-century theatre, and Griffith's conception of the man's
tragic persona, and at the same time his mythical will, was faithfully
reproduced by both John Cromwell for *Abe Lincoln in Illinois* (1939),
starring Raymond Massey, and John Ford with *Young Mr Lincoln* in
the same year.[9]

One of the best ways to understand how Griffith initiated a more
personal biographical portrait is by examining the differences in
sequential narrative technique and cinematic styling with a comparison
of the assassination of Lincoln in both *The Birth of a Nation* and
*Abraham Lincoln*. As Vlada Petric observes in a detailed study of both
five-minute scenes (they are almost identical in length in each film),
Griffith attempts a 'vertical' exploration of the events in *The Birth of a
Nation* that locks the Booth assassination into a montage sequence
fully integrated with the related strands of the narrative throughout
the rest of the film.[10] In *Abraham Lincoln*, however, the sequence is
viewed 'horizontally' as a narrative chronology reproducing the events
without further context and thus, according to Petric, giving a rather
flat, undynamic rhythm to the sequence.[11]

Griffith strove to be 'faithful' to his subject-matter with such a
technique and in doing so produced a far less contentious work than
his 1915 epic, but one that advanced very typical notions for the
cinematic life story of the causation of events and decisions in life and
of, as Door notes, 'those rhythms of life in which positive moments
evolve (quite miraculously) from negative moments'.[12]

The very act of visual representation is thus in itself a statement of intent about practice and presentation. Political biography, which in the 1930s was most obsessed with the legacy of the 16th president, attempted to infuse scenes and spectacle with the means to convey destiny and prophecy. Although later films about American presidents would establish policy and administrative management in the fore-ground of their treatments, similar sentiments of philosophical deter-minism and the shadow of some unforeseen greatness that hung over the personality of their subjects would be an equally critical investment in both character and story. This is no better demonstrated than in the film that, nearly thirty years after his comments about *The Birth of a Nation*, became the epic portrayal of the 28th president's own life, in Henry King's sprawling filmography *Wilson*, made in 1944.

In one sense *Wilson* was the political biography to end all political biographies. Filmed in Technicolor, with a towering central performance by Alexander Knox who was uncanny in the role, the film took a sedate and diverting tour around the life of the former academic and pro-gressive Democrat, beginning the story as late as his presidency of Princeton and following him through the brief sojourn as Governor of New Jersey to the White House in 1912, and the battle over the League of Nations in 1919. Reviews focused on the idealised magnificence of King's vision, and the *Motion Picture Herald* in particular identified the nostalgic imagery of the film as being as significant a reading of the Wilson legacy as any analysis of Knox's performance in the central role. 'It comes forth upon the screen in sequences of great pageantry and interludes of poignant intimacy stranded together with skill and over spread with the patina of glamour that only Hollywood can achieve', recorded Terry Ramsaye.[13]

Such lavish showmanship in *Wilson* tended to build on the film's nationalistic sentiments, reminiscent in themselves of the second half of *Gabriel over the White House*, the ideological undercurrent of *The President Vanishes*, and the broadly fascistic sentiments of *Meet John Doe*. As one that was filmed and directed at a wartime audience though, the picture's patriotic entreaty resembled nothing so much as Oliver's English counter-epic, *Henry V* (1946).

*Wilson* undoubtedly got the flavour of political rhetoric and bombast associated with the coming of modern electoral campaigns in America in the early part of the century, but the President's southern upbringing, his controversial charges such as William McAdoo, and his potentially scandalous quick remarriage to widow Edith Bolling Galt in 1915 following the death of his first wife, Ellen, in August 1914, are framed within constantly supportive contexts.[14] Director King followed a pattern of composition arrived at by Griffith, but Lamar Trotti's screenplay was inspired by his work on *Young Mr Lincoln* only a few years before. It was Trotti, pushed on by producer Darryl Zanuck, who sought to re-create the mythology of plain decency in Woodrow Wilson that had served him so well for the young Abe, and Zanuck and Trotti's influence upon this character building is excellently observed by Leonard Leff and Jerold Simmons in their analysis of *Wilson*.[15]

Like the two Lincoln biopics, the contrast between personal dilemmas and public responsibility shaped the political character of Wilson for Trotti and director King; their effort to establish complex and paradoxical demands upon politicians was one that few other political films found the emotional depth to carry off in 1940s' and 1950s' Hollywood. Of those few examples, both *Citizen Kane* (1941) and *All the King's Men* (discussed in Chapter 3) perhaps not insignificantly appeared in the same decade as *Wilson*. These films too, in their sense of euphoric rise and turbulent descent, directed political fortunes through the underlying ethics of personal emotions and the human condition. In *Wilson* all this was set against the background of sepia-tinted nostalgic excess such as football games, period songs and visits to the theatre.[16] As Leff and Simmons observe, scenes such as Mr and Mrs Wilson's helping with a Red Cross canteen outside Washington for 'doughboys' about to be packed off to France in 1917 emphasised a common touch that was less identifiable in real life, but heavily played upon in the film.[17] This was an ideological precept and overloading of contemporary iconography allied to personal psychosis that informed director Oliver Stone's construction of the life and times of Richard Nixon some years later, but other examples prior to this took an alternative route to biographical representation.

In 1939, director Ford had embarked on his own biography of the Civil War president with *Young Mr Lincoln*. But Ford's work would include no war or assassination scene because he went no further than the initiation of Lincoln's early political career. Although Ford's iconic political symbolism could stretch to both the democratic significance that was to come in Lincoln's career, and the debt he also owed as a filmmaker to the influence of Griffith – by including similar shots of the Lincoln Memorial at the end of his film as Griffith had done nine years earlier – this work really predicted greatness, forecast adoration, and signalled the Lincolnian strengths of honesty, hard work and perseverance as the roots of greatness.

Ford establishes these traits in the young Lincoln right from the off as first love Ann Rutledge is claimed by the perishing Illinois winter, and Abe then resolves to make himself into a lawyer and journeys to Springfield intent on forging a reputation for himself. The common-sense decency of the man sees him preach fairness and urge restraint in first the attempted lynching, and then the trial of brothers Matt and Adam Clay, accused of murder at the Springfield Fair. But it is the determined manner of the confession that Lincoln extracts from J. Palmer Cass and the actual as well as anticipated rivalry that is shaped through the narrative by the presence of Lincoln's political *bête noire*, Stephen A. Douglas, that capture a ruthless and politically astute streak in the man.

Almost fifteen years later, the same pretensions and similar structure adorn Henry Levin's film *The President's Lady* (1953), this time following the early life of Andrew Jackson. As played by Charlton Heston, Jackson is a robust, vigorous lawyer but also pioneer of the American west in the early part of the republic. His treatment and attitude towards Native American tribes is stereotypically racist, though still reflective of contemporary judgements during the 1950s, and the controversies over some of Jackson's military exploits – including his permission for military executions – are virtually abandoned in favour of his enduring love affair with divorcee Rachel Donaldson Robards (Susan Hayward).[18] Any political scheming or sense of his ideological causes is left to the condensed final section following Jackson's triumph at New Orleans in the War of 1812. For Levin instead, the moral lesson and philosophical enlightenment of the future president is offset by a scandal brought on by his illegal marriage and his fight for the recognition of Rachel in higher social circles, driving him on towards the presidency but also personal tragedy as he assumes office.[19] Reviews acknowledged the sense of early American history passing before the protagonists' eyes as well as their shaping of it (the passage of time is accompanied by some rather dubious make-up for Heston and co-star Hayward in the latter part of the film) for the course of generations to come.[20] The final section of the film makes some play of the emerging 'western' tradition and the suspicions and dismissive flavour of eastern reaction to a frontiersman like Jackson emerging in Washington. The brief campaign scenes feature crowds who accuse Jackson on the stump of murder and stealing another man's wife, in effect of bringing the kind of lawlessness to the capital that exists out on the frontier. In *Young Mr Lincoln*, as Tag Gallagher has noted, director Ford manages also to acknowledge the underlying ideals of the age – in the confines of the 1830s' Jacksonian era, where the film is set – by fusing together the Lincolnian traits with a spiritualism and truth garnered from nature, and thus to hint at the transcendalist philosophy and Second Great Awakening, incorporated in the contemporary writings of Thoreau, Emerson and later Whitman, that was in turn so admired by Lincoln himself.[21]

Even more so than *Young Mr Lincoln*, however, *The President's Lady* was a literal and figurative representation of the political times in which the film was produced. Although attempting no real critique of the dynamics of political change and the need for a more determined party leadership that was at the heart of democratic reform during Jackson's era, it remains a film very much about exclusion, about preconceived notions of personality, and it is about sacrifice. For a production made at the tail-end of the McCarthyite witch-hunts and the HUAC investigations in Hollywood, those were themes of immense importance to the kind of community Hollywood, and the wider America, had become during those years.

Ford's film offers some illusion to contemporary attitudes during the New Deal era as well, and its setting, within a small-town communitarian backdrop, accentuates the sense of a populist *mise-en-scène* that kept Lincoln as a close spiritual acquaintance to President Roosevelt in the 1930s. It would seem no coincidence that the director's next film was *The Grapes of Wrath* and where he would invoke a similar religious ethos and historical symbolism closely related to America's earliest philosophies, most notably Winthrop's city upon the hill.[22]

In 1960, it was the turn of Roosevelt himself to become the subject of biographical treatment in Vincent Donehue's adaptation of Dore Schary's play *Sunrise at Campobello* (1958). Once again forsaking a straightforward biographical narrative, the film takes a snapshot of Roosevelt's career, and boosts up the 'poignant and inspirational' qualities of the man.[23] The story focuses around Roosevelt's contracting of polio in 1921, and his physical and political recovery that would lead him to nominate Al Smith as Democrat candidate for President in 1924, signalling his own later 1920s' triumph winning the governorship

of New York. By now cinematic political biography had a clear delineation of expression and treatment. Personal sacrifice, the overcoming
of fateful odds, and the strength of character gleamed by family and
friends identified a set of moral and social concerns that perceived
political intuition and the pursuit of a successful career as being just
around the corner. The life-affirming properties that great political
figures were immersed in could not help the potential at the box office
for this picture, however, and political biography in general continued
to be regarded as unsuitable fare, reflecting a dubious financial history
for such projects. Griffith's *Abraham Lincoln* failed to draw in audiences
and *Wilson* was only a limited hit at a time when people sought a break
from wartime conflict in theatres where they had watched newsreel for
four years, and particularly at a moment in World War Two (August 1944)
when the breakthrough had been achieved and victory was at hand.[24]

But also, for many critics sceptical of the Hollywood connections to
the political process, political biography all too readily assumed a
propaganda purpose that seemed at the behest of the attitude of the
studios and moguls alike. The release of *Wilson*, for example, was met
by debate in Congress and strong partisan claims that it was 'fourth
term propaganda' for the Roosevelt administration.[25] The film was even
banned for showing by the War Department because it infringed the
Soldier Voting Act which forbid distribution of work classified as
propaganda within the armed forces.[26] In 1960, *Sunrise at Campobello*,
although certainly not propaganda for the Massachusetts senator, did
give a boost to the Kennedy campaign for office, made apparent by a
presidential candidate who had a striking admiration for FDR and
intended to build on the legacy of the New Deal.[27]

In the 1970s and 1980s, political biography's attraction was largely
relegated to the TV mini series, and although the popularity of *Kennedy*
(starring Martin Sheen and shown around the twentieth anniversary of
the assassination in 1983), *LBJ: The Early Years* (1987, starring Randy
Quaid) and adaptations of Nigel Hamilton's work on the early years of
John Kennedy proved successful within their limited confines,
Hollywood shied away from any notable evaluation of political careers.
Robert Altman's *Secret Honor* (1984) was an honourable exception but
was only one of a series of low-budget pieces that the director filmed
during the decade, here with Philip Baker Hall giving a rendition of
Richard Nixon as a foul-mouthed, alcoholic liability.

It was left to Oliver Stone in 1991 to breathe new life into the legacy of biographical presentation with the much vaunted and dazzling *JFK*. Although the style that Stone used owed its allegiance more to the conspiracy thriller realm and any 'representation' of Kennedy is brief, indistinguishable and broken by actual documentary footage (see Chapter 4), the film also constructed narrative sequences and drew upon several cinematic techniques, most notably time-lapse photography and documentary recovery of old film which has become a Stone signature, and montage sequences that slowly built up a legacy of power relations and events that were in themselves stories of the Kennedy years in the White House and before. What Stone added in visceral terms to both this picture and *Nixon* was a layering of *film noir* that aided their conspiratorial feel, but alluded once again to the biographical trait of destiny.[28]

With *Nixon* (1995) the resultant structure saw Stone recapture more readily a flavour of the epic political biography from earlier in Hollywood's history. As Gavin Smith observed:

> Nixon's manic-depressive secret history is composed from the fragments of a century of cinematic technique, encompassing Griffithian associative superimposition and *Forrest Gump* digital compositing, Soviet montage and Wellesian *mise en scène*, the 60s American avant-garde and *March of Time* newsreels.[29]

The mood of destruction at the heart of the administration is in addition offset by scenes of increasing darkness and night-time sequences that allow Stone's cinematographer, Bob Richardson, to roam the hallways of the reconstructed White House, establishing the mood for the demons that Anthony Hopkins's Nixon conjures up in his own mind. With no pretence at a chronological treatment of its central figure, the film in addition offers sequences and events from Nixon's life that are subject to not only flashback, but to a series of composite scenes, most particularly in the White House discussions surrounding Watergate, the array of technique and composition allowing for the distortion of logic, and the breakdown and pressure of concealment thus acts as a physical presence destroying the administration in its last two years. While directors like Griffith and Ford professed greatness and the spirit of American renewal cut short by tragedy, Stone's 1995 film signals descent and a greater personal affliction, repetitively preying on Nixon and leading to an inevitable political tragedy to follow.

The flashback, black-and-white dreams of Nixon's childhood confer much of the responsibility on him and his future that is also a part of the spectacle in Ford and Levins's earlier political biographies. Nixon's 1930s' California is paraded by Stone as the last frontier of America, while the passion of his mother, the anger of an omnipotent father and the deaths of his two brothers, Arthur and Harold, constitute symbolic staging posts on the young Richard's ladder of ascent. But in fact the restiveness and desolation that Stone feeds into the concluding part of the film, contrasting the early optimism by later parading Nixon as a broken spirit listening to the Watergate tapes in the Lincoln room, visited by the apparition of his mother, Hannah (Mary Steenbergen), is an identification of the collapse of dreams and political goals closer in tone to Henry King's eulogy to a broken Woodrow Wilson, his health wrecked by his fruitless campaign to approve successfully the Versailles Peace Treaty dwelt upon at the conclusion of *Wilson*.

Further similarities between the two films are also very much apparent. The emphasis on the role of strong women in the life of each (Wilson's two wives, Nixon's mother and wife Pat) is part of an evolving dynamic in political biography notable in the Lincoln trilogy for the prominence given to Mary Todd, and in *The President's Lady*, the very title and focus on Rachel Donaldson Robards being the deliberately conceived subtext of political ambition and drive. Yet in *Wilson* and *Nixon* the notion of political partnership and of the fusion of ideals and ambitions is more striking than in other films, underscored by Joan Allen's emotionally brittle performance as Pat Nixon, supportive and influential in early years, but later despairing and cast-off alone in the White House.[30]

At the heart of the film remains an auteur vision that is difficult to displace in political biography. Stone has always felt susceptible to charges of fabrication and delusion. The experience of *JFK*, by his own admission, profoundly shocked him to the extent that defence and justification of history had to be his strategy to comprehend a piece of art, as he told *Time* magazine at the height of the furore.[31] As if to anticipate such criticisms actor James Woods noted, on returning to work with Stone on *Nixon*, almost a decade on from having first been directed by him on *Salvador*, that the style had become more loose, scenes and dialogue were constantly subject to change and alteration, and the capacity to research more material was never-ending.[32] Stone, and screenwriters Christopher Wilkinson and Stephen Rivele, produced an annotated screenplay and historical companion to the film, edited by Eric Hamburg, that was as equally detailed and refined as the Zachary Sklar book for *JFK*.

Yet the focus on the film-projector scene and salesman's pitch, watched by the Plumbers (Watergate burglars) at the beginning of *Nixon*, has always suggested a 'fabricated and disassembled' structure to history making.[33] Stone's illusion to 'pop art' techniques in weaving the real and constructed historical record together into what might be construed as pastiche, is an important self-deprecating awareness for him of the reducibility of history in an age where image is king.[34] Stone was not the first to engage in the kind of detailed historicism that has become his trademark, for likewise on *Wilson*, screenwriter Lamar Trotti spent two years reading as much source material on the President as possible, and further engaged the assistance of the leading Wilson scholar of his generation, Ray Stannard Baker.[35] But Baker and Trotti were happy with an extrapolation of persona that played up to the wider concepts of patriotic and nationalistic sentiment encoded throughout the film.

One might have expected Stone to follow the same Manichaean line of *Wilson* where the president's opponents are berated for bipartisan spite in refusing the Versailles Treaty, and the dying president is subsequently cast in glowing reverential terms, except of course following a reverse, detrimental position. Yet as Stryker McGuire and David Ansen commented at the time, *Nixon* discovers ambiguity in the man and a twisted humanity and tortured history that professes personal tragedy and likens itself in this way to other non-political biographies in Hollywood history. The result for Stone was a considerably more ambiguous ideological agenda and one that was in some ways reflexive of the criticism levelled at *JFK*.[36]

The film highlights Nixon's staff as more than co-conspirators, as active impresarios in the unfolding events. Haldeman (James Woods) and Ehrlichman (J. T. Walsh) acquiesce to the role of grand schemers while Mitchell, Magruder and Dean remain dubious, concealed, unreliable and ultimately treacherous comrades in Nixon's unfolding war, as Theodore White concurred in his own work on Watergate.[37] The film debates the critical aspects of the falsities and deceptions inherent in the grasp for power. *Nixon* is no one-note film, however, for the enveloping crisis of Watergate is a counterpoint to Stone's parade of Nixon's achievements in opening up relations with the Soviet Union and with China. Stone's confrontations between the President, Soviet premier Leonid Brezhnev and Chinese leader Mao Zedong may have a tone of historical obligation to the story, but they register achievement and empathy in any case.

Nevertheless in conclusion, *Nixon* still returns to the enduring features of political biography. Stone envisaged the film as part Greek, part Shakespearean tragedy because like other films discussed here the need is always to drive political and ideological discourse through the archways of ambition and character and the attention given to the self. The illusional quality at the heart of political biography typifies the adjuncts we the audience can never come to terms with in leaders and great figures. What drives them, what makes them want to sacrifice their privacy, what forces rational, intelligent individuals sometimes to make misguided or dangerous choices? What all these films argue for is the need to be recognised, to be appreciated, and to find a mandate for one's actions. That is why the treatment of the 'common folk' in political biography movies is so important to an understanding of ideology. They remain static players, an amalgam of hopes and beliefs waiting for guidance, hoping for a prophet. The films show those leaders in the process of becoming and in time destroying that mercurial facade. Some question the value at all of a messianic portrayal of leaders within the genre. As Oliver Stone himself said of Richard Nixon: 'In the end . . . It's tough not to feel some compassion for a guy who just never thought he was good enough to join the establishment, even when he emblemised that very entity.'[38]

## NOTES

1  Bosley Crowther, '"Wilson," an Impressive Screen Biography, in which Alex Knox Is the Star, Has Its World Premiere at the Roxy', *New York Motion Picture Critics Reviews*, 7 August 1944, p. 284.
2  Chris Salewicz, *Oliver Stone: The Making of His Movies* (London: Orion, 1997) p. 113.
3  Richard Reeves, 'Oliver Stone and History', in *Do the Media Govern? Politicians, Voters, and Reporters in America*, ed. Shanto Iyengar and Richard Reeves (New York: Sage, 1997) pp. 43–9.
4  Allan Lloyd Smith 'Is There an American Culture?', in *Culture*, ed.

Jeremy Mitchell and Richard Maidment (London: Hodder & Stoughton, 1994) p. 312.

5   Thomas J. Knock, '"History with Lightning": The Forgotten Film *Wilson*', in *Hollywood as Historian*, ed. Peter Rollins (Lexington: University Press of Kentucky, 1983) pp. 88–108.

6   In Dixon's novel, Stevens is christened 'Thaddeus Stoneman' and has a clubfoot indicating a brooding and implacable character. See Everett Carter, 'Cultural History Written with Lightning: The Significance of *The Birth of a Nation (1915)*' in *Hollywood as Historian*, ed. Peter Rollins, pp. 9–19.

7   John H. Door, 'Griffith's Talkies', *Take One*, vol. 3, no. 8, Nov/Dec 1971, pp. 8–12.

8   Richard Schickel notes that the 'obvious falsity' of the setting raised 'the merely realistic toward the mythic level'. See Richard Schickel, *D. W. Griffith* (London: Pavilion, 1984) pp. 557–8.

9   Tag Gallagher, *John Ford: The Man and His Films* (Berkeley: University of California Press, 1986) p. 171.

10  Vlada Petric, 'Two Lincoln Assassinations by D. W. Griffith', *Quarterly Review of Film Studies*, Summer 1978, pp. 347–69.

11  Ibid. p. 348.

12  Door, 'Griffith's Talkies', p. 10.

13  Terry Ramsaye, 'Wilson: 20th Fox – Romanticized Political History', *Motion Picture Herald*, 5 August 1944, p. 63.

14  Bosley Crowther pointedly comments on Wilson's refusal to seek assistance from Senate colleagues when framing the Versailles Peace Treaty as being idealistically whitewashed by the script's comment about too many practical men writing too many treaties. Loneliness, he asserts, is also brought forward as a reason for his marriage to Edith Bolling Galt. See Crowther, 'Wilson', p. 284.

15  Leff and Simmons argue for the promotion of 'plain Woodrow Wilson' in the film much as 'plain Abraham Lincoln' had been the motif for Ford's film. As they say, Zanuck intended to put a little bit of humanity back into Wilson. See Leonard J. Leff and Jerold Simmons, '*Wilson*: Hollywood Propaganda for World Peace', *Historical Journal of Film, Radio & Television*, vol. 3, no. 1, March 1983, pp. 3–18.

16  Critics who either liked or were more critical of the film observed that the lush spectacle delivered a sensory relocation of thoughts and emotions back to those years around World War One. See Crowther, 'Wilson', p. 284; Howard Barnes, 'Wilson', *New York Herald Tribune*, 2 August 1944, reproduced in *New York Motion Picture Critics Reviews*, 7 August 1944, pp. 284–5.

17  Leff and Simmons, '*Wilson*: Hollywood Propaganda for World Peace', pp. 3–4.
18  See Robert V Rimini, *The Election of Andrew Jackson* (New York: Harper & Row, 1963) p. 154.
19  The scandal was largely uncovered by Charles Hammond, editor of the *Cincinnati Gazette*, who exposed the sham of a marriage that Jackson had entered into. Ibid. pp. 151–3.
20  The *Monthly Film Bulletin* was less kind to the film, seeing it as just another costume romance, adding that 'due to grotesque make-up, both players age rapidly, particularly Susan Hayward, who also takes to knitting long, shapeless articles'. See review of *The President's Lady* in *Monthly Film Bulletin*, vol. 20, no. 232, May 1953, p. 70.
21  Gallagher notes Abe's courting of Ann, and her later passing away, as key to these themes within the narrative. See Gallagher, *John Ford*, pp. 167–9. Whitman would write a number of works devoted to the presidency and subsequent passing away of Lincoln, most notably *When Lilacs Last in the Dooryard Bloom'd* and *O Captain! My Captain!* See Walt Whitman, *Complete Poetry and Selected Prose*, ed. James E. Miller, jun. (Boston: Houghton Mifflin, 1959) pp. 233–40.
22  In *The Grapes of Wrath*, Tom Joad (Henry Fonda again) walks away from the bandstand to the top of the hill beyond, just as Abe does in *Young Mr Lincoln*, the future obligations signposted by the dramatic sky overhead. See Colin Shindler, *Hollywood in Crisis: Cinema and American Society 1929–1939* (London: Routledge, 1996) p. 77.
23  See review of *Sunrise at Campobello* in *Variety Movie Guide, 1993* (London: Hamlyn, 1992) p. 676.
24  The film did extremely well in the big theatres of New York and Los Angeles but lost a great deal of momentum as it travelled through the heartland of America, even given its ten Academy Award nominations for 1945. The film was a major grossing product for Twentieth Century Fox but lost $2 million in the end set against costs. See Knock, 'History with Lightning', pp. 103–6.
25  Ibid. p. 89.
26  The film's internationalism was subject to special attention by reviewers and seemed to be complaisant with the post-war agenda Franklin Roosevelt was campaigning for in an election year. See Leff and Simmons, '*Wilson*: Hollywood Propaganda for World Peace', p. 12.
27  Although Brian Neve comments that the film had little impact in the campaign itself, it seemingly encouraged liberals in hiding from the purges of the 1950s to make a cautious move towards political involvement. See Brian Neve, *Film and Politics in America: A Social Tradition*

(London: Routledge, 1992) p. 212.

28   Stone underlined the fact that beginning the film with the pistol whip-
     ping of Jack Martin by his boss Guy Banister on the stormy night of 22
     November 1963, just as Garrison did in his book *On the Trail of the
     Assassins*, gave a Raymond Chandler-esque feel to the events as they
     unfolded. See James Riordan, *Stone: The Controversies, Excesses, and
     Exploits of a Radical Filmmaker* (London: Aurum, 1996) p. 352.

29   Gavin Smith, 'The Dark Side', *Sight and Sound*, vol. 6, no. 3, March 1996,
     pp. 6–9.

30   Stryker McGuire and David Ansen, 'Stone Nixon', *Newsweek*, 8 January
     1996, p. 42.

31   'Whenever you start to dictate to an artist his "social responsibility" you
     get into an area of censorship', replied Stone when asked whether a
     filmmaker should have any responsibility to historical fact. See Susan
     Mackey-Kallis, *Oliver Stone's America 'Dreaming the Myth Outward'*
     (Boulder, CO: Westview, 1996) p. 41.

32   Woods sat through weeks of research with Stone for the film, convincing
     him that he could play the part of H. R. Haldeman. See Salewicz, *Oliver
     Stone: The Making of His Movies*, pp. 111–13.

33   Smith, 'The Dark Side', p. 7.

34   Ibid. p. 9.

35   Baker's eight-volume study *Woodrow Wilson, Life and Letters (1927–1939)*
     won the Pulitzer prize in 1940 and he travelled to Hollywood to work
     on the script with Trotti in late 1943, through early 1944. See Knock,
     'History with Lightning', p. 91.

36   Stryker McGuire and David Ansen, 'Stone Nixon', *Newsweek*, 8 January
     1996, pp. 39–45.

37   White said: 'The villains were clear-cut – Haldeman and Mitchell and
     Magruder and Dean, and the lesser hustlers of the underground.' See
     Theodore White, *Breach of Faith* (London: Jonathan Cape, 1975) p. 34.

38   Michael Singer, 'Interview with Oliver Stone', in *Nixon: An Oliver Stone
     Film*, ed. Eric Hamburg (London: Bloomsbury, 1996) p. xvii.

*Chapter 6*

# HOLLYWOOD AND POLITICS
# IN THE 1990s

———⊃⊂———

Ask not what your country can do for you, you have nothing to fear but
fear itself, if you can't stand the heat get out of the kitchen, live free or
die, and in conclusion, read my lips.

> Acceptance speech, Thomas Jefferson 'Jeff' Johnson
> in *The Distinguished Gentleman*

In December 1998, the actor Tom Hanks announced publicly that he
regretted contributing the maximum $10,000 to the legal defence fund
that was fighting the allegations of sexual impropriety made by former
White House intern Monica Lewinsky against President Bill Clinton.[1]
Hanks, along with other Hollywood stars like Barbra Streisand and
Michael Douglas, as well as directors Steven Spielberg and Ron
Howard, had been known as a close supporter of the President since
he came to office and had stayed over in the White House on a number
of occasions.

The public notice of disapproval at the President's actions over the
affair, from one of Hollywood's most respected stars, was a minor
embarrassment for Clinton; but it arrived at the end of a year when
few public figures could have ever survived even the first onslaught
of attacks and revelations, let alone the Grand Jury testimony,
Congressional investigation, and articles of impeachment that were to
follow Kenneth Starr's lengthy inquiry into Clinton's behaviour.
Although by no means a haven from criticism and accountability,
the President's bridge to the stars in Hollywood probably sustained a
greater belief and tolerance in his administration than any other leader
could have had a right to. From that now famous appearance on the
Arsenio Hall Show in the 1992 campaign all the way to public PR
stunts with the likes of Spielberg and Oprah Winfrey, Clinton always

understood how to 'connect' with the voters he liked to court. The accounts in this book have relayed the way Hollywood and American politics have become closer bedfellows over the years, more so than perhaps ever seemed imaginable. In John Kennedy, Washington had a president who was a film buff and looked like he could be in movies; with Ronald Reagan, there was at last an actor in the White House; but in Clinton, public service finally found an artisan who understood exactly how to shape the mythology Hollywood services for his own indefatigable ends.

That relationship had begun to mature long before the Lewinsky scandal broke, with Hollywood supporting the President's agenda as far as it dared, and tapping into his predilection for film culture. As Martin Walker commented: 'Even more than in the days of Ronald Reagan, the Clinton White House thrills to Hollywood. Not surprising for a man who spent the 1992 election day watching John Wayne movies with his daughter, Clinton casts political crises in film terms.'[2] The President has been an aficionado of the art of visual histrionics and, in giving screenwriters all the material they needed, his administration raised the ante for the appreciation, relationship and portrayal of politics in film during the 1990s.

As a consequence the more intriguing aspect of Hanks's revelation was not his rebuke of the President but his answer to the now pre-dictable question relayed to almost any movie star about whether he would ever consider a run for public office. The interest in asking this man the almost requisite blasé question about famous figures cashing in on their name and profile would be fascinating enough, but, as *The New Yorker* magazine put it so bluntly, the enquiry was not whether Hanks would run for *any* public office, but whether he would run for *the* public office; the White House itself. His answer is quite simply the reason why Hollywood is a contributor to the profile, and an influence on the ideology, of American politics at century's end.

> My image is a really good one. I made a nice acceptance speech on TV a couple of times. I handled myself pretty well in the flare of the entertainment media. The actual ideology that anyone can glean as projected by my appearances on TV is that America is good because we are all so different and respecting each other is not such a hard thing to do. Not a bad platform, I suppose, to run for some office.[3]

With brush strokes as broad as this, and a view of American society that could only be described as 'neat', even Hanks's most celebrated character, Forrest Gump, would have no trouble accepting such beliefs. But the truth is, platitudes this general are valuable assets; in fact they are assets that are sold all over the United States every day by politicians for whom the fixation of their perceived image is the saleable commodity that will perpetuate a political career in the modern age. As Michael Kelly has observed:

In this new faith, it has come to be held that the sort of people politicians actually are and what they actually do is not really important. What is important is the perceived image of what they are and what they do. Politics is not about objective reality, but virtual reality . . . It exists for only a fleeting historical moment, in a magical movie of sorts, a never-ending and infinitely revisable docu-drama.[4]

Hanks, in this context, has a raft of characters to call upon: from Gump through astronaut Jim Lovell to Captain John Miller in *Saving Private Ryan* (1998); all of whom could fill the image gap for an expectant public. But perhaps what he does not have is a political character of his own – Hanks has never played a politician on screen – one that defines his image to the American people and fleshes out a personality from which his 'ideal politics' can flourish. President Clinton, by contrast, has had the luxury of being a real political figure for whom Hollywood has deigned to construct a whole host of fictional characters in the 1990s, all of whom have resembled his political technique, and peddled his values and beliefs, with a mimicry little observed since the days of Kennedy himself.

Indeed, right at the beginning of the Clinton administration in 1993, Martin Walker reflected on the fact that Hollywood in the early 1990s had paved the way for the emergence of Clinton by being a standard bearer of typically heroic Kennedy mythology in films such as *Love Field* (1992) with Michelle Pfeiffer, *Matinee* (1993) with John Goodman, and of course *JFK* (1992) starring Kevin Costner.[5] Clinton's iconic presentation, in the 1992 campaign, of his brief handshake with JFK in the year he died was, as Walker asserts, symbolic of the generational torch-passing that Hollywood itself finds so endearing. As a result, no sooner had Clinton walked into the Oval Office than Hollywood was seeking to rediscover storylines with an innocence and strength of character that had been all but missing from its political films since the 1940s.

In Chapter 1 I argued that a whole new generation of films – *The Distinguished Gentleman, My Fellow Americans, Primary Colors, Bulworth*, but most especially *Dave* and *The American President* – took their cue from, and paid homage to, the screwball idealism of directors from this classic era like Preston Sturges and, in particular, Frank Capra. Walker maintained that American audiences fifty years on were 'ready to believe again', encouraged by what appeared to be a new 'New Frontier' around Washington, but that Clinton's 'own dangerous fascination with movie culture' ought to have warned us all that the credibility of symbolism was now in the hands of the arch prevaricator of 'spin'.[6]

Whether by accident or design, Clinton's Hollywood agenda has both welcomed the stars into the White House and, almost imperceptibly, sidled film dialogue into press conference usage and garnered brief appearances for the President in pictures themselves – Clinton footage from CNN is incorporated into the Robert Zemeckis film *Contact* (1997) for example, his elegy to Richard Nixon at his funeral in 1994 is used at the end of Oliver Stone's *Nixon* (1995), and another speech during the 1996 campaign is shown on TV screens in Warren Beatty's *Bulworth* (1998) – thus reorientating the public back to the methods and critical imagery of cinematic illusion. The 'Hollywoodisation' of public affairs has been no idle buzzword in the 1990s. On the one hand groups like The Creative Coalition and Cause Célèbre have emerged, 'so the power of the entertainment industry can be effectively mobilised in appropriate campaigns', as they put it, while at the same time Clinton has often appropriated the position of a fan, publicly remarking on one occasion, for instance, how he got Glenn Close to accept the role of the vice-president in Wolfgang Petersen's *Air Force One*.[7]

Clinton's now legendary political infallibility has in itself even stretched over onto celluloid because, as Chapter 4 pointed out, the increasing fascination with the White House as subject-matter in 1990s' movies has not simply been confined to pleasing comedic pieces about triumph over adversity. The renewed interest in conspiracy and paranoia fixed the political dial firmly to a recipe of cover-up, lies and deceit. *Absolute Power, Murder at 1600* and *Shadow Conspiracy* all inculcated their fictional presidents, and the executive as an institution, in murder, blackmail and sexual liaisons. Probably by *both* accident and design, the Clinton White House has never failed to disappoint in all these areas, particularly with Hillary Clinton charging right-wing conspiracy against her husband's accusers as the Lewinsky scandal dragged on; and consequently the implied criticisms have merely become knowing references for the public rather than hard-edged critiques. In short, Clinton's persona, his intuitive feeling for his public, for minorities, for those less fortunate and excluded from society, makes him stand out as a Dave Kovic or Andrew Shepherd in 1990s' Hollywood parlance; alternatively his private life and political wheeler-dealing away from Washington also offer him as prime candidate to be Presidents William Haney from *My Fellow Americans* (1997) or Alan Richmond from *Absolute Power* (1997).

Moreover, Hollywood in the Clinton era has been able to reincorporate a third sub-genre into its stable of political films: the satire. Films on politics have always had at least a tinge of the satirical about them, as *The Manchurian Candidate* demonstrated, *Advise and Consent* reinforced also, and *Dr Strangelove* most certainly revealed. But in the 1990s the shrewd absurdity of satire as an inflated weapon of our thoughts about the world is now outmoded. *Bob Roberts* – already extensively discussed in Chapter 3 – and more recently *Wag the Dog* and *Bulworth* have found a way to represent uncannily that which is both absurd but also frighteningly true to life about contemporary American politics and society. The combination of recognisable real actions and scarcely believable narratives has urged the American public to watch on with grim fascination. After all, until this decade, who in real life would credit a political candidate who sings folk songs, one who has a relationship with a woman many years younger than himself actually in the Oval Office, or one who would deliberately manufacture a foreign conflict just to disguise the problems befalling him at home? As if the point needed labouring when, in 1998, Clinton ordered retaliatory strikes in the Sudan following the bombing of American embassies in African cities during the height of the Starr inquiry, it was the Republican Senate Majority Leader himself, Trent Lott, who evoked the spirit of Barry Levinson's *Wag the Dog*.[8]

Timing and rationale are everything of course, especially in this era where the most obvious of cultural references can be broken by the speed of change in news and communication. The spatial distance between real and supposedly conceived plots, the response and wider

political reaction of experts, and, most poignantly, the public anticipa-
tion and analysis of events, only serve to elucidate once more the
notion that film and politics appear kindred spirits in an age where the
discourse of our lives is played out on mediums once reserved for
nothing more than our entertainment of distant fantasies.

It should remain clear to us, however, that Americans are not so
wrapped up in the fawning of the rich and famous that they hang on
the every word of any Hollywood star, director or producer who
happens to make a film that includes a political motif. It is also apparent that American politics has operated, and crucially been perceived
to operate, in a state of perpetual crisis since Vietnam and Watergate,
to such an extent that any fictional/factual/factional presentation of
American democracy in film can and has been met by a public well
versed in cynicism and easy dismissal. Political films have therefore
continued to find box-office popularity difficult to come by.

But it is important to underline that the public has also been open
to suggestions about its polity in Hollywood culture because it has
for so long felt duped by a Washington culture – a place that Kevin
Phillips summarised in his book as an 'arrogant capital' – that it could
afford to be induced by a little homespun populism, or even concocted
paranoia. Oliver Stone recently commented that he never felt there
was a ready-made audience for a political film like *JFK*, the movie
simply generated its own excited interest and raged critics who felt that
its widespread appeal produced outlandish misconceptions among
the public about the theories it was propagating.[9]

Reflecting on the disingenuous atmosphere that Americans perceived
as being part of the federal process in the 1980s and early 1990s
Phillips argued that:

> Most Washington opinion moulders embraced a particularly
> delusionary and deceptive pretense – that the electorate was only
> temporarily disaffected, that no historical crisis was involved, that
> the disarray in Washington, the party system, and the process of
> government was little more than a matter of 'gridlock'.[10]

His isolationist and alienating critique for the nation's capital seems
appropriately apt given the Hollywood portrayal that is being analysed
in this chapter.  Film culture in the 1990s has been able to move
seamlessly from critical endorsement of this parochial detachment

(*The Distinguished Gentleman* and *Murder at 1600* do this effectively within their own narrative strands of comedy and detective thriller) to a moral rebuttal of the very same position that instead urges inclusory understanding and celebrates the robust nature of politics (*Dave* and *The American President* once again) without ever seeming to lose its faith in democratic credentials.

That allegiance to the tenets of American democracy is never really eroded because Hollywood can play the exact same game that the political establishment does in the late twentieth century: it can sublimate its sense of reality for a process of euphemism and evasion. As Robert Hughes has opined in his own tract on 1990s' America, 'The art of not answering the question, of cloaking unpleasant realities in abstraction or sugar is so perfectly endemic to Washington by now that we expect nothing else . . .'[11] In Hollywood politics similar principles naturally apply. The critical point here is that where once democratic rhetoric within film might have been interpreted as satirical, demonstrating the wide open spaces between real and fictional language in politics, they can no longer be as simply compartmentalised.

In 1993, for instance, the producer of Tim Robbins's film *Bob Roberts* was requested by the Democratic Party to write a script and produce a film for the President himself. Forrest Murray was asked by the western states finance director of the Democratic National Committee, Darius Anderson, how he had got the campaign mannerisms in his film to be so accurate. Murray replied self-effacingly that he had just made it up, and was promptly hired to make a short feature for the California State Democratic Party convention.[12]

These pictures also further endorse the fact that political language in film has continued to emphasise the individual traits of American political theory that this book has considered. The themes of individualism, liberalism and communitarianism shine through in these portraits, yet they do so from a perspective where ideology is being consciously dissipated, as any mainstream Hollywood product is reasonably expected to be, partly to simplify political discourse within film, but also partly to re-evaluate the consensual nature of American politics in Hollywood. Where once films of the 1930s and 1940s included journalists as sole bastions of political dialogue and propagandist messages when required, in the current age they are represented virtually as a fringe sect lost in a visual (and virtual) world of global media spectacle, message, communication, and therefore ideological thought. As

Christine Williams has observed of American elections:'The expansion of media outlets, formats and technologies has varied the message and audience of political campaigns.'[13] But, she also warns, 'the personalisation, professionalization and policy degeneration . . . [have] marginalised political parties and redefined the basis of governance'.[14] This final chapter is interested in exploring the way political films have sought to grapple with these alternative presentations, new modes of communication and the changing experience of values, while seeking to reaffirm and locate a place and context for the debate on these values in the late twentieth century.

In theoretical scholarship the battle of competing views is no better expressed than by Michael Foley's contention that the position of political ideas in society has three distinct responses: first, that the organic nature of America's historical development and political practice defies ideological placement; second, that political ideas are actually defiantly salient to the American experience as exemplified by 1960s' conflict and protest; and thirdly, that there is almost a middle-ground ambivalence to ideological determinism that sees ideas as endemic to the United States but the country only periodically concerned with the usage of such ideas.[15]

Hollywood has come to act as both messenger and message-giver to the wider populace, and this requires it to accept habitually that third position of signifier without thrusting an idolatry of values the way of the audience. How film, as the dominant cultural medium, resolves the dilemma of accepting the public disillusionment with institutions and processes while having to position itself as a historical bastion for American democracy, which has been its long-standing twentieth-century role, is the necessary enquiry of this chapter.

Dismay runs high in public life – even as reliable past indicators like foreign policy and the economy show excellent prospects for Americans – and there has certainly been no shortage of takers waiting to evaluate the outgrowth of crisis and dislocation in the political system.[16] Summing up a litany of literature that has considered the philosophical question inherent in American politics during the decade, British commentator Gavin Esler recently observed: 'Concerned Americans . . . see all around them the crisis of confidence in America's political system, apathy towards politics, ignorance of the issues, angry social and cultural trends, and an increasing gap between the rich and the poor.'[17]

Writing about the various scandals and fallout from Washington life since the Watergate era that have at least partly influenced the attitudes Esler is talking about, Robert Williams accepts that the media (principally television news) have had a significant impact in directing public attitudes towards their government. But, he asks, what really drives American politics? In this day and age, party identification, ideology, even pragmatic policy initiatives are harder to determine than ever. What dictates the public reaction – indeed what drives the media sensationalism and emphasis on reportage – Williams correctly observes, is character.[18] Commentator E. J. Dionne agrees: 'It's true of course', he asserts.

> Voters have always paid a good deal of attention to the personal 'character' of candidates, especially candidates for president. Character surely matters in a leader, which is why interest in Colin Powell mushroomed. But the definition of 'character' has become narrower. We focus more and more on sex and money, and less and less on a constancy of belief, a commitment to public purposes, a capacity to lead.[19]

In these remarks Dionne spots the dangers for a reformulation of political credibility in the public's eyes that the chapter on elections also reflected upon; it all begins to gravitate down to perception, 'doing it with mirrors'. At the head of the queue on political character, with the means and rhetoric to sail above the storm happening below, is a modern political figure, as Esler states, like William Jefferson Clinton.[20] And once you establish character as your central political theme, then riding the wave of controversy – as Clinton has successfully done – becomes a much more reasonable prospect for determining political achievement.

Character, therefore, is plainly at the forefront of many of the ideals that this book's reflection on American politics through the eyes of Hollywood has been about. In this context it becomes less surprising to find Clintonian style and image at the heart of Hollywood accounts in the 1990s. But equally as important, I asserted in Chapter 1 that as well as an embedded fusion of democratic ideals at the heart of American political film history, there was also an endorsement of those ideals through the visceral depiction of political symbols. In other words, the verisimilitude of doctrines and ideology within iconography was an important, if paradoxical, consideration if one was to attain some sort of consensus about Hollywood depictions over time. Political films in the 1990s have adopted the canvas of institutional symbolism even more wholeheartedly than in previous generations. In this final chapter it is therefore crucial to return to that hypothesis as a way to investigate the contemporary approaches to politics, politicians and political institutions.

## WASHINGTON: WHERE THE INNOCENTS GO

If there has been one defining popular reaction to 1990s' Hollywood films it has probably been that it is OK to trade in one's cynicism for innocence once again. As proselytised by Robert Zemeckis' wildly popular and apolitical *Forrest Gump* (1994), American film has striven to rediscover a collection of values and source of enlightenment that are articulated as both timeless and yet deeply theological to any understanding of the nation's experience. Yet it has done this in a post-modern framework where the collage of such symbols and ideals from across the ages has tended to make these views (and political films are as representative of this as anything Hollywood has produced) kitsch, subservient pastiches of earlier, and in critical terms, better pictures.

As Mark Steyn asserts, the theme of presidential films over the years has been redemption; the ability to find strength in calamity, disaster or poor judgement.[21] Rob Reiner's 1995 film *The American President* is no different in this respect. Andrew Shepherd (Michael Douglas) is a chief executive apparently heading towards a political climbdown with an election only a year away. The crisis of 'spin' in his administration is generated by a series of pictorial images and perceived impressions disclosed to the public by his likely presidential opponent, Bob Rumson (Richard Dreyfus), concerning his relationship with environmental lobbyist Sidney Ellen Wade (Annette Benning). Shepherd's lesson is in not responding to the 'spin', not being alert to the battles played out on the airwaves in the name of his personality. It is actually not a dissimilar lesson to the one that Jefferson Smith has to learn in *Mr Smith Goes to Washington* when, at his first informal press conference, he is duped into making bird noises and giving off-the-cuff remarks that are quoted out of context in the following morning's papers.

The difference, however, is that Capra's Smith really did inhabit if not an innocent then certainly a comparatively simpler world where honesty could be made to prevail if only it could be exacted upon a political system that was meant to safeguard those values. From the same era, Preston Sturges' *Hail the Conquering Hero* has Woodrow Truesmith (Eddie Bracken) reveal his deception as a fake war hero to a special town meeting called to debate his candidacy for mayor, but is then told by the judge, and perennial candidate Doc Bissell – at the railway station as Woodrow is about to leave town disgraced – that the public love honesty and will accept that courage of revelation even if they don't know why. Honesty can not only be crafted into political success, but is the rock on which politicians must be judged, argued Sturges fifty years earlier. In Reiner's updated version of this fable, integrity certainly matters, and Shepherd's final address in the White House press room is proof of that, but *The American President*'s closure is not about resolution or triumph of the system, but about the greater value of presentation *and* self-confession in the modern age.

Screenwriter Aaron Sorkin allows doubt to creep into Shepherd's

Fig. 8 *Andrew Shepherd (Michael Douglas) in* The American President. *Honesty and integrity are the hallmarks of Michael Douglas's performance (BFI Films: Stills, posters and designs).*
The American President © 1995 Castle Rock.

Fig. 9 *Classic romance and screwball comedy pay homage to the 1930s' and 1940s'*
*Hollywood traditions in Rob Reiner's* The American President
*(BFI Films: Stills, posters and designs).*
The American President © *1995 Castle Rock.*

mind when reflecting on whether the premature death of his wife
brought out the sympathy vote for him in the first presidential race,
and whether his foreign policy initiative bombing of Libya, to destroy
weapons' capability, is in any way a courageous or edifying thing to
do. But, as reviewer John Wrathall reflects, Shepherd's re-emergence at
the closure as a toughened political operator, his pay-off lines about
the citizenry needing to want democracy as much as they want a
commodity like soap detergent, and especially the parting soundbite,
'My name is Andrew Shepherd and *I am* the president', is no more
than highbrow rhetoric, a creditworthy, idealistic notch above Rumson's
contention that the President had allowed his personal life to get in the
way of the politics.[22]
   Reiner's film therefore works perfectly on the two most crucial
levels of 1990s' politics: it is an endearing homage to the 1930s' and
1940s' screwball comedic tradition and incorporates both Capra references and a clip of the Spencer Tracy/Katherine Hepburn vehicle

*Adam's Rib* for good measure; and it is also a virtuoso endorsement of personal character remaining central to political success. To misquote Richard Maltby's earlier contention about Robert Redford in *The Candidate* (see Chapter 3), the sincerity of Michael Douglas's performance in this film *is* the theme of the movie, and a winning one it proved.

The same objectives litter Ivan Reitman's earlier *Dave* (1993), a film that initiated the Clinton era in Hollywood.[23] Even less so than Reiner, Reitman had anything but a political background coming to this film – he is more famous for directing comedies like *Ghost Busters* (1984), *Twins* (1988) and *Junior* (1994) – and the narrative, as reviewer Philip Strick commented on, passes up on any of its opportunities really to invoke questions about the power structure in Washington.[24]

Dave Kovic is a happy-go-lucky guy who runs an employment agency but is content to see life just drift by. He also just happens to be the spitting image of President Bill Mitchell (Kevin Kline playing both parts), and thus the Secret Service take him on as a double at a high-profile event while the President is involved in a liaison with his secretary. The plan falls apart when Mitchell ends up in a coma and the White House seek to delay the inevitable media storm by having Dave impersonate the President for even longer. Chief of Staff Bob Alexander (Frank Langella) sees his chance to become the main man while the earnest but weak Vice-President Nance (Ben Kingsley) is out of the country, and battle ensues as Dave transforms presidential approval ratings and wife Ellen (Sigourney Weaver) is won over to someone she quickly realises is not her husband.

Amid the pure comedic value though, something again quite significant was happening. The intentional farce in sub-plots that have accountant friend Murray (Charles Grodin) come over and trim the budget with nothing more than his calculator, and the fairly loose concoction of financial impropriety that Mitchell is meant to have been involved in and which Alexander threatens Dave with, is all rather superfluous to dedication, decent values, and once more the honesty of owning up to one's misdemeanours. Dave, in the final scene inside the Capitol Building, tells the representatives and the watching public at home what a good man Nance is even though he has zero screen presence for a leader of the free world in the late twentieth century, and his speech is a goodly reminder of ideals, decency and moral fibre – a president confesses all in the full glare of the media – after which he fakes (Mitchell's) death on the floor of the House, and wanders away only to become infected by the desire to serve and run for the local council, with the now widowed Ellen at his side.

*Dave* is an engaging enough comedy and in its own way details the pressures of modern society and the scrutiny any public figure can expect to find themselves a victim of. But its political agenda – and this is crucial because it is as significantly a cloaked ideology as that which exists in *The American President* – runs through a montage of good photo-opportunities passed off as symbolic of presidential leadership, it equates goodness and morality with political intuition, and yet it also serves that which it mocks. The inclusion of a host of real politicos in the film – Chris Dodd, Tom Harkin, Tip O'Neil and so on – makes the play for authenticity but only reconfirms who is in charge again at the end of the film, while the scripted-into-the-plot inclusion of the *McLaughlin Group* TV show, and Oliver Stone's willingness to self-parody his own conspiracy agenda (correctly of course for this story) further demonstrates the Hollywood desire to reference its own mythic and cultural claims. In fact this is a notion that has been built upon in a number of political pictures during the 1990s. In Peter Segal's film *My Fellow Americans* (1997), ex-president Matt Douglas (James Garner) tells his Secret Service detail at one point just to leave him alone and go and rent *In the Line of Fire* again. It's a funny line but only co-opts a mythical plot that has itself appropriated history for its own storyline (see Chapter 4). Hollywood has thus begun to reheat its own political narratives and use them as signifiers of ideals and discourse.

Jonathan Lynn's *The Distinguished Gentleman* (1992) adopts a similar posture but fashions its references in a more historical context. Eddie Murphy plays Jeff Johnson, a small-time crook from Miami who also just happens to have the same name as the recently deceased congressman in the district where he lives (a cameo again by James Garner). Johnson decides that there is money to be made in Washington and runs for office on the ticket of the independent Silver Foxes party. British director Lynn (who helped create the *Yes Minister* series for the BBC) and screenwriter Marty Kaplan play the Murphy vehicle for laughs – probably his best performance since *Trading Places*, a quite similar comedy – but with both having political connections their observations about American democratic convention is also very sharp in places. The whole premise of 'voting for the name you know' – Johnson does no advertising with himself in shot, only the name – is richly documented in American electoral history; and most effective of all Jeff's acceptance speech is a hugely engaging motif of political soundbites down through the ages, lost on an audience who vaguely remember the words but cannot place the context.

Electoral apathy, third-party politics and the initiation of freshmen congressmen are thus all incorporated in *The Distinguished Gentleman*, albeit only superficially, and if the second half diverts itself into romance and Jeff's emergence as a man of principle – campaigning for a young girl who is the victim of the carcinogenic effects of power lines – then it too only imitates that which it seeks to emulate.

The real problem with these three contemporary films in particular is not that they are broad elliptical parodies of modern politics – in almost all cases they have some precise and copied observations to make about the present-day system – but that, like so many other films in this era of Hollywood channelling mainstream product towards some average, median audience, they are at pains to ignore that which is most contentious and most threatening to the values and ideals on offer. In *The American President*, for instance, Andrew Shepherd is allowed to enquire on the nature of political existence without his wife – a plot that has echoes of Woodrow Wilson's loss in the White House in 1914 – but not on the social and emotional ramifications of the way his family was torn apart (is his daughter hounded by the press at school for example?) and how he lives out an existence permanently in the public glare. In *Dave*, Ellen Mitchell is a capable, intelligent and smart woman but one who in conclusion is still given the cautious role of addendum to a new husband/politician, a 'trophy' wife, when she appears perfectly astute enough to make a career for herself in politics.

Most particularly, *The Distinguished Gentleman*, even in comic mode, only tentatively addresses multiculturalism in Johnson's campaign – his trawl around the diaspora of Miami suburbs on the campaign trail in one scene, for instance – and misses any chance to question the current-day role of black politics. As one aspect of this, Murphy's pointed Martin Luther King impression as representative of NAACP (National Association for the Advancement of Colored People) ideals in the 1990s is funny and throwaway in one respect, and yet clichéd and anachronistic in another. Veteran African-American representative and activist Elijah Hawkins (Charles S. Dutton) becomes Jeff's walking moral conscience in congress and yet his standpoint and dignified upholding of minority views are used only as a point of isolation for an institution that is represented as permanently 'on the take'.

The film, of course, remains at heart a comic and inflated portrayal of relationships and decision-making in Washington, and the difficulty of translating black culture and politics overall in Hollywood pictures has subsequently been underlined by Warren Beatty's satirical piece, *Bulworth* (1998). Beatty attempts to parade the sectional exclusion of Los Angelean African-American society in his film through both an emphasis on the positivism of ghetto music and culture, and a dialectical play for class as much as race division in American life. 'White people have more in common with black people than they do with rich people', he says, juxtaposing his scenes in South-Central with his character Jay Bulworth's attack on the affluent filmmaking community of Beverly Hills. While the film is nearly a first for its realisation of the electorate (or non-voting electorate as the case may be) as anything but a homogeneous entity, it still finds it difficult to break with a polemic of unity in the face of what is really a cultural salad bowl rather than the melting pot once so courted in Bulworth's past. As Richard Kelly remarks, Beatty's framing of 'too many shots of "I-like-what-the-man-says" expressions on beaming black faces' is pressing hard for the realisation of a liberal dream come true.[25] The periodic intervention of a soothsayer tramp, played by black writer Amiri Baraka, entreating Bulworth to be 'a spirit not a ghost' is also a sacred symbol of togetherness rather wished upon than realised, as Linda Holt argues.[26]

It is not only with race, however, but gender as well that political films have had to confront tricky societal norms. As portrayed by Celia Kirby (Victoria Rowell) in *The Distinguished Gentleman*, Sidney Wade (Annette Benning) in *The American President* and Nina (Halle Berry) in *Bulworth*, the woman's role in 1990s' films has been somewhat updated since the 1930s, and they now get to be lobbyists, fighters of causes, and even assassins, but are less often to be seen in control of events. Their characters channel the feisty, independent, level-headed attributes of previous female leads in political movies we have examined – Alice Wylie (Constance Cummings) in *Washington Merry-Go-Round*, Clarissa Saunders (Jean Arthur) in *Mr Smith*, Barbara Stanwyck (Ann Mitchell) in *Meet John Doe* – but only Glenn Close in *Air Force One* (1997) has had the power of office in her hands when she played Vice-President Kathryn Bennett. Virtually none have the authority and hard-nosed sense of someone like Kay Thorndyke (Angela Lansbury) in *State of the*

*Union* and thus the most resolute upholding of female influence in 1990s' political films remains the portrayal of a real figure, Pat Nixon. In Oliver Stone's portrait of the President, Joan Allen's performance stands out as one that, even if it overextends her own depressive nature which many critics of the film who were in the Nixon White House at the time have suggested, truly seeks to investigate the elements that make a political partnership and the sacrifices that are invested in such a relationship.

In other areas of Hollywood political portrayals, much broader brush strokes of character have been drawn in this era. *Independence Day, Deep Impact* and *Air Force One* are all films that include tough resourceful presidents, backed by unified administrations with only the merest hint of dissension in the most abject of crises (kidnapping of the president, blowing up of the world). In Mimi Leder's *Deep Impact* (1998) Morgan Freeman is able to unite his countrymen threatened by an asteroid on collision course with earth as (the first?) black president of America. Bill Pullman is a former air force pilot called upon to return to action as leader of a united *world* in repulsing an alien invasion in Emmerich's *Independence Day* (1996), while Harrison Ford is also an ex-military man (an interesting contrast to the actual incumbent) fighting terrorists on his own aircraft in Petersen's film.

These films are all comic-book capers of course that present leaders and authority figures as a one-dimensional cut above mere mortals. As mentioned in Chapter 4, only in the re-emergence of paranoia and conspiracy films has Hollywood really tested the moral and personal efficacy of political figures, albeit again with rather unconvincing staged plots. Presidential culpability in murder and blackmail are the root of *Absolute Power, Murder at 1600* and *Shadow Conspiracy*, and though their exaggerated narratives plaster the themes of accountability and secrecy at the heart of politics all over the plot, yet again real events appear to confirm their resonance with public attitudes more than the cosy resolution of stories in other pictures.

Only a few films in the 1990s have really advanced alternate structures or given a varying slant to the actions of Washington's beltway mentality, the first being the Peters and Segal comedy *My Fellow Americans* (1997). While leaving the complexities of decision-making and institutional operations to one side, the comedy manages to take a dig at both wings of the political spectrum while in effect representing Democrats and Republicans as one and the same thing.

It initiates a plot that puts two ex-presidents, Russell Kramer (Jack Lemmon) and Matthew Douglas (James Garner), outside the Washington establishment and plays with the notion of public reaction to renowned ex-leaders while having to gauge their response on the wrong side of the loop to an impending crisis with incumbent William Haney (Dan Ackroyd), who is about to unveil the alleged misdemeanours of these two as previous occupants of the office.

Kramer and Douglas take in a truncated jaunt across east-coast America on their way back to Washington (the presidential helicopter crashes with them initially on board believing that the president is trying to kill them) allowing the film to engage in a direct contact with the people message, again a rather sugar-coated lesson in listening to what voters want, and realising how the smallest decisions impact on the lives of the citizens. Although the film has a convenient slapstick ending, the twist in the narrative reveals that the architect of the plots to remove the ex-presidents and implicate the incumbent is none other than the simplistic Dan Quayle-like figure of Vice-President Ted Matthews (John Heard) who has put on an act all along with the intention of ending up in the Oval Office. Deception through presentation is the order of the day, and an analysis of the film might be stretching the detachment of the electorate a little too symbolically; nevertheless it is not a radically different message from that which Washington has really been grappling with throughout the 1990s.

By contrast these broad sweeps of political power, rarely diverted from in recent Hollywood portrayals, have been challenged by one picture attempting to go beyond a 'federal' critique of politics in the 1990s: Harold Becker's vehicle for Al Pacino, *City Hall* (1996), is much more of an old-style political tract. Attempting to re-create the urban city machine scenario of the earlier legal/gangster genre of the 1930s, and giving at least a nod to modern inspirations like Sidney Lumet's tackling of New York institutional systems (*Q&A* (1990), *Night Falls on Manhattan* (1996)), Becker's film at least encases its political themes within a closeted framework, that is, not everything involves the freedom, destruction and breakdown of the institutional structure of America. It dives into the murky political world of New York public affairs, with a similarly driven and idealised character, Kevin Calhoun (John Cusack), who as deputy mayor finds himself chasing a line of corruption that involves dead vice-cops, municipal building contracts, organised crime and compromised circuit judges. Al Pacino gives Mayor John Pappas a religious gravitas that few Hollywood portrayals have managed, indicative of earlier characters like Willie Stark and Judson Hammond.

Becker's film is one where old-fashioned personality and political legacy drive the empire on, and where the road to the highest offices and the means to realise one's goals are achieved only through circuitous routes. The language of the film is similarly circumlocutional and weighty, as one would expect from a writing team that includes Nicolas Pillegi and Paul Schrader. The unveiling of deception and the betrayal of the relationship between Pappas and Calhoun concludes with a distinctly underplayed paternalistic conversation and is contrasted with the move by the protégé into the master's shoes as Calhoun in the finale runs for a council seat in New York's Sixth District.

In Barry Levinson's *Wag the Dog* (1998), the past, records of achievement, and the fabric of the constitution and even law and order itself are minor irritations in a world where the president of the United States can guide the tribal masses in messages of distraction, and manipulation, and where honour and responsibility are fall guys in a relentless pursuit of media spin. While the film, as Robin Dougherty has commented, may be recollected in the distant future as serendipitous, the notion of 'pitching' a foreign policy crisis to the public – for that, in the wake of a sex scandal engulfing the President, is exactly what spin doctors Winifred Ames (Anne Heche) and Conrad Brean (Robert De Niro) enlist the help of the marvellously named Hollywood producer Stanley Motss (Dustin Hoffman), for – and the difficulty of Levinson and screenwriter David Mamet coming up with a scenario sufficiently different from real-life alternatives, means they offer up familiar slices of sex, soundbites and technical wizardry.[27] The film is also on dangerous ground when attempting to conclude with farce rather than any suspect condition of either community, but this suggests that Hollywood and Washington are finally at a crossroads in their relationship. The two have infiltrated each other's subconscious to the extent that depth of field, ideological conscience and critical analysis are not something they trust to the audience. *Wag the Dog* brilliantly conceives of the notion that spin is king, but after that Stanley Motss' catchphrase sums it up, 'This is NOTHING!'

CONCLUSIONS

Speaking in January 1998 about the problems befalling his embattled foreign secretary Robin Cook (who had had an affair, left his wife, and subsequently remarried his secretary), British Prime Minister Tony Blair commented on national television that 'Britain could be heading for the same type of political agenda as they've now got in the United States, where everything is like an extension of Hollywood. I don't think it's very sensible for us to go in that direction'.[28]

The comment was naturally off the cuff and largely unspecific in which aspect of the Cook affair could be given 'Hollywood' status. Yet such a remark is symptomatic in the modern age of the indeterminate reach and persuasive agenda that Hollywood wields. In Britain it seems instructive to remark on how one of the chief advisers to the Chancellor of the Exchequer in late 1998 (Charlie Whelan) could seamlessly pass through the process of managing the nation's finances in one week to writing a column in a national newspaper on football the next. If Britain is surreptitiously learning means and methods of conducting politics from the United States, then regardless of the Prime Minister's comments, it is doing this because in America, as Philip Davies notes, 'The culture of celebrity in politics and in the media significantly connects Washington and Hollywood'.[29]

In the United States the clear delineation of that relationship has increasingly been taken for granted. During 1998, the citizens of Minnesota elected Jim Janos as their new Governor. Janos had a colourful past, including being an army frogman in Vietnam, a bodyguard for the Rolling Stones, and then latterly an all-in wrestler on the WWF series that is so popular in the United States. By now he had changed his name to Jesse Ventura, and he went on to win 37 per cent of the vote in a state known for its radical sentiments.[30]

Ventura has been dismissed as one of those quirks of fate that American politics throws up from time to time. Minnesota hardly seems representative of the greater political heartland of America it's argued, and certainly not of a cultural philosophy that would consciously link entertainment and politics as natural bedfellows. But the connection to a television-friendly entertainment like WWF should not be dismissed in a nation where many TV stations boast the 'sport' as one of the leading ratings winners.[31] In reality Ventura only replicates that which has gone before in American politics. The attention afforded Clint Eastwood's stint as Mayor of Carmel in California, the rise and popularity of singer Sonny Bono in the same state, each professed the coming of media heroes to politics and a backlash against professional careerism in public life. In one sense these examples remain sparse, and yet it is no longer the desire of personalities but the demands of the political system that mean that Hollywood and Washington will continue to gravitate towards each other.

In the immediate aftermath of the Senate Impeachment trial in January 1999, attentions were focused on the future for the President and the First Lady. The instructive element of this star-gazing was that while Hillary Clinton could ponder the rumours – not denied – about her imminent run for Daniel Patrick Moynihan's Senate seat in New York in 2000, the President's team were left to scotch incessant claims that he was going to accept a position at his friend Steven Spielberg's DreamWorks SKG studio in 2001.[32]

The possibility of such a move is at best slight and fraught with dangers for all concerned, and yet is the product of a society where hopes, fears and aspirations are never one's own property for very long. According to E. J. Dionne the problem emanates from the fact that the distinction between the public and private realm in society has been lost.[33] The mystery between those who govern and those who are governed loses its allure when human nature is to err and leaders are judged according to those distinctions and, crucially, their handling of those character flaws. The 'talk-show presidency' of Bill Clinton came in for much criticism early in his administration when the traditional media outlets were superseded by direct communication like electronic mail being installed in the White House.[34] Slowly though the emphasis on personal expression and revelation has allowed room for Clintonian style and a strong sense of Hollywood-type imagery to shine though. The counterbalance to this was that in Hollywood films of the 1990s these personal qualities of self-esteem and indeed self-absorption became the framing devices for the majority of examinations of the efficacy and durability of the system.

In April 1999 that most conservatively styled of American journals, *The Nation*, devoted a whole issue to Hollywood and American politics. One of the arch *uber*writers of American cinema himself, Peter Biskind, edited the issue and speculated that never had the time been more ripe for an exposé of a relationship that had once subconsciously, and now ever more blatantly, expedited an umbilical cord between the 'offworlds' of Hollywood and Washington, producing an extroversion of their common ideals. As Biskind enquiringly stated: 'If politics has become no more than a mere epiphenomenon of entertainment, a shadow play of a shadow play, why not go to the source?'[35]

The edition also featured an article by Carl Bromley questioning the direction – left or right – of Hollywood ideology in this era. Citing 1998's two blockbuster 'asteroid movies', *Deep Impact* and *Armageddon*, Bromley notes how the industry has managed to cut it both ways, representing militaristic, hegemonic drives forward for freedom (the latter) versus cross-cutting multicultural, progressive unity with a black president and diverse crew aboard the space shuttle (the former).[36] The theme is 'co-optation'. 'There is some leeway for progressive cultural politics', says Bromley. 'But ultimately they are subsumed by the corporate agenda. The similarities with the Clinton White House are uncanny – one understands why Hollywood and Clinton are such a good fit.'[37]

One can begin to comprehend, in such an environment of cinematic production, the way the two strands first discussed at the beginning of this book have come together. Ideology is no longer detached from the iconographic meaning inherent in the symbolic edifices that adorn political films. The symbolism has become meaning, and while in the past icons might have been redolent of iconoclastic tendencies within the political culture, today they may be perceived as empty vessels that no longer signify, but are merely *meant* to signify, universality and sin-gular ideals in a political state where that ideology has been condensed and political debate minimised.

Albert Boime's work on the cultural appropriation of America's national monuments, including a comparison of the use of the Lincoln Memorial in films, provides an interesting analogy between the political sentiments encased in earlier films discussed here, such as *Mr Smith Goes to Washington* and *Young Mr Lincoln*, and recent incorporation of those values in *JFK*, *In the Line of Fire* and *Nixon*.[38] For Boime these later films offer more testing observations about national ethos, set as they are within narratives that challenge conventional patriotic codes. Yet it seems instructive to observe that all of these recent pictures have skimmed the historical memory for interrelated cultural signals, and thus even Oliver Stone has our historical senses on overload as Nixon, played by Anthony Hopkins, walks up the steps of the monument at one point in the film, to the backdrop of fading Civil War photographs and a mushroom cloud looming out of the sky.' National icons preserve historical, religious, and biographical memory', states Boime. 'And these awesome operations alone may be sufficient to invest them with a powerful appeal.'[39]

The appeal of memory, I would conclude, and the induction into a subliminal world of political gentrification are the critical legacies and forceful ideological agendas dictating Hollywood's history of films about politics. Those films that I have included here go to the source of that appeal, they emblematise the trends of ephemeral pastiches, of materialistic and moral vacuums, but also of a deep-seated coagulation of traditional signs and pedagogy. Emotive response and the recognition of democratic language are the signals and transference of belief in all these films. Thus the pecuniary nature of these two forces of American life, cinema and politics, the insignias that betray their hands at work in society, are at century's end inseparable edifices, syncopated by values and goals that infringe as well as inform the politics of our time.

## NOTES

1 Michael Ellison 'Wholesome Hanks Turns His Back on Clinton', *The Guardian*, 1 December 1998, p. 18.

2 Martin Walker, 'Star-spangled Banners', *The Guardian*, 30 November 1995, pp. 2–3.

3 Ellison, 'Wholesome Hanks', p. 18.

4 Michael Kelly, 'The Game and The Show', *The Guardian*, Weekend, 20 November 1993, p. 6.

5 Martin Walker, 'Clinton's Hollywood', *Sight and Sound*, September 1993, pp. 13–14.

6 Ibid. pp. 13–14.

7 Matthew Campbell, 'Hollywood Rules Roost in Washington', *The Sunday Times*, 30 November 1997, p. 20.

8 Peter Biskind, 'When Worlds Collide', *The Nation*, vol. 268, no. 13, 5/12 April 1999, pp. 11–12.

9 'On Movies, Money & Politics', ed. Peter Biskind, *The Nation*, 5/12 April 1999, p. 18.

10 Kevin Phillips, *Arrogant Capital: Washington, Wall Street, and the Frustration of American Politics* (Boston: Little, Brown & Co., 1994) p. 6.

11 Robert Hughes, *Culture of Complaint: The Fraying of America* (London: Harvill, 1994) p. 27.

12  Eugenia Bone, 'Mr "Roberts" Goes to Washington', *Premiere*, September 1993, p. 38.
13  Christine B. Williams, 'The Media and the Message', in *Political Issues in America Today: The 1990s Revisited*, ed. Philip John Davies and Federic A. Waldstein (Manchester: Manchester University Press, 1996) pp. 79–95.
14  Ibid. p. 93.
15  Michael Foley, *American Political Ideas* (Manchester: Manchester University Press, 1991) pp. 214–17.
16  Included amongst an extensive list during the last decade have been J. E. Chubb and P. E. Peterson (eds), *Can the Government Govern?* (Washington DC: Brookings Institution, 1989); E. J. Dionne, *Why Americans Hate Politics* (New York: Simon & Schuster, 1991); and W. Greider, *Who Will Tell the People?: The Betrayal of American Democracy* (New York: Simon & Schuster, 1992).
17  Gavin Esler, *The United States of Anger* (London: Penguin, 1998) p. 289.
18  Robert Williams, *Political Scandals in the USA* (Edinburgh: Keele University Press, 1998) pp. 129–31.
19  Dionne's reference to Colin Powell seemed especially apt during the 1996 presidential election. In the end Powell never declared himself a candidate or even ground out any distinctive manifesto yet remained high and often in the lead with approval ratings that asked the question, 'which person would you most *trust* in the office of president?'. See E. J. Dionne, *They Only Look Dead: Why Progressives will Dominate the Next Political Era* (New York: Touchstone, 1997) p. 29 & p. 276.
20  Esler, *The United States of Anger*, p. 289.
21  Mark Steyn, 'Whiter than White House', *The Daily Telegraph*, 6 December 1995, p. 19.
22  John Wrathall, review of *The American President* in *Sight and Sound*, vol. 6, no. 1, January 1996, p. 36.
23  Walker, 'Clinton's Hollywood', p. 13.
24  Philip Strick, review of *Dave* in *Sight and Sound*, vol. 3, no. 11, November 1993, p. 40.
25  Richard Kelley, review of *Bulworth* in *Sight and Sound*, vol. 9, no. 2, February 1999, pp. 41–2.
26  Linda Holt, 'Is this how White People Rap?', *The Times Literary Supplement*, 29 January 1999, p. 29.
27  Robin Dougherty, review of *Wag the Dog* in *Sight and Sound*, vol. 8, no. 3, March 1998, p. 57.
28  Michael White, 'Blair Backs "Superb" Cook', *The Guardian*, 11 January 1999, p. 1.
29  Philip John Davies, 'The Media and US Politics' in *Developments in*

*American Politics 3*, ed. Gillian Peele, Christopher J. Bailey, Bruce Cain and B. Guy Peters (London: Macmillan, 1998), p. 339.

30  See Michael Ellison, 'The Governor', G2 Section, *The Guardian*, 28 January 1999, pp. 2–3.

31  Ibid. p. 3.

32  Incumbent Senator Daniel Moynihan announced he would not seek re-election for his seat in New York in the 2000 election, and in the early months of 1999 Hillary Clinton was widely reported to be organising a campaign team that might take a run at the seat also courted by New York mayor Rudolph Giuliani. DreamWorks marketing chief Terry Press, meanwhile, commented that he had been asked the question about Clinton coming to work at the studio 8000 times and it still wasn't true. See Matthew Campbell and Tom Rhodes, 'Rabid Rudy Waits for Horrid Hillary', *The Sunday Times*, 21 February 1999, p. 21; Nancy Gibbs, 'What's Next for Bill and Hillary?', *Time*, 15 February 1999, p. 34.

33  Dionne notes that when the barriers between public and private life are broken down, then democracy itself is at stake. See Dionne, *They Only Look Dead*, pp. 28–31.

34  John Hart, 'The Presidency in the 1990s', *Developments in American Politics 2*, ed. Gillian Peele, Christopher J. Bailey, Bruce Cain and B. Guy Peters (London: Macmillan, 1994) pp. 127–8.

35  Biskind, 'When Worlds Collide', p. 11.

36  Carl Bromley 'Celluloid Family Values: Are Studio Films Liberal or Conservative?', *The Nation*, 5/12 April 1999, pp. 40–3.

37  Ibid. p. 43.

38  Albert Boime, *The Unveiling of National Icons: A Plea for Patriotic Iconoclasm in a Nationalist Era* (Cambridge: Cambridge University Press, 1998) pp. 5–7.

39  Ibid. p. 7.

# INDEX